1 359398 0

C000177936

£12.00

Borough Government and Politics:
Reading 1835-1985

Borough Government and Politics:
READING 1835-1985

ALAN ALEXANDER
Lecturer in Politics, University of Reading

London
GEORGE ALLEN & UNWIN
Boston   Sydney

George Allen & Unwin (Publishers) Ltd,
40 Museum Street, London WC1A 1LU, UK

George Allen & Unwin (Publishers) Ltd,
Park Lane, Hemel Hempstead, Herts HP2 4TE, UK

Allen & Unwin, Inc.,
Fifty Cross Street, Winchester, Mass. 01890, USA

George Allen & Unwin Australia Pty Ltd,
8 Napier Street, North Sydney, NSW 2060, Australia

First published in 1985.

359398 01
352 0422 93 ALE

British Library Cataloguing in Publication Data   *823693*

Alexander, Alan,
    Borough government and politics: Reading 1835-1985.
1. Reading (Berkshire) – Politics and government
I. Title
352.0422′93   JS3870
ISBN 0-04-35211-7

Library of Congress Cataloging in Publication Data

Alexander, Alan, 1943-
    Borough government and politics.
Bibliography: p.
Includes index.
1. Reading (Berkshire) – Politics and government.
I. Title.
JS3865.R43A78   1985   320.9422′93   85-1265
ISBN 0-04-352117-7 (U.S. : alk. paper)

Set in 10 on 12 Plantin by
Columns of Reading
Printed and bound in Great Britain by
Biddles Ltd, Guildford and King's Lynn

Contents

List of Plates

1 George Lovejoy (1808-83), campaigner for audited
  Corporation accounts.
2 Lorenzo Quelch, Socialist Councillor and Alderman.
3 Reading Corporation in 1879,
  Mayor H. B. Blandy presiding.
4 Dr Stokoe and boys, Reading School, 1877.
5 John Rabson succeeds William Henry Short in 1927,
  accompanied by Town Clerk C. S. Johnson.
6 Municipal enterprise in Reading,
  the first electric tram, July 1903.
7 The last electric tram, Mayor W. E. C. McIlroy
  driving, May 1939.
8 (a) George William Colebrook, Mayor 1880.
  (b) Arthur Hill, Mayor 1883-7.
  (c) John Wessley Martin, Mayor 1892 and 1910-11.
  (d) Edith Mary Sutton, Reading's first
      woman Mayor 1933.
9 A graphic view of Caversham's hostility to Reading.
  Berkshire Chronicle, 3 October, 1908.
10 Cartoonist's view of Caversham's obduracy after the
   issue in 1910 of the Provisional Order extending the
   borough boundaries (John Burns was President of
   the Local Government Board), *Berkshire
   Chronicle*, 7 May, 1910.

*(Plates 1-8 are reproduced by courtesy of Berkshire County Library:
Reading Local Collection)*

To my children, Kate and Neil,
who said it was their turn.

Preface

In 1981 the Borough Council of Reading asked me to consider writing a history of the government of the town, to be published to coincide with the 150th anniversary of the Municipal Corporations Act 1835. This book is not a continuous history of a century and a half of municipal government: that would have required a book twice as long. Rather it is an attempt to convey the development of government in a developing town and, in particular, to illuminate the governmental capacity of a form of local government Britain no longer has: the all-purpose or unitary local authority. Not every service the corporation has ever provided is recorded here and no doubt some of those who have served the borough will be disappointed by my emphases. I have tried to illuminate as well as record and some records have been ignored because they shed little light. Moreover, illumination becomes less reliable as the account approaches the present day: there is a risk of distortion because of lack of perspective, especially when the light is shone by one who has been an active participant in a short and fairly recent period of the town's political history.

Much of the basic documentary research was done by my research assistant, Jan Eastham. In many respects the book is as much hers as mine and I am happy to record my appreciation of her year's work. I must also thank the Archivist and his staff at the Berkshire County Record Office for their unfailing helpfulness and co-operation. The staff of Reading Reference Library who, as the book is published, have just moved into a new library first mooted by the borough council in 1912, spared no effort in searching for the more obscure items in the borough's Local Collection and in fetching for me the weighty volumes of local newspapers which, in cramped and unsuitable surroundings, they have tried to preserve from the ravages of time, damp and, by the look of things, mice. Members of the Town Clerk's Department, including Town Clerk Harry Tee, have helped in a number of ways, not least by providing space for me to consult documents sensitive enough not yet to have found their way into publicly accessible archives. In particular, Carol Charles, the Town Clerk's personal assistant, ensured that the final typescript was produced with exceptional efficiency and accuracy. The book owes something to all of them.

About half of the book was written, and the rest planned, during an enormously pleasurable and productive month as a Scholar-in-Residence at the Rockefeller Foundation's Villa Serbelloni overlooking Bellagio on Lake Como. My thanks here cannot adequately express my appreciation of the foundation's institutional generosity or of the many personal kindnesses of Bob Celli and his staff. I must also thank the University of Reading for granting me leave of absence for the month at Bellagio and its Research Board for a contribution to my travel costs.

My wife Morag encouraged the book's completion, read and listened to my drafts, and showed great forbearance as my temper grew short as deadlines approached and passed.

All errors and omissions are, of course, my sole responsibility.

Alan Alexander
Wokingham, Berkshire
August 1984

Borough Government and Politics:
Reading 1835-1985

1

Clearing the Roost

Members of the same family have happened to belong to the
Corporation for the last fifty years [and] their conduct is
viewed by the inhabitants with a degree of jealousy and
dissatisfaction.

> Report of the Municipal Commissioners, 1833,
> *Corporation of Reading*, p. 17

It was not the men but the system which brought these
gentlemen into disrepute; they having the power naturally
exercised it in favour of their own party, which was
Conservative.

> W.S. Darter, *Reminiscences of Reading*, 1888, p. 187

We clear the roost from top to bottom – Town Clerks and
all – abolish all the old names except Mayor and Town
Clerk – give a simple Town Council . . . one third to go out
annually.

> Joseph Parkes (Secretary to the Municipal
> Corporations Commission (to Lord Durham, 1 June 1835

In common with about two hundred other towns in England and
Wales, Reading dates its modern institutional history from its
inclusion as a municipal borough in the schedules to the Municipal
Corporations Act 1835. The significance of the system of local
government created by that Act lies chiefly in the fact that it
imposed upon urban England the principle of directly elected local
institutions to replace the ancient medieval corporations, many of
which, as the Municipal Corporations Commission of 1833 had
shown, had become self-electing, self-perpetuating and corrupt. To
be fair, the commissioners found it possible to apply only the first
two of these adjectives to the Corporation of Reading, although the
tone of the report, to quote Childs (1910, p. 30), was 'the faint
praise which damns'.

Until 1835, Reading's government was based on a series of royal charters dating back to the Middle Ages, the most important being that granted by Henry VIII in 1542. This charter was the first to recognize the Town Council as a body corporate as distinct from the Merchant Guild, and all subsequent charters had the effect of developing the pre-modern institutional arrangement of local government by a Corporation of Burgesses and various specified officers such as Sergeants-at-Mace, Capital Stewards and Recorders. Like most other unreformed corporations, Reading's was a self-perpetuating oligarchy, Conservative in politics and completely inaccessible to the people of the town, upon whom it levied a rate. The reports of the Municipal Commissioners told many stories a good deal worse than that of Reading where the members of the corporation were probably moderately venal rather than deeply corrupt. Even so, to quote the commissioners, the very suggestion of corruption was 'in itself, proof of the practical inconvenience produced in the town of Reading by the system of self-election, and close management, to which cause it seems mainly attributable, that the motives and actions of the corporate body, even where they are unexceptionable and meritorious, are constantly regarded with distrust'.

Distrust was compounded by dissatisfaction with the activities of the corporation. As with most unreformed corporations, Reading's was in the business of managing assets rather than providing services and the list of things which the members did was, by modern standards, very short indeed: they granted licenses, acted as trustees of local charities (some of which they grossly mismanaged), managed the corporation's property and looked after the bridges within the borough boundary. Probably because of the complacency bred of oligarchy which 'by harmonious action enjoyed a flourishing monopoly' (Darter, 1888, p. 192), the unreformed corporation showed no desire to acquire, by special Act of Parliament, additional powers to improve the physical environment of the inhabitants of the town. As in most other towns, the modern services of paving, lighting and watching came to be provided by what Sidney and Beatrice Webb called 'statutory authorities for special purposes', and the public utilities such as water and gas (and, much later, electricity and public transport) were initially provided by private enterprise companies acting under private Acts of Parliament.

Before 1835, and for a considerable time thereafter, public services of an environmental kind were provided in Reading by the Paving Commissioners, first established under the Reading Improvement Act 1785. The powers of the commissioners were greatly extended by the Reading Improvement Act 1826, a major piece of private legislation nicknamed by its opponents, in a controversy that foreshadowed that between the 'improvers' and the 'economizers' twenty-five years later, the 'All-Perfection Act'. The full title of the Act was 'An Act for the Better Paving, Lighting, Cleansing, Watching and Otherwise Improving the Borough of Reading'. It conferred on the commissioners, who comprised the Mayor and corporation, the local vicars, county justices resident in the borough and 197 other named individuals, very wide powers, including those of compulsory purchase of buildings for the purpose of improvement. Childs's magisterial judgement that the commissioners' 'administration lagged some-what in arrear of their pretentious title' is confirmed in other sources (Lee, 1850; Daltry, 1933; James, 1954) and in statistics of mortality and morbidity that show (see Chapter 2) Reading to have been, in the first half of the nineteenth century, a notably insanitary and disease-ridden borough.

In this regard, however, Reading was little different from other towns in the period between the onset of the Industrial Revolution and the triumph of the public health reformers after 1850. The obstacles in the way of effective improvement were both institu-tional and financial. For not only was there considerable overlap of jurisdiction between the corporation and the Paving Commis-sioners, as well as the cross-membership specified in the 1826 Act and rendered more important by the fact that only a small minority of the commissioners attended meetings whose mood was 'acri-monious' and procedure 'haphazard' (James, 1954, p. 11), but also there was a reluctance to pay the rates that the Paving Commissioners were empowered to levy. As elsewhere, a re-luctance to pay, given the influence of those liable to rates upon those able to charge them, was often reflected in inactivity on the part of statutory authorities with the power to make improve-ments.

It is important to note that this was a period when the provision of local services depended entirely upon the strength of local initiative. Powers of improvement were granted by Parliament in response to petitions raised locally, and even when powers had been conferred there was no obligation on commissioners to exercise them. There was no central direction, no power of inspection, no central intervention against defaulting authorities, no prescription of appropriate standards. The Reading Improvement Commissioners, whose powers passed to the Local Board of Health in 1850, succeeded in paving some streets and in clearing and opening up the most insanitary and congested parts of the town, but their relative lack of impact may be gauged from the report in 1809 that 'every inhabitant must long have witnessed with regret the shameful state wherein the streets are suffered to remain the year through' and from the comment in the *Reading Mercury* in 1823 that there was 'no town in England where there was less attention paid' to keeping the streets clean, in good order, and passable to traffic (Childs, 1910, p. 31).

The powers of the commissioners in paving, cleansing and lighting facilitated the early relationship between the public authority and private enterprise companies formed to supply what later became universally regarded as natural government monopolies: gas and water. The first Reading Gas Company was formed in 1818 and began to supply gas for street lighting the following year. Illuminating the main thoroughfares, originally by specifying that each householder should hang a light outside overnight and later by the direct provision of lights by the commissioners, not only was in pursuance of the commissioners' powers of lighting, but also helped in the 'watching' or policing of the town in the hours of darkness, a function undertaken, until the formation in 1836 of the Reading Borough Police, by about a dozen watchmen.

Reading's first water company was set up in 1696 and entered a covenant with the corporation to supply water to the borough for a thousand years. Such a commitment was wildly optimistic, for the works at Mill Lane proved inadequate to the task of pumping water up to the town centre and they quickly fell into disuse. The company, having been revived in 1802, was incorporated by Act of Parliament in 1826 as the Reading Waterworks Company and was given powers compulsorily to purchase specified properties needed for the use of the company's works on the River Kennet at St Giles Mill near the centre of the modern town.

Thus, on the eve of the Municipal Corporations Act 1835, the government of Reading was fragmented, shared among an oligarchic corporation, a moribund Paving Commission, and two private companies contracting with corporate bodies for the supply of water and gas. There were also, as there continued to be for almost a century, the separately elected Poor Law Guardians charged with the administration of the Elizabethan Poor Law as amended by the Poor Law Amendment Act 1834. Such fragmentation was to continue for many years, as it did throughout England, but the passing of the Act of 1835, and the establishment of Reading as a municipal borough, created the institutional framework for the gradual development of a unitary, all-purpose borough council. The remainder of this chapter considers the provisions and limitations of the Municipal Corporations Act, suggests the governmental possibilities it contained and examines the composition of the first reformed corporation of Reading. It concludes with a sketch of the kind of town Reading was at the start of its modern municipal history.

The Municipal Corporations Act was one of the earliest achievements of the first reformed Parliament, and its authors clearly saw an intimate connection between national and local institutional change. Joseph Parkes, the enthusiastic, campaigning and deeply committed Liberal who was Secretary to the Royal Commission on the Municipal Corporations saw 'municipal reform [as] the steam engine for the mill built by parliamentary reform'. Parkes's letters (Buckley, 1926, ch. 7) show the clear political motivations of those who saw the reform of the close corporations as a possibly final nail in the coffin of English Conservatism. The power of the corporations in parliamentary elections would be reduced, perhaps eliminated, and Britain, it was argued, would not have a Conservative government again. The philosophical underpinnings of the Act are clearly expressed by Finlayson (1966, p. 674) when he says that 'for radicals, corporation reform would represent a breach in the old system: a triumph for Benthamite principles of democracy, utility and efficiency'.

The reform of the municipal corporations was as much an expressive as an instrumental act, as much symbolic as practical. The commissioners did not approach their task of examining the corporations with an open mind: they were chosen for their radicalism and they set out to discover the abuses that would justify an institutional reform to symbolize the onset of a more democratic age. Reading was a part of that age. The passage of the great

Reform Act in 1832 had been received in the town with dancing and dining in the streets, and the new corporation celebrated its first meeting by passing an Address to the King, expressing thanks for his assent to the Municipal Corporations Act and welcoming its establishment of 'the great principles of free election and democracy of our local governors and their responsibility to their constituents'.

Oligarchy was out, democracy was in. In Reading the roost was cleared in the first elections to the new corporation when 'Reform' candidates won fifteen out of eighteen seats. Only six of the twenty-two members of the old corporation stood for election of whom four were defeated. At least one of the latter, Alderman Letchworth, declined to be elected as an alderman (to occupy one of the six places on the new council to be filled by indirect election, with the elected councillors comprising the electorate) on the grounds that having been rejected by the voters of the town he would not join the new corporation by the indirect aldermanic route (Darter, 1888, p. 193). The domination of Conservatives was replaced by a preponderance of Liberals. The early elections to the reformed corporation were highly competitive and partisan. Reading was, like most of urban England, a town where the parties competed for municipal office and for the prestige and patronage associated with it. Party competition has had its ups and downs in the 150 years of Reading's modern municipal history, but its presence in 1835, and its resilience over time, cast doubt upon the existence, often claimed by modern opponents of party politics in local government, of a golden age when the calibre of the individual rather than the party label determined whether candidates would be elected to the council.

The early manifestations of partisanship were, however, less concerned than in modern times with the issue of what the council should do and how it should do it. In the first elections, partisanship centred on the attitudes to the politics of reform. It was non-programmatic, concerned about the politics of who should be elected rather than the content of the measures that should be implemented. The powers passed by the old corporation to the new were extremely limited, extending only to the management of corporate property, the maintenance of bridges and the trusteeship of the Reading Free Grammar School. The one new statutory obligation laid on the reformed corporation was the duty to

organize a police force to replace the watchmen of the Paving
Commissioners. In institutional terms, this duty led to the
beginning of the committee system because the new corporation set
up a Watch Committee to oversee the police force and to appoint
and pay its officers.

Derek Fraser, a perceptive historian of nineteenth-century urban
England, contrasted the municipal reforms of 1835 and the Local
Government Act 1888 by saying that the first was a 'change of men'
and the second 'a change of system'. Although that might be said to
understate the symbolic importance of the elective principle in the
1835 Act the fact that the new corporations did little more than the
old lends considerable weight to the judgement. In the Reading
case, Darter's comment, with the hindsight of half-a-century, that
'the new Corporation consisted of a considerable majority of
Liberals, some of whom had no claim to the office . . . but the
feeling of the public was so decided against the old order of things
that some excuse might be made for so sweeping a change' reflects
a general view that what the reform produced was 'a more or less
different body of people doing the same things as before in the
same way' (Ashworth, 1954, p. 70). Yet here again, too little regard
is paid to the significance of direct elections and the openness to
press and public that came with it. For while the expressive and
symbolic quality of the reform is emphasized by the restricted
range of powers of the new bodies, and by the failure to transfer to
them the powers of other local authorities, their democratic
character made them the natural recipients of increased powers
conferred by general legislation. It also gave them a legitimacy
when local demands for improvement necessitated an approach to
Parliament for a local Act to authorize the provision of extended
local public services. The accretion of powers to the corporation in
the fifty years after 1835 is explored in Chapters 2 and 3.

At the time of the passage of the Municipal Corporations Act,
Reading stood on the threshold of its development as a modern
industrial, service and communications centre. Its population was
about 17,000 and rising quite rapidly. There had been just over
16,000 inhabitants in 1830, and the returns at the two decennial
censuses after reform showed rises to 19,000 in 1841 and to almost
21,000 in 1851. Although the figures are not large in absolute
terms, they show an increase, in each of the two decades before the
effects of the major public health reforms upon rates of mortality

began to be felt, of about 10 per cent.

This population was confined very largely to those areas of the three parishes of St Giles, St Mary and St Laurence that converged on the modern town centre, and although some development had taken place between the town centre and the Abbey Ruins and along the Oxford Road, the town had not spread across the meadows to the south bank of the Thames. The configuration of Reading in the early nineteenth century has been described as roughly triangular, with Friar Street as the base and London Street/Silver Street and Southampton Street, meeting at the top of Mount Pleasant, as the two other sides. As Hinton (1954, p. 133) points out, some development had begun to take place as 'a fringe of short roads [appeared] along each of the triangle's sides' but 'most of the population [was] still housed within the triangle'.

A map of 1813 shows the boundaries of the three parishes extending to the river on the north, to Tilehurst and Southcote in the west, and to the Wokingham Road in the east. The availability of undeveloped land in the defined area of the borough ensured that the social, economic and physical expansion of the middle decades of the nineteenth century would be achieved without changes to the boundaries. As will become clear in Chapter 4, the need for extensions came much later, in 1887 and 1911, and was related to the link between efficient and effective local government and the natural expansion of the local community.

The eve of the development of modern local government in England coincided with the beginning of the railway age, the boom in investment that was to provide the country, in the space of twenty years, with a network of lines that, by ending the age of stagecoach and canal, revolutionized communications and transport. Reading was already a major crossroads in the communications of central southern England. It was a staging post on a number of roads from London to the west and the south Midlands and from the south coast northwards. The completion of the Kennet and Avon Canal in 1810 gave Reading water-borne connections with Bristol, Birmingham and London. It was suggested in 1814 (Childs, 1910, p. 15) that this not only improved the commercial prosperity of the town but also gave it a commercial advantage over London, in that goods from the west – the West Indies, America and Ireland – would reach the town for distribution without the perilous journey along the length of the English

Channel and into the Thames Estuary. Such a judgement probably overstated the growing commercial significance of Reading and the dangers of Channel navigation but the fact remains that an estimate of the town's trade in 1835 put the gross import and export at 50,000 tons carried by canal and river and only 100 tons by road. An impression of the suddenness with which the canal trade was overtaken by the railways may be gained from the fact that only five years separated the building of a new dock and wharf at Reading in 1828 and the publication in 1833 of the first prospectus of the Great Western Railway.

The coming of the railway was, of course, a major landmark in the history of the town. Although the Great Western Railway Bill passed into law before the Municipal Corporations Act, the impact on Reading was not felt until after 1840, when the line reached the town, and 1841, when it was completed to Bristol. By 1849 Reading had direct rail connections with London, Bristol, Southampton and Newbury, and with the South Western Railway via a spur to Farnborough.

That Reading was a communications centre both before and after the coming of the railways owes much to its geographical position. Gilbert (1934) gives a clear account of how both geographical and geological factors influenced the development of the town. Reading stands at the confluence of the Kennet and the Thames, and at the junction of two ancient roads, those from London to Bristol and from Southampton by way of Winchester and Basingstoke to Reading and onwards to Oxford and the Midlands. Geologically the town developed on a gravel escarpment between the Kennet and the Thames, a position that afforded good drainage and protection from flooding, but which presented continual difficulty in the provision of a reliable water supply, a difficulty not entirely overcome until long after the transfer to the ownership of the Local Board of Health of the Reading Waterworks Company in 1868.

In 1835 Reading was much more a commercial than an industrial centre. As Childs put it (1910, p. 21), 'the age of cloth was over, the age of seed and biscuit still to come'. The preponderance of 'trade' over 'industry' was reflected in the occupational composition of the first reformed corporation. The *Reading Mercury* (6 January 1836) reported the results of the first elections to the new council, identifying the successful and unsuccessful candidates by their political affiliation (Reformers or Tories) and by their occupation and status.

Of a total membership of twenty-four (eighteen councillors and six aldermen), only four were manufacturers, while eight were in 'trade', broadly construed to include shopkeeping, brewing and merchandising. Among the elected councillors, those in 'trade' included a miller, three grocers, a brewer and a wine merchant, while the manufacturers comprised the maker of 'Reading Fish Sauce' and two ironmongers (a category that might equally well be included among the 'trade' but which probably indicates small ironfounders). There were also two builders, a solicitor, a land surveyor and four 'gentlemen'. Cook (1970) shows how the changing economic profile of the town was reflected in the composition of the council throughout the nineteenth century, with representatives of its two most famous and economically dominant firms, Huntley and Palmer and Suttons Seeds, serving on the council throughout most of the second half of the century. This important connection between society and government is explored in Chapter 6.

2
'A Clean, Orderly, and Well-Governed Town'?

Reading is a clean, orderly and well-governed town.
> John Weedon, Mayor of Reading, on his election, 1847

Basic questions about the legitimate use of power . . . were involved in the mundane subjects of water and drains.
> Derek Fraser, *Urban Politics in Victorian England*, 1976, p. 10

It takes three centuries to carry anything out in Reading: one to think about it, another to talk about it, and another to carry it out.
> John Okey Taylor, Mayor-elect of Reading, 1862

To write about the governmental history of a single town inevitably risks either a descent into preciousness and special pleading or a retreat into the particularization from the general that sees the town simply as a local case of general political, institutional and governmental history. To avoid these extremes demands a degree of artifice, an approach that recognizes the distinctiveness of a growing town as a community, a political system and a social entity within the context of a national governmental system in the midst of rapid change and, importantly, irresistible centralization. Towns and their governments were part of the Victorian administrative state, but their incorporation in 1835 not only confirmed their independence of their surrounding counties, but also provided a legal and constitutional foundation for the expression of localism. Localism was a value in itself as well as a bulwark, if sometimes only a symbolic one, against centralist meddling in local affairs.

The significance of incorporation in the development of urban government may be emphasized in two ways, by reference to events at the beginning and the end of the period covered by this book. First, the importance attributed to the principle of incorporation by local notables is shown by the enthusiasm and urgency with which the pursuit of borough status was approached in those urban areas which, because they had developed after the era of the conferment of royal charters, found no place in the schedules of the 1835 Act. Many of the major towns of the industrial north of England, including Manchester, began their modern institutional history with a campaign for the incorporation which would establish their local government independence and foster the development of a local politics that was elective and democratic, free of the oligarchic patronage of county government, and which would eventually take over from special purpose authorities and select vestries.

Second, the abolition of the county boroughs in 1974, and the continuation of borough status for ceremonial purposes only, has been argued to be the most profound change in the history of the constitutional relationship between local and central government. As Michael Elliot argues (in Young, 1983, pp. 44-5):

> The constitutional significance of the [1972 Local Government] Act lies . . . in the fact that it removed from local government units the last vestiges of a power that did not derive from parliamentary grant. . . . The royal charters and power derived from them provided . . . a reminder that at least some units of local government possessed powers which were not wholly at the disposal of the centre.

To these may be added, as will be seen in Chapter 3, the symbolic and practical importance attached by local politicians and their professional advisers to ensuring that Reading would qualify for the continued independence of the surrounding county that was guaranteed by the grant of county borough status under the Local Government Act 1888.

Despite the corporate independence implied by borough status, however, the immediate capacity of the council to affect the life of the town was strictly limited. In terms of service provision, the only new statutory duty laid on the corporation was that of organizing a police force. The Metropolitan Police had been established under Home Office control in 1829, and it was convenient to employ the first piece of general municipal legislation thereafter to extend to other urban areas, but under the control of the corporations, what was regarded as a successful innovation. Paradoxically, however, the addition of the police power might be argued to have weakened rather than strengthened the influence in the town of the corporation, for the Watch Committees were authorized to supervise the police force subject to *report to* rather than *approval of* the whole council. When Reading attempted, in its major Local Bill 1887, to extend this form of wide delegation to other committees, the proposed clause was struck out of the legislation on the recommendation of both the Home Office and the Local Government Board.

Thus, apart from the management of corporate assets and the trusteeship of local charities and of the Reading Free Grammar School, the corporation's powers were limited to the provision of a police force and the maintenance of certain streets and nineteen bridges specified in the Elizabethan charter only six of which, according to a report of the Finance Committee to the council on 29 January 1836, were likely to cause considerable expenditure, the others having been recently repaired.

As indicated in Chapter 1, then, the modern incorporation of the Borough of Reading did not create a multipurpose authority able to deal comprehensively with the prospects, problems and needs of the town. Rather, it ensured the conditions for the development of the council into such a body. Thirty-five years after the Municipal Corporations Act, the President of the Local Government Board, on the eve of the passage of the Public Health Act 1872 which, according to an early academic student of Reading's public service history, was 'the first step towards unification, simplification and compulsory regulation' (Daltry, 1933, p. 2), characterized the local government system as 'a chaos as regards Authorities, a chaos as regards rates and a worse chaos as regards areas'. Although the effects of that chaos had been exaggerated between 1835 and 1870 by the fact that special powers had been given to such new bodies as Local Boards of Health, gas companies and water companies and by the conferring of additional powers on existing bodies by both public and private legislation, its existence is easy to trace in 1835. Even if the administration of the Poor Laws is omitted from the description, the local government of Reading was complicated by the existence of the Paving Commissioners, the Vestries of three parishes, the Reading Gas Company and the Waterworks Company. Although the latter two undertakings were private companies, they were incorporated by Act of Parliament and they were closely related to municipal activities by two important linkages.

First, they were in contractual relationships with both the Paving Commissioners and with the corporation; and second, linkages based on individual local notables were ensured by the prevalence of cross-memberships. Not only were all members of the corporation also Paving Commissioners, but also some of them were directors of the companies which contracted with the corporation. Nor was there any distinction similar to the modern one between members and officers of the council. It is easy to forget that the fastidiousness about declarations and conflicts of interest, ineffective though it sometimes is in preventing the gaining of uncorrupt advantage, is a fairly late development in Britain's municipal history. As will be discussed later, some local Reading notables in the middle decades of the nineteenth century, in particular J. J. Blandy and Thomas Rogers, had fingers in so many local pies as to give them a personal influence in the affairs of the town that exceeded the sum of their various official and semi-official powers.

But the difficulties in the way of the establishment of the borough council as a multipurpose authority leading the way in the development and government of the town were not merely structural. There was also, in the early years after municipal reform, an absence of will. B. J. Barber (1980, p. 301) in his study of municipal government in Leeds suggests that one of the objects of the Municipal Corporations Act was the reduction of municipal expenditure and he notes that 'many of the new corporations inaugurated their regimes with acts of ostentatious parsimony'. If the traditional tension in British local government, whether in the days before the creation of multipurpose authorities, or in the modern period of intense party competition, has been between economizers and spenders, between those concerned with the level of local taxation and those concerned with the level of local services, it was the economizers who had the whip hand in the early days of the reformed Reading Corporation.

It would be an exaggeration to apply the adjective ostentatious to the continuous efforts to reduce expenditure that are revealed by the corporation minutes in the ten years after 1835. Not surprisingly, since the provision of a police force was both the most important and the most expensive of the duties of the corporation, the attention of the economizers was continuously directed towards the activities of the Watch Committee, as well as to other expenditure falling under the general heading of the administration of justice. In the year 1836, for example, the Watch Committee on two occasions acceded to the advice of the council to reduce the number of police officers in order to save money, and by February 1837 the new force, having been established at thirty men a year before, had been reduced in two stages to twenty-four and then to eighteen men. Over the next few years, moreover, further economies were achieved by the demotion of an inspector to the rank of sergeant and by replacing a dismissed inspector by a sergeant.

It is clear that the motivations of councillors in making these changes were primarily to reduce the charge on the borough fund. For there is evidence that at the same time, if somewhat inconsistently, the corporation regarded its police powers as highly symbolic of its independence and status. On 8 May 1840 the council decided to present to Parliament a very strongly worded petition against a Bill to amend the law relating to the administration of local police forces. The Bill would have amalgamated the county and borough forces and the borough based its strong opposition on two aspects of its status. As might have been expected, the corporation stood very much on the dignity of its municipal history 'in resistance to the contemplated invasion of municipal rights', arguing that 'the . . . Borough has always possessed an independent and exclusive jurisdiction'. Less convincingly, in view of its attitude to expenditure in the previous five years, the petition went on to say that 'the Police Establishment of this Borough forms the main charge on the Borough Fund; and its regulation and control constitute by far the most important and responsible functions of the Corporation'. The corporation claimed to see the intended co-operation with the county police as almost apocalyptic: 'It is inconsistent with the very principle of our Municipal Institutions and will leave little more than the form and name of self-government.'

That policing and the administration of justice were by far the most important of the corporation's duties and the heaviest call on the borough fund is revealed by the summary figures for 1840 which show the income and expenditure of the council balanced at £3,692 10s 0$\frac{1}{2}$d of which £2,529 was raised by the borough rate. The principal items of expenditure were as follows:

Police and constables	£1045	9s	10$\frac{1}{2}$d
Jail, prisoners, etc.	£519	1s	1d
Administration of justice	£309	10s	4d
Public works, repairs, etc.	£422	10s	5d

Thus, over half the expenditure of the corporation was accounted for by matters arising from its policing, judicial and penal responsibilities.

As the new corporation concerned itself with economy, police and a minimalist concern with the state of the bridges and roads, pressures were building which would alter the balance of the council's work. Even in these earliest days, the physical environment of the town and its generally insanitary condition begin to obtrude on the deliberations of the council and its committees. In 1839, for example, the council decided to draw to the attention of the surveyors of the three parishes 'the disgraceful state of the public streets and highways within the Borough from accumulated mud and dirt and that when the streets are scraped the heaps formed thereby are allowed to remain without being removed'. At this time, however, the corporation appears not to have considered taking action itself, though as a body corporate it could presumably have entered into a contract to have the work done. It could also have used the access given by cross-membership to put pressure on the Paving Commissioners. Instead, the council requested the surveyors of the parishes to take immediate action.

As the figures in Chapter 1 indicated, Reading's population was growing steadily in the 1830s and 1840s and it continued to do so throughout the nineteenth century. This growth was in itself a pressure towards the development of municipal activity because, as the town's population increased, so the inevitable by-products of urban living had to be coped with. Quite simply, the primitive sanitary arrangements of a town of fewer than 10,000 inhabitants in 1801 were manifestly unsatisfactory as the population exceeded 20,000 in the 1840s. As Hennock (1973, p. 2) says, 'the growth of the urban population depended . . . on constant improvement in sanitary administration'. In Reading the time between diagnosis and satisfactory treatment was extended by controversies that say much about mid-Victorian values, about conceptions of the role of government and about the proper balance between the public and the private.

W. M. Childs, writing in 1910, detected 'about the years 1843 and 1844 . . . an old order of ideas and practice being submerged by the rising tide of innovation'. Certainly there is evidence in the 1840s of a growing concern in Reading, as there was in the country at large, with vital statistics, with the possibility that men working through their modernized local institutions might extend the lives of individuals and make individual lives more tolerable. These were the years running up to and including the investigations and report of the Health of Towns Commission, of the zealous propagandizing of Edwin Chadwick, Thomas Southwood Smith and the Bishop of London, of the practical application to perceived social evils of the utilitarian principles of investigation, report and innovation. In 1846 the Sewers and Drains Committee of the corporation presented to the council an extensive report on 'the alarming evils consequent on the defective sanitary arrangements of the borough'. Until this time, the role of the council in respect of sanitation had been generally reactive rather than active. Particular nuisances would be suppressed, offenders occasionally prosecuted, but local administration was not generally regarded as a matter either of prevention or improvement. Although few opponents of improvement went so far as to argue, as Alderman Brown was to do as late as 1859, that the prevention of fever was 'impious' and that to say that a good drainage system would prevent disease 'was saying more than mortal man ought to do', there was not until the 1840s any clear recognition of the link between sanitation and ill-health. In some ways it is surprising that this should have been so in Reading, for even before the town became part of the general public health reform movement in the 1840s, there was evidence of activity in the medical field of an enlightened kind. On the voluntary side, the People's Dispensary had been set up in 1802 by Doctors Thomas, Salmon and Barry, an Eye Infirmary was opened in 1826 and the Royal Berkshire Hospital was established in 1839, supported by public subscription despite antagonism from a section of the community who felt that the existence of the hospital would attract 'delicate and sick people' to the town (James, 1954, p. 17).

Additionally it had long been recognized that the natural environment of the town, surrounded by low-lying marshy ground between two rivers, was particularly conducive to epidemics of 'fever'. The connection between the discharge of sewage into the rivers and the health of the population that depended on these same rivers for water was not made until rather later. On the official side, the capacity of public institutions to contain the effects of infection had been experienced in Reading as elsewhere by the appointment, as early as 1831-2, of a Local Board of Health to deal with the cholera outbreak of that year. This board was composed of 'the Magistrates, the Medical Gentlemen, the Clergy, the Dissenting Ministers, and six other gentlemen from each Parish'.

In the 1840s it was the 'medical gentlemen' on the council, together with a letter from Mr Hooper (a surgeon and apothecary who was also an assessor to the Paving Commission) and 'a powerful memorial from other members of [the medical] profession resident within the town' that led the Sewers and Drains Committee to request from Mr John Billing a report on the sanitary condition of the town. On the basis of this report the committee, in December 1846, recommended that the council should seek an extension to their powers. This led to the Reading Improvement Bill controversy of 1847 and, eventually, to the application to Reading in 1850 of the provisions of the Public Health Act 1848 by which the corporation became the Local Board of Health. These developments are examined later in this chapter.

The information contained in Billing's report amounted to apparently irresistible pressure for action to improve the public health of the town. In 95 per cent of the borough there was no drainage of any kind, with domestic and commercial effluent discharged into cesspools that eventually soaked off into the streams and rivers and which commonly overflowed. Dr Southwood Smith, of the Royal Commission on the Health of Towns which produced the report that preceded the passage of the major public health legislation of 1848, described Reading in 1847 as 'nothing but an extended cesspool'. Of 4,155 houses, almost 2,000 had no water supply, and while 390 houses depended on the Kennet for water, almost three times that number 'with their privies, slaughterhouses, pig-styes etc., drain to these streams; consequently the water thus obtained [was] filthy and altogether unfitted for domestic uses'.

More compelling even than Billing's graphic description of the filth and squalor were his comprehensive statistics on mortality and morbidity showing how unfavourably Reading compared with other localities in what would now be called the quality of life. Billing's particular comparisons were with four other areas of Berkshire. His figures were impressively presented, clearly influenced by the passion for statistical information that characterized Victorian social reform movements. They showed that on all the major vital measures – death-rate, infant mortality, life expectancy – Reading's position was worse than that of the other areas. A resident of Reading could expect to live five years fewer than his neighbour in Easthampstead, Cookham and Wokingham. Later comparisons with towns in other parts of the country and with national vital statistics confirmed the unhealthiness of the borough. In the 1840s, for example, the general death-rate, as reported by the Registrar-General, was sixteen per thousand of the population. In Reading the figure was twenty-four per thousand in 1841 and thirty per thousand in 1849.

Other related factors can be seen to have been pressing the council in the same direction, towards a government initiative on 'improvement' of conditions. All three parish graveyards were already full to overflowing, and although there were a few other small burial grounds together with a new graveyard opened by the Reading Cemetery Company in 1843, there were no regulations to prevent continued use of the old churchyards. An observer at St Mary's is quoted by Daltry (1933, p. 128) as describing 'a gravedigger, spade in hand, chopping up a half-decomposed corpse, in order to make room for another grave'. Also, even without the impetus that would be given by the public health reforms, the town's population was already increasing as agricultural depression and industrial growth affected Berkshire much as it affected the rest of the country. In 1846 Huntley & Palmer employed only forty-one workers at their biscuit factory in Reading and, even before the immigration that the growth of the business would stimulate, George Palmer was writing to the *Reading Mercury* on 19 September protesting about the sanitary state of the town and supporting moves towards the promotion of a drainage Bill, by then under consideration by committees of the council. By the time of the 1851 census, 30 per cent of those Huntley & Palmer employees identifiable from the returns had come to Reading from

Berkshire, Oxfordshire and Hampshire (Corley, 1972, p. 98). However, the industrial development of the town was not far enough advanced for industrial pollution to contribute materially to the insanitary conditions in which the population lived. In 1850, William Lee in his *Report to the General Board of Health* (p. 12) concluded that 'there is no great staple trade employing the mass of the people, and that none of the occupations are such as to affect the health of those employed, much less to account for the excessive general rate of mortality'. In short, the nature of Reading's problems was clear by the mid-1840s. The attempts to find a solution were to occupy the politicians and political institutions for a quarter of a century.

The procedures for securing a private Act of Parliament in the mid-nineteenth century were such that Parliament would act only upon the receipt of a favourable report from a local inquiry conducted by surveying officers of the Commissioners of Her Majesty's Lands and Forests. The functions of such an inquiry were twofold. First, it had to examine the merits of the plan contained in the Bill, its practicability and the capacity of the promoters of the Bill, in Reading's case the corporation, to exercise the powers being sought. Second, the inquiry could assess the extent to which the promoters of the Bill were expressing the wishes of those they purported to represent. In this procedure may be seen the interplay among the values of representative local democracy, parliamentary sovereignty, local initiative and, in embryo, national standards. In terms of its effect on the government and politics of the locality to which the proposed new legislation would apply, the inquiry procedure guaranteed a forum, much like a modern planning inquiry, where local currents of opinion could be tested against each other.

Even before the inquiry was held in 1847, it was clear that the community was deeply divided on the issue of the drainage and sewerage scheme proposed in Billing's report and accepted in 1846 as the basis for the application for increased powers. Opposition to the scheme may be categorized as public and private. There was, as always, public hostility to any proposal which, however desirable in general terms, would cause an increase in the rates. More significantly, however, there was private opposition from vested interests which feared that they would be materially and financially disadvantaged by the new legislation. The Bill proposed, following

Billing's report that it was essential to obtain 'a constant supply of pure filtered water at high pressure', to empower the corporation to construct its own waterworks, drawing a supply from the Holy Brook. Such a proposal was bound to bring opposition from the existing Waterworks Company, especially since the Bill contained powers for the corporation to lease or acquire the works and property of the company.

Nor was the corporation unanimous in its pursuit of the new legislation. In March 1847 Alderman Thomas Rickford, a former Mayor and a long-serving member of the corporation who had also served on other public bodies (including the Poor Law Guardians and the Local Board of Health of 1831-2), resigned from the council because he would not 'be a party to the distressing taxation which [would] be entailed upon . . . the rate payers by the measures which a part of the Council are now taking'. His description of the 'monstrous powers' included in the Bill were a clear expression of hostility not only to the specifics of the proposed legislation but also to the extension of governmental power they implied, especially in respect of private property rights. This division on the council was to have repercussions long after the Improvement Bill controversy was over and was the source of some of the most acrimonious exchanges witnessed in the Council Chamber in the middle years of the century. W. S. Darter who was elected to the council in 1847 as an 'anti-sewage' candidate, later described his view of the council at this time: 'Nothing could be more disagreeable than our Corporation meetings . . . my aversion to them reminded me of my boyish feeling when going to school with the certainty of being thrashed' (Darter, 1888, p. 203).

Darter had, in fact, been active in the public opposition to the Improvement Bill and he was instrumental in calling a public meeting on the subject in December 1846. The *Reading Mercury* of 21 November 1846 contained a letter from Darter in the following terms:

I conceive as paramount . . . that a public meeting should be called to ascertain the feelings of the ratepayers as to whether they will allow themselves to be taxed . . . to meet the enormous outlay . . . upon a fresh act of Parliament and an entirely new system of drainage.

That meeting was held at the Town Hall on 22 December 1846 and it marked the point at which the public or ratepayer pressure against the Improvement Bill was joined to the private or commercial opposition. The motion against the Bill was moved by Edward Vines, a lawyer who was clerk to both the Reading Waterworks Company and the Reading Union Gas Company, and there were allegations that the water company had packed the meeting with its supporters. The motion was couched in terms which did not deny the need for some sanitary improvements but which doubted the wisdom of a private Act when it was anticipated that the government would soon introduce general legislation in response to the report of the Health of Towns Commission. The Reading Bill was, according to Vines's motion, 'premature and injudicious . . . calculated to subject the inhabitants to unnecessary expense and risk and [demanded] the decided opposition of this meeting'. After a debate notable more for its personal vilifications than its mature consideration of the issues, the motion was carried by a good majority. The flavour is conveyed by a *Berkshire Chronicle* report (26 December 1846) accusing one participant, Mr J. B. Monck, a shareholder in the Waterworks Company, of 'a barefaced attempt to disguise his pesonal interests under the cloak of indignant patriotism' and by an editorial deploring the public meeting as 'a melancholy exhibition of private interests and special pleading combining for the obstruction of the public good'.

It would be mistaken, however, in the context of the 1840s, to see private interests and public good as entirely separate and distinct. Behind the apparently self-interested opposition to interventionist legislation there often lay a genuine conviction that the role of public authorities could not properly be extended from the management of common assets and the punishment of offences into the promotion of public welfare. Conflict in localities between 'clean' and 'dirty' parties, between 'sewage' and 'anti-sewage', between 'improvers' and 'economizers' was common in the 1840s and 1850s throughout the country and there was a strongly held view among the conservative economizers that it was their duty not only to minimize the rate burden but also to defend the inalienable rights of Englishmen. The point is well made by Gill (1952, p. 273) in his history of Birmingham, when he comments that, for these extreme believers in *laissez-faire*, 'respect for an Englishman's home

extended to the drains' or, he might have added, to his right not to
have any drains at all. At this time also, *The Times* was thundering
against attempts to have the people 'bullied into health' and the
Berkshire Chronicle (26 December 1846), though not perhaps fully
comprehending the reasons for the embitterment of the controversy, was aware that something quite important was afoot: 'The
Town . . . is agitated to its centre – not as usual by the great issues
of religion and politics – but by a Bill for the improvement of the
Town.' As Fraser (1976, p. 10) perceptively noted, 'basic questions
about the legitimate use of power . . . were involved in the
mundane subjects of water and drains'.

In his report to the General Board of Health in 1850, William
Lee concluded that because the surveying officers who conducted
the month-long inquiry in February and March 1847 decided that
the corporation's scheme was impractical, 'the whole time occupied, and the money expended, was productive of no beneficial
result'. Certainly the Reading Improvement Bill and the comprehensive scheme of drainage and sewerage it proposed died with the
negative report of the surveying officers. However, the arguments
advanced both by the proponents and the opponents of the
corporation's scheme would influence the course of Reading's
municipal politics and government for two decades. Nobody was
actually against measures to improve the health of the town. In the
1840s, and on many occasions thereafter, opposition, as the
Berkshire Chronicle, then the press champion of improvement in
apparent contradiction of its general stance as a Conservative paper,
drily commented in 1846, was based on 'the short-sighted
objections of those who look only to the pounds, shillings and
pence view of it'. Of course, those who took such a view were
strategically placed as ratepayers, councillors and local notables to
influence the course of local policy.

The detailed and specific opposition to the Improvement Bill
1847 was based on criticism of the technical merit of Billing's plans
and on his estimates of the likely costs. On the face of it, the
technical and financial sections of the report to the Sewers and
Drains Committee on which the decision to apply for a new Act
was based are less convincing than the statistical section on the
health of the town. It is worth emphasizing here two factors about
John Billing. First, he was not a full-time official of the
corporation. There were no full-time salaried officers until the

appointment of John Marshall as Surveyor to the Local Board of Health in 1856. Billing was a local contractor who became Borough Surveyor in 1849. According to Lee (1850), he had, together with his father, for many years done most of the corporation's business. He was not, therefore, disinterested. He probably stood to gain major contracts under the proposed legislation and it would have been in his interests to minimize the likely costs and maximize the probable benefits.

Opponents were particularly critical of Billing's claim that the utilization of sewage for agricultural purposes (that is, as fertilizer) would 'effect a diminution rather than an increase in the burdens of the town'. At the inquiry no evidence was produced to support the assertion that farmers would buy the sewage, and while it is true that the sewage farm or irrigation method of purification and disposal was eventually adopted by the council in 1870, the process could be argued to be self-financing only in revenue terms, the capital costs being submerged in the overall debt of the corporation. The same criticism could clearly be levelled at Billing's estimate of the costs of sewage works under his scheme which exactly balanced the cost of servicing the loan needed by the revenue from the sale of sewage manure. Any shortfall in revenue would, of course, have been a charge on the borough rate.

Also, as John Berry Clacy, Billing's rival for the post of Surveyor to the Local Board of Health, was quick to point out in 1851, the surveying officers had commented very unfavourably on the inadequacy of the proposed water supply in the Billing scheme. Clacy said that the 1847 scheme was 'characterised by a recklessness of expenditure almost beyond credibility' and regretted, perhaps a little piously for one currying favour with a board dominated, as a direct result of the 1847 controversy, by anti-sewage economizers, that the scheme had created 'an aversion to even the necessary sanitary requirements . . . [and] much dissension and ill-feeling'.

It was true that in the elections of 1847 and 1848, the supporters of the Improvement Bill had been routed. As the *Berkshire Chronicle* (5 October 1850) acutely observed when it had become clear that the corporation would be designated the Local Board of Health under the 1848 general legislation, the Improvement Bill controversy had so split the council as to render any positive response to the new arrangements problematical. There were three 'parties' in the corporation: the 'most numerous section' which opposed all sanitary measures; the opponents of the 1847 Bill who claimed to favour a general Act but, having been 'carried triumphantly into the Town Council upon the strength of anti-sanitary agitation' now had to be 'advocates of a general measure'; and the promoters of the 1847 Bill who now took 'no public or active part in bringing the General Act into operation'.

The protagonists of the Reading Improvement Bill were, to some extent, impaled on the Morton's Fork of their own localism. Their counsel at the inquiry, Samuel Warren, had played the localist card in arguing against legislation that might involve oversight by national inspectors, 'strangers to, and unconnected with, the town'. It was infinitely preferable to vest 'the powers and authorities . . . in the responsible governing body of the town . . . whose interest in the welfare of the town is identical with that of their fellow ratepayers and inhabitants'. Thus, despite their enthusiasm for improvement, they were in some difficulty in supporting the application of the Public Health Act 1848 to Reading, involving as it did the supervision of the corporation as the Local Board of Health by the national General Board of Health. Localism, then, took two forms: that of *laissez-faire* liberals opposed to all extensions of government; and that of those opposed only to the invasion by central government of what they regarded as inalienable municipal rights.

The bitterness engendered by the controversy simmered on for years after the immediate issue had been resolved, and beyond the designation in 1850 of the corporation as the Local Board of Health. During the dispute over the Bill, the opponents had turned up a Chancery Division precedent that seemed to suggest that in the event of the legislation failing, the costs of the promotion of the Bill and of the inquiry associated with it should be borne, not by the council as a body corporate but by the individual members of the council who had supported the application to Parliament. The costs, as detailed in a reply to a question from Councillor Hobbs who, before his election, had raised the issue of liability for costs in a letter to the *Reading Mercury* (10 June 1848), amounted to just under £3,000.

Almost £2,000 of the total was for professional fees to the Town Clerk, J. J. Blandy, who eventually issued a writ for payment against the corporation. It seems clear that the issue of whether the

corporation or Blandy as an individual should bear these costs
became confused with another dispute involving the retention by
Blandy of moneys paid to the corporation by the Great Western
Railway Company. The point at issue was that the Town Clerk
held £975 of the corporation's money at a time when the
corporation found it necessary, in 1846, to raise a temporary loan of
£300. The costs of the Improvement Bill were finally paid by public
subscription, but the dispute was symptomatic of what James
(1954, p. 47) refers to as 'the lack of administrative machinery and
men with administrative training' in mid-nineteenth-century public
authorities.

The difficulties associated with the Reading Improvement Bill
show an authority grappling with problems with which it was ill-
designed to cope. The line between the public and the private was
unclear and continuously shifting: J. J. Blandy was a prominent
solicitor who charged his professional rates when acting for the
corporation, but as Town Clerk he had certain ancient rights and
privileges as a member of the body corporate. The matter of the
money paid to the council, through the Town Clerk, by the Great
Western Railway Company was resolved by the simple procedure
of referring to a minute of 1846 which had authorized the Town
Clerk to receive such payments on behalf of the corporation. In the
mean time, however, confusion was apparent in the council's
request to the Town Clerk to advise them on the course to be
adopted in the matter of his own action against them. Wisely,
Blandy declined to do so. The effects of the Improvement Bill
controversy can hardly be better illustrated than by this passage
from Blandy's answer to charges against him which were 'devised
less by a zeal for the interests of the Borough than by the envious
hostility of professional rivalry'.

> The Tribunal before which I appear, and by which I shall be
> judged is now in some measure composed of those whose
> accession to office has been facilitated by the active and
> persevering dissemination of those very charges on which it
> now becomes their duty to adjudicate.

The first major legislative triumph of the public health
movement was the passage in August 1848 of the Public Health
Act. In national terms its significance lay in the fact that it

established, for a five-year term in the first instance, a national body whose job it would be to inspect and supervise the work of local institutions. The powers, duties and functions of local authorities could now be enlarged, without recourse to a local Act of Parliament, by action of the General Board of Health which could establish a Local Board of Health on the petition of at least 10 per cent of the residents of a local authority area or after a request from the corporation of a borough. In boroughs, normal practice was to designate the Town Council as the Local Board of Health, subject to election to it, for sanitary purposes only, of representatives from any area included in the jurisdiction of the Local Board of Health (LBH) but lying outside the municipal boundaries. An LBH, as soon as it was constituted, had all the powers given to such bodies by the Public Health Act 1848, a consolidating as well as innovating measure which contained, as an automatic grant of powers, the many 'model clauses' which, up to 1848, had to be included in private Acts in order to make them effective in a particular locality.

Perhaps not surprisingly, given the divisions created by the Improvement Bill, the Town Council was not prepared to take any immediate initiative to have the new measure applied to Reading. When opinion is deeply divided, the soft option for any political body is to do nothing. Also, in the absence of any major change in public opinion, there was an apparently democratic basis for the anti-improvement views of the majority of the council as identified by the *Berkshire Chronicle* at the conclusion of the dispute over the Bill. In the months after the failure of the corporation's Local Bill, however, there occurred certain changes of attitude and allegiance which had an effect on the course of institutional change in the town. As with the issue of the Bill, however, these developments stemmed both from public interest and from concern with private rights.

The most public change was in the attitude of the *Reading Mercury* which, throughout 1846 and 1847, had been the spokesman of what its rival and competitor, the *Berkshire Chronicle*, called 'the filth and fever interest'. Quite suddenly in January 1849 the editorial line of the *Mercury* changed completely and began to support an immediate application for the Public Health Act – sometimes called the Health of Towns Act – to come into force in Reading with the corporation as LBH. Explanations for this volte-face need to be a little tentative, but contemporary sources suggest that, once again, the confusion between the public and the private was significant. When it occurred, the editor of the *Berkshire Chronicle* was clearly enraged. Having consistently supported sanitary reform, the *Chronicle*'s contempt for its new ally was obvious: 'Its [the *Reading Mercury*'s] venal columns were prostituted to support the presumed interest of a trading company . . . [and] the cause [of improvement] was seriously damaged.' The allegation was made that Edward Vines, then Clerk to the Reading Waterworks Company, had written the anti-Improvement Bill copy for the *Mercury* in 1846-7 and that in 1849 he was writing the material in favour of the establishment of a Local Board of Health. In the interim, however, he had been the leading figure in the establishment of a new company, the Reading Union Water Works Company, which had begun the process of seeking private Act powers to allow it to operate in Reading in competition with the old company. The inquiry of 1847 had revealed the inadequacy of the existing water supply and had emphasized that although it regarded the corporation's scheme as impracticable, there was an urgent need for remedial measures in the town. First among such measures would be the provision of a reliable and continuous supply of pure water. It was easy to infer that the establishment of an LBH, the members of which would be the Town Council of whom a clear majority opposed increasing direct municipal expenditure, would be likely to create a major commercial opportunity for a company able to guarantee supply, both for domestic use and for drainage in any comprehensive scheme which might be implemented under the direction of the LBH. Thus the success of the new water company, whatever the specific statutory basis upon which it was set up and permitted to trade, was intimately connected with the application to Reading of the provisions of the 1848 legislation. What had to be avoided was the construction by a new LBH of its own waterworks. For whatever reasons, both of the local newspapers by early 1849 favoured the application to Reading of the new public health legislation.

During 1849 the pro-improvement party was at work, collecting signatures for a petition to the General Board of Health in favour of bringing Reading under the provisions of the new Act. Eventually, about one-third of the inhabitants expressed support in this way and the General Board of Health appointed William Lee to produce a report with recommendations on the possible establishment of an LBH. Thus the second government inquiry in three years into the public health needs of the borough was undertaken and its findings constituted the basis for a major extension to the powers, if not of the activities, of the corporation.

The Town Council, though unwilling or unable to take the lead in the matter of the Public Health Act, could hardly ignore the fact that the procedures specified in the legislation had been set in motion by the petition, especially since the outcome was likely to be a substantial increase in its powers as a corporate body. On 3 February 1848 a resolution in support of the Health of Towns Bill and therefore by implication its application to Reading was moved in council and passed by fourteen votes to three. Despite this the opinion was later expressed by the Mayor that the measure was 'an imperfect attempt to improve the sanitary conditions of the country and did not meet the requirement of [Reading's] inhabitants for there was no provision for an unlimited supply of water which . . . would render the whole scheme abortive'. This statement is, perhaps, an example of another strand of thought among those civic leaders of Reading who consistently opposed the execution of major sewerage works until action was forced on the council by the Thames Conservators in 1868: that the public authority ought not to do anything because it could not do everything.

William Lee in 1850 drew heavily on the information presented to the 1847 inquiry, and he fully endorsed its conclusion that major sanitary works were both necessary and urgent. There was no doubt, therefore, that he would recommend the application to Reading of the Public Health Act 1848, with the council as the Local Board of Health. In one particular, however, Lee's recommendations can be seen, in the perspective of history, to have cast a long shadow before them. Both in the body of the report and in the recommendations relating to the creation of the Reading LBH, Lee recognized a problem that would be a recurrent one in the government of Reading for the next century and more: the lack of correspondence or 'fit' between Reading as a local government area and Reading as a social and economic entity. As the report put it, 'a consolidation of existing jurisdiction is very desirable, both for economy and efficiency'. That consolidation was partly institutional, with the powers of a Local Board of Health vested in the corporation and the remaining powers of the Paving Commissioners under the Acts of 1785 and 1826 transferred to the new body. But it was also concerned with boundaries, with a recommendation that, 'for the purpose of drainage, the Hamlet of Whitley shall be included within the district to be brought under the operation of the Public Health Act'. This involved the election to the LBH, for these purposes only, of three representatives from Whitley, and it was the first official indication that Reading's municipal boundaries might be obsolescent. It also created a confusion that could be used by those members of the corporation who sought ways of limiting the activities of the LBH.

It must be noted here that the appointment of a Local Board of Health was in no way a guarantee that anything would be done. An inspector's report might identify the problems, recommend the solutions and ensure the creation of the necessary institutions. It could not oblige the new board to act. Although the Public Health Act 1848 is rightly regarded as an important victory in the battle for public health and a key point in the development of the local government system, it was passed at a time when the conflict between a pre-modern conception of localism and local self-government, on the one hand, and a scientifically based view of the duty of government to promote the general welfare, on the other, had not yet been resolved in favour of the right of the centre to oblige local authorities to act. The legislation, because of this, shows signs of the compromises necessary to get it passed. The General Board of Health was established to supervise but not to control, its enforcement powers being virtually non-existent except in conditions of epidemic; it was to last for only five years, further legislation being necessary to prolong its life. (In fact, it lapsed in 1858, in the last great parliamentary victory of the localists.) Parliament, despite the *dirigisme* of the public health reformers, trod warily where ancient rights of self-government were argued to be at risk. And that wariness made it possible for the less progressive of councils, of which at least until the 1870s Reading was one, to respond to the new arrangements in a way which was, at best, grudging and minimalist.

The application to Reading in August 1850 of the Public Health Act 1848 created, in legal terms, a new local authority with power to levy a rate. But, as in the other boroughs, the LBH was identical (or nearly so) to the corporation and it will be simplest to refer to the body from now on as the council or the corporation. It will normally be clear from the context in what capacity the body was acting – corporation or Local Board of Health – and, when it is not, specific clarification will be given. The institutional distinction between the two, as will be seen later, disappeared almost entirely with the Public Health Act 1872, although the legal necessity of levying (though not collecting) the borough rate under the Municipal Corporations Act and the general district rate under the Public Health Acts endured until 1926.

The recommendations of Lee's report were detailed and specific. Although the council was dilatory in carrying them into effect, they helped to create the conditions under which the responsibilities of the corporation would eventually be extended beyond the promotion of the public health into the provision of services, the protection of the environment and the planning of urban development. The provisional order by which the LBH was created empowered the council to acquire one or both of the existing gas companies. It recommended that the application of the Reading Union Water Works Company to have included in its private Act a power to levy a water rate be opposed because it would leave the LBH without adequate power to insist on the extension of supply to most of the houses in the borough or to ensure, in Lee's words, 'a PROPER supply of water *within the maximum fixed by the Public Health Act*' (emphases in original). It suggested that the waterworks 'should be capable of extension to meet the future requirements of the inhabitants, without taxing the present generation for the benefit of posterity'. When the Reading Waterworks Act was eventually passed in 1851, it represented an attempt at balance between the public and private interest in that while investment and supply would be privately organized, the sale of water both to the public and to the council, would be subject to maximum charges specified in the Act. The cost of water was, in fact, substantially reduced after 1851, and the supply became more reliable. However, the incorporation of the new company, and the application of the Public Health Act maximum charges to it, effectively secured the objective of preventing the council from constructing its own works, ensuring that the only alternative to controlling supply statutorily and contractually would be the eventual purchase of the company, an outcome delayed until 1868.

Others of Lee's recommendations amounted to a possible agenda for environmental action by the council. There were references to the provision of new cemeteries (left in the hands of the Reading Cemetery Company, which the council did not seek to acquire until 1887), improved paving and street cleaning, opening up the town by building new streets that would allow 'better public and private ventilation' and dealing with what was by then a perennial Reading problem, the proliferation of slaughterhouses in the centre of the town. All of these implied a greatly enhanced role for an active corporation and the last made possible an extension of the trading activities of the council when, in 1860, the corporation provided public abattoirs to replace those private slaughterhouses that were closed down by regulatory by-laws under the Public Health Acts.

The legislation, however, was permissive rather than mandatory and, despite the presence on the council of some improvers, including George Palmer, an outspoken and consistent supporter of sanitary reform, who was first elected in 1850, the majority of the corporation were intent in the 1850s on doing as little as possible. Some members, like Councillor Brown, denied the necessity of any measures to improve sanitation, drainage or sewerage. Others, such as Thomas Rogers and William Hobbs, relied on more subtle delaying tactics. Rogers was nothing if not inventive in reconciling his public support for general legislation with his private distaste for doing anything that would cost money. At the first meeting of the council sitting as the Local Board of Health, in September 1850, he proposed that the board should investigate 'the general character and extent of its powers' before doing anything, including the appointment of officers. When this was defeated, by two votes, Rogers refused to recognize the appointment of J. J. Blandy, the Town Clerk, as Clerk to the Board, whereupon a motion was carried unanimously to the effect that the serving officers of the Paving Commission should act for the LBH until permanent appointments could be made. (The omnipresent J. J. Blandy was, for the moment, unaffected by this manoeuvre, since he was also Clerk to the Paving Commission. His position, however, was vulnerable, as will be seen later.) At this point the council reversed its earlier decision and unanimously passed Rogers's original motion. At the same meeting, apparently in justification of his delaying motion, Rogers objected to the council acting corporately as the LBH until members were acquainted with the nature of their duties. Hobbs, for his part, signalled the intention of many of his colleagues to hasten slowly by saying, after objecting that the petition in support of the Public Health Act had not been made available for public inspection, 'It is now law, and we must obey it, though I shall take my part in it most reluctantly'. A month later Rogers objected to the making of the general district rate on the grounds that 'it was being forced on with undue haste . . . to give an impetus to the opposition [to the implementation of the Act]' in order to affect the municipal elections due to take place in November.

Throughout all this, Rogers can be seen to have been pursuing his own interests as well as working to minimize the activities of the council under the Public Health Acts. Between November 1850 and July 1851 he progressed from the office of councillor, to that of alderman and finally to the position of Clerk to the Local Board of Health, an office he held until 1873, combining it for the final seven years, after the death of J. J. Blandy, with that of Town Clerk. It is difficult to disagree with Cook's judgement that by the end of the 1860s Rogers had become 'the sole potentate in the town' (Cook, 1970, p. 115), a description given added point by the fact that from 1852 he was also Liberal Party agent for parliamentary elections in Reading.

Rogers's rapid transit to the office of Clerk to the LBH was facilitated by the effects of the multiple office holding of the other outstanding local notable of the mid-nineteenth century, John Jackson Blandy. Blandy was in 1850 Town Clerk (an office he held for thirty-three years, 1833-66), Clerk to the Paving Commission, Clerk to the Reading Waterworks Company, Clerk to the Reading Gas Light Company, Coroner, Clerk to the Charity Trustees, and much else besides, of both a commercial and a philanthropic kind. He had also been for short periods a member of the Corporation, serving as Mayor in 1831. It was, however, his commercial connections with the Waterworks Company that attracted criticism. As early as February 1850, before Lee's inquiry and before the designation of the Council as LBH, a motion had been moved in Council to the effect that Blandy's position as solicitor to the Reading Waterworks Company was 'incompatible with his duties as Legal Adviser of the Corporation . . . especially in reference to . . . the Health of Towns Act and the rival claims of [the two water companies]'. Although this motion, which implicitly denied the distinction between the corporation and a Local Board of Health, was defeated by fourteen votes to three, it raised the issue which led in January 1851, after only three months in office, to his removal as Clerk pro tem to the LBH. The issue of conflicts and dualities of interest was rather complex at this time, but there seem to have been some conflicts that were unacceptable, particularly those where a pecuniary interest was associated with a contractual relationship with the public authorities, as was the case with both the water company and the gas company. For a short period after Blandy's removal, Joseph Whatley, Clerk of the Peace to the Borough Quarter Sessions, acted as Clerk to the LBH until Rogers's election in July. Blandy, however, continued as Town Clerk since despite the near identity of the corporation with the LBH, the contractual relationships for gas and water supply did not involve the borough council in its corporate capacity. This outcome meant that Reading began the period of extended local jurisdiction under the Public Health Act unable to comply with one of the earliest Minutes of Instruction from the General Board of Health to local boards that 'for the sake of unity of functions and economy, the General Board would recommend the appointment of the Town Clerk in all cases'. The minute went on to say that 'the policy of the Act, throughout, favours the consolidation of offices'. Such consolidation had to await the death of J. J. Blandy in 1866.

The judgement as to what constituted a conflict of interest did not, however, extend to what a correspondent to the *Berkshire Chronicle* in July 1851 described as appointment decisions in which the council showed itself to be 'wanting in independence and guilty of unseemly favouritism'. For not only was Rogers appointed Clerk before his resignation as an alderman, the only other office under the Local Board of Health filled at this time went to John B. Clacy who had to resign as a councillor in order to accept appointment as Surveyor to the Board. The picture is completed by noting that several other members of the council were directors or shareholders in the utility companies including the Mayor, William Silver Darter, who was on the board of the new Reading Union Water Works Company.

Given the local political background, and the state of opinion on the council at the time when it became the Local Board of Health, Reading can hardly be said to have made an auspicious beginning to local government under the Public Health Act. An already unpromising political climate was further complicated when serious doubts were raised about the legal powers of the council and the soundness of the provisional order under which the Act was applied to Reading. (The Provisional Order procedure was a form of delegated legislation much used by the General Board of Health, and its successors as the supervisory department for local government. Orders had immediate effect and were provisional only in the sense of requiring later ratification by Act of Parliament, a requirement that was usually met by the passage of omnibus Provisional Order Confirmation Acts dealing *en bloc* with a large number of orders.) The legal doubts were raised soon after the establishment of the LBH, and they related to that part of the provisional order that extended the boundaries of the drainage and sewerage district to the Hamlet of Whitley. The argument was that the council might be acting *ultra vires* if it executed drainage works outside the borough boundaries because of a possible conflict between the provisional order and the terms of the Act under which it was made.

It is possible to take two views of the council's difficulties over its legal position. On one reading, it was perfectly reasonable and responsible to proceed cautiously, to act only in the certainty of legality, to be sure of the new board's powers and duties. On another, the legal issue, supporting as it did Rogers's pleas at the first meeting of the Local Board of Health that the board should be clear about its powers and its members fully acquainted with their duties, may be seen as a pretext or justification for delay on the most pressing issue facing the authority, the need for a comprehensive scheme of sewerage and drainage. The issue became public in August 1851, having exercised the board in Committee of the Whole throughout the preceding year. A report was published replying to charges in the press that the council were 'culpably neglecting their duties and even deliberately intending not to fulfil them'. Attempts to have the position clarified by the General Board of Health had been unsuccessful, and it seemed that the intention of the government was to extend the boundaries of the town, but only for drainage purposes. The report recommended that, pending clarification of the powers of the board in respect of Whitley, the authority 'should proceed with improvement within the Borough' where no doubts existed about its jurisdiction. James attributes the lack of urgency with which the board reached this apparently simple and obvious conclusion to the inadequacy of institutional arrangements and an absence of 'administrative training' (James,

1954, p. 47). There may also have been, once again, an absence of will. This possibility is given some credibility by the timing and the content of the LBH report of 22 August 1851. The possible significance of the timing arises from the 'veritable storm of abuse' which, according to the *Berkshire Chronicle* on 16 August, had been directed at the board's inactivity, particularly in the matter of sanitation. The minimalists on the council had, throughout the bitter controversies of the previous five years, shown some sensitivity to public opinion. The substance of the report was hardly radical. Its recommendation to proceed within the borough, pending clarification of the Whitley issue, was accompanied by a series of recommendations for remedial and improvement works of a more or less minor nature. Significantly these included a proposal to conduct a full 'map survey' of the town before major works could be undertaken. None of this reads like the product of a year's deep deliberation. Despite its moderation, some members, when the request was presented, opposed carrying out any works under the Public Health Act on economic and financial grounds. Provincial towns, like Reading, it was argued, had been badly affected by depression and were not therefore in a position to lay out large sums of money.

In the event, the council managed to postpone major capital expenditure on drainage and sewerage works until 1870, and the issue occupied council members and ratepayers recurrently for two decades. After the establishment of the Local Board of Health and the resolution of the legal doubts about its powers, the government of Reading became less subject to the acrimoniousness that had characterized the period between 1846 and 1851. The council as LBH set about organizing itself for the business indicated in the report of August 1851 by establishing three committees – finance, surveyor's and inspector's. These committees were given no delegated powers, all of their decisions being subject to approval by the whole board, but their establishment is significant because committees, unlike the council itself, met *in camera*. Writing in 1888, William Silver Darter, Mayor in 1850-1, graphically makes the point about the difference between open meetings of the council and closed meetings of its committees. When describing the bitterness of the conflict over improvement he says: 'Reference to the Reading papers will abundantly prove this, although they do not report the proceedings of committees, where the real business of the town is conducted, and, therefore do not furnish any notice of the altercations which so frequently occurred there.' Out of these altercations, and the discussions and deals associated with them, local policy was made and only the most important issues saw the light of public debate when council or board was divided on the recommendations brought to it by committees. Committee reports were dealt with by a process of exception: council would approve them with the exception of any item on which members indicated, by amendment moved in open meeting, a wish for a debate and a separate vote. Also, there was frequent recourse, throughout the nineteenth century, to the device of resolving council into Committee of the Whole, a procedure which had two consequences, one beneficial, the other potentially pernicious. It may be said in favour of the practice that it allowed all members to participate in the discussion of a matter too important to be considered only by a committee without the procedural limitations of debate in full council, where members could speak only once on any motion and, indeed, where discussion was possible only upon the basis of a formal resolution. On the other hand, it was not uncommon for the device of Committee of the Whole to be used to get round the provisions of the Municipal Corporations Act and the Public Health Acts that meetings of the body corporate should be open to the press and public. The issue of public access to civic decision-makers was a recurrent one in Reading, not resolved until it became mandatory, under the Local Government Act 1972, to open all meetings to press and public, except where matters of a sensitive or personal nature were under consideration.

The big issues, then, came to council, were fully debated and were extensively reported in the press. But the scope of government in Reading was being extended incrementally by decisions of committees, ratified by council and sometimes, where the publication of by-laws was involved, subject to central government approval. The concerns of the Local Board of Health, as indicated in the 1851 report, can be divided into two categories roughly corresponding to the modern distinction between revenue items and capital items. In respect of the first, the council would finance any expenditure out of the rates, with the consequent duty to balance income against expenditure. For capital items, it was necessary to raise a loan, for which government approval was required, and in respect of which the supervising department would specify the repayment period. Interest charges were paid from rate revenue and until the council found itself obliged to undertake the major sewerage works it so long postponed, the disposition of the majority was, almost invariably, to avoid increasing the municipal debt. Where the raising of a loan was unavoidable, the council tried to negotiate the longest possible repayment period, thus reducing the immediate call on the rate fund and avoiding the necessity for large increases in the level of the rate. The loan application procedure could also be rather irksome for the council, for it was a major access point through which central control could be exerted over local government. In 1852, for example, the council sought permission from the General Board of Health to borrow £6,000 for expenditure, recommended in the 1851 report, on paving, gutters and other environmental improvements. The response was to grant approval for a loan of £5,000 with a repayment period not exceeding fifteen years, with no reason given for either decision. The council decided to reapply. A further example of the conservative financial policies of the council in the middle decades of the nineteenth century occurred in 1864 when, because of a new system of metering the supply of gas to street lamps, the council found itself with a windfall saving of about £400 per annum. The Finance Committee recommended that the money should not be used to reduce the rates but for the 'execution of those special works of town improvement which have for a long time been pressing . . . and which in any other event must either be left unperformed or the expenses discharged by further loans upon the Rates'. The committee's view was that further debts should be avoided 'unless it be for an object of magnitude or very special importance'. This decision also demonstrated a lively perception of the unpopularity of rate increases. It showed considerable sensitivity to the fact that a decision not to reduce the rates is always less controversial than a decision to raise them.

The growth of government in Reading in the period between the establishment of the Local Board of Health and the major drainage scheme of the early 1870s then, was promoted in committee and financed, in the main, from revenue. In particular, the Inspector's Committee and the Surveyor's Committee gradually but inexorably increased the impact of the council on the life and character of the town. Even though it steadfastly refused to execute the drainage works declared to be essential as early as 1847 (an account of the council's consideration of the issue between 1850 and 1870 is given later in this chapter), the corporation, sometimes as a means of avoiding the more expensive initiatives, sometimes in response to external pressures, sometimes on the recommendation of its own officers, continuously extended the range of its functions. As a consequence, the nature of civic government gradually changed in the direction resisted by the economizers and still opposed by a minority of councillors. The corporation, as the Local Board of Health, promoted the public good in various ways from flushing the streets to providing recreation grounds, while the corporation, acting under the Municipal Corporations Act, ran the police, managed municipal assets and got itself caught up in an endless and ultimately unresolved wrangle about corn tolls, the Corn Exchange and, once more, the proper limits of public enterprise. The remainder of this chapter, before turning to the question of drainage and sewerage, examines the activities of the corporation in various policy fields and considers the institutional arrangements necessitated by the fact that, to quote a report submitted to the council in 1869, 'the business of the Corporate Body in [its] double character [had] assumed very large proportions'.

Improving the Environment

By the time that the Local Board of Health was established, and took over the functions of the Paving Commission, there was no shortage of information about what had to be done to improve the physical condition of the town. The 1847 inquiry, supplemented by Lee's Report of 1850 and the board's own plan of action of August 1851, constituted an agenda for improvement even for an authority determined to proceed cautiously, and as inexpensively as possible. Concern for the ratepayers, and sensitiveness about its own position as the rating authority, were continuous themes behind all of the council's activities. The *Berkshire Chronicle*'s view, when commenting on the defeat in Castle Ward in 1851 of a candidate pledged to a policy of improvement, that 'the minds of the ratepayers had been so imbued with the irrational anti-sewage feeling . . . that they would vote against anyone who supported those public improvements which required a consequent rate', probably underestimated hostility to local taxation and failed to perceive the identity of

interest between those who levied the rates and those who paid
them. The consequences of poor sanitation, except when they
fostered epidemics of serious disease such as typhoid and cholera
which respected no social barriers, were felt by the poor and
unenfranchised working class who neither counted as burgesses for
local electoral purposes nor paid rates in support of local
expenditure. The borough council at this time was overwhelmingly
middle class, composed, to quote Hennock (1973, p. 10) writing
about other towns, of 'those who could spare the time, who had
arrived where they were content to be'. In Reading there were also
those who saw some personal advantage, both direct and indirect,
accruing from their membership.

Sensitiveness about the rates is evident in the anxiety of the
LBH, in October 1851, that 'the ratepayers should distinctly
perceive what expenses are attendant on the special provisions of
the [Public Health] Act and what those are which arise out of the
consolidation of former authorities in one body'. The point here
was the incorporation in the general district rate, set at 2s in the
pound, of the former paving rate and highways rate. (There is a
similarity here with the concern, when Reading lost its municipal
independence in 1974, that the ratepayers should know what
proportion of their rate demand was accounted for by the county
council precept.) Also, as a prelude to the frequent memorials from
ratepayers pressing expenditure control on the council which were
presented throughout this early period, the council had received,
on the eve of its designation as the Local Board of Health, a
resolution from the St Mary's Vestry Meeting expressing the hope
'that it is and will be the study of [the] Council to reduce
expenditure of the Borough as much as it is in their power to do'.

The environmental activities of the council may be characterized
under three broad headings, though these do not represent
watertight, discrete categories. First of all, and of particular
significance to the changing conception of the role of government,
the council after 1850 steadily increased its powers and duties in
the fields of regulation and licensing. The 1851 report to the Local
Board of Health recommended by-laws to fix the number of lodgers
permitted in any registered common lodging house and to allow
inspection of such premises. In October 1851 the General Board of
Health drew to the council's attention its powers under the
Common Lodging Houses Act 1851 and the Labouring Classes

Lodging Houses Act 1851. In reporting to the LBH, a Committee of the Whole Board said that these Acts should be carefully considered and, in a tone of moral absolutism that chimed well with the sometimes slightly sanctimonious paternalism of mid-Victorian social reformers, noted that 'these statutes . . . are directed against a very chief source of physical pestilence as well as moral depravity among the labouring classes'. Concern about the physical and moral conditions of lodging houses in the borough had formed part of Lee's report on the application to the town of the Public Health Act, with the conditions in Silver Street particularly singled out 'for there the evils were aggravated by numerous lodging houses for prostitutes, thieves, tramps and Irish'. Quite apart from what these comments say about Victorian social attitudes, the registration, inspection and licensing power which they were employed to justify represented an extension to the regulatory power of local government.

Similarly the 1851 report directed the board's attention to the problem of the large number of slaughterhouses in the populated areas of the town. Not only was this insanitary in itself, but also it was associated with various trades of a noxious character such as blood-boiling, bone-crushing and fell-mongering, all concerned with the manufacture of animal by-products. The environmental pollution from slaughterhouse trades occupied the Inspector of Nuisances throughout the 1850s, and the council moved first to prevent the licensing of any new slaughterhouses and the registration of existing ones and then, in 1855, to a decision in principle to erect public abattoirs which would allow action to close private slaughterhouses and so oblige butchers to use the new public facilities. The public abattoirs were opened in 1860 and since fees were charged for their use, their provision represented not only the logical conclusion of the council's regulatory powers but also an extension to its trading activities.

A third regulatory recommendation of the 1851 report related to the removal of refuse and the times and manner of cleansing and emptying waterclosets, privies and cesspools and proposed, as in the case of lodging houses and slaughterhouses, that the appropriate mechanism for control was the publication of by-laws that had to have the sanction of the Home Secretary before coming into effect. Council action in this field led, later in the period under consideration, not only to an increase in the regulatory powers of the public authority but also to an extension in the services provided, directly or under contract, by it. In 1861 it was decided to organize scavengering (as it was still called as a legacy from the Paving Commission) and the watering, repair and maintenance of roads on a continuous basis by dividing the borough into three districts and inviting tenders from outside contractors. Three years later, in a particular example of a general practice whereby elected members were, in the early modern period, more directly and formally involved in day-to-day civic administration, three groups of three members were appointed 'to inspect and report periodically on the condition of roads in their district'. This was a time before the development of a large full-time professional local authority staff and therefore the modern distinction, imperfectly perceived though it sometimes is, between the proper roles of officers and members had not developed. Hennock (1973, p. 317), commenting on Leeds and Birmingham, notes that 'it was still assumed in the 1860s and early 1870s . . . that the members . . . had a duty personally to inspect the town for nuisances'. In Reading, too, what in modern local government parlance is called the 'site visit' was a common feature of the work of members and not, as it tends to be today, an exceptional procedure resorted to only in cases of particular difficulty. In 1863, in what may be seen as the beginning of the employment by the council of its own workforce, the Local Board of Health decided that 'the works hitherto executed under contract should in future be undertaken by [the] Board and carried out by men to be employed by [the] Board under the direction of [the] Surveyor'. Thus the council began further to affect the life of the town as it became a direct employer as well as a service provider and a regulatory authority.

In the first fifteen years of the Local Board of Health, regulation was extended to cover obstruction of the highways and footways by shopkeepers displaying their goods (in respect of which, significantly, the council decided in 1855 to meet the defence costs of an action against the Inspector of Nuisances for seizure of goods) and to the licensing of hackney cabs and cab ranks in 1854. The council's power in these two areas, as well as in others, was extended by the Local Government Act 1858, which also increased the role of local government in local planning and building regulations. Finally, under the heading of regulation, the LBH acted in 1851, after a further report by Inspector Lee, to close the burial grounds of the three parish churches, despite opposition from the parochial authorities. From 1851 the Reading Cemetery Company, to which the ubiquitous Thomas Rogers was solicitor, had the monopoly on burials, interments taking place at its cemetery between the Wokingham and London Roads just outside the eastern boundary of the borough. Cemetery Junction is still a major Reading landmark, though the cemetery is no longer used.

In addition to the various statutory extensions to the regulatory powers of the corporation, there was some evidence of a developing view that the council ought to assume a role of moral leadership, that civic leaders should be allowed to exercise civic power in the interests of spiritual as well as physical improvement. In 1853, for example, Councillor George Palmer, in a debate on police expenditure, said that 'the main source of evil [is] in the numerous beer shops and public houses' and called upon the council to petition Parliament for their closure on Sundays. Again, in 1866, a special meeting of the council failed to produce a two-thirds majority in favour of the application to Reading of the Public Houses Closing Acts of 1864 and 1865, a decision that was reversed nine months later, despite a petition from wine and spirit merchants. On other occasions too, the council showed itself to have moved away from the restricted conception of its role that emerged after the passage of the Municipal Corporations Act 1835 and persisted for about two decades thereafter. In 1860, for example, the council, in response to a letter from the Wholesale Drapers' and Grocers' Society concerning the influence of the Railway Directors' Association in the House of Commons on the content of railway legislation, said that it would be 'happy to co-operate in any lawful measures [to prevent that influence being used] adversely to the interests of the community'. Statements of that kind, though not entailing either action or expenditure, reveal something of the view the council had of itself in relation to the town.

The second heading under which the activities of the council may be examined in this period is that of recreation, leisure and amenities. Although the major initiatives in this field – the adoption of the Public Libraries Act, the establishment of a municipal museum, the laying out of King's and Hill's Meadows and the acquisition of Prospect Park – came later in the century and early in the next, it is possible to see in the business of the council in the 1850s and the 1860s a further aspect of concern for the spiritual well-being of the community. In 1854 the corporation decided to purchase land at Forbury Hill to be opened to the public for pleasure and recreation. This was subsequently (in 1857) supplemented when the Local Board of Health decided to lay out an ornamental approach from the Forbury Pleasure Gardens to the Abbey Ruins and to raise money by subscription to pay half of the £1,000 cost of restoring the Abbey Gateway (members of the council starting the ball rolling with contributions of £100). The significance of these initiatives lies in the fact that they were entirely discretionary, with no obligation on the council to make such provision. The council, however, was slower in implementing its plans to provide public baths and wash-houses. A petition asking the council to use its powers to provide these facilities, financed by loans on the security of the rates, was presented in 1854. The *Berkshire Chronicle* reported that the petition 'when unfolded reached all round the council table' but by 1863 the LBH was still considering the matter.

By far the biggest impact on the life and environment of the town and its people during these early decades of expanded local government came from the efforts of the Local Board of Health to improve the physical conditions of life. The new corporate body was, after all, concerned with the *health* of the town and despite its reluctance to execute the main drainage and sewerage works, much was achieved between 1850 and 1870. By 1865, when the Survey and Highways Committees reported jointly on the general state of the health of the town and the measures taken to prevent epidemic disease, they were able to say that

> a good deal has been accomplished towards securing a satisfactory condition of the town. Nuisances of various kinds such as those arising from ill-drained courts and other places and overflowing cesspools and deposits and accumulations likely to become prejudicial to health have been overcome.

It went on to say, in a phrase that would have met with indignant opposition from many members fifteen years before, that 'compulsory steps' were taken when co-operation was not forthcoming from the residents.

Between 1851 and 1870 the council steadily grew in the

confidence with which it was prepared to deal with the most obvious manifestations of physical decay and unsalubriousness. Streets were widened by the acquisition of land for the purpose. Middle Row, the most notorious slum in the town, was acquired by the Local Board of Health partly by agreement with the corporation and partly by the use of compulsory purchase powers under the Public Health Act 1858, and demolished by unemployed men taken on for the purpose by the Public Relief Fund Committee administered by the Mayor. The council, in an early move into the fields of both building regulation and urban planning, decided in 1852 to acquire the site of the Oracle, the former centre of the long-defunct cloth trade, because its owners, the governors of Christ's Hospital, intended to 'grant the site on building leases which would lead to the erection of a large number of dwelling houses of an inferior class and thereby preclude the hope of effecting any improvement in that part of the borough'. In 1856 the process began of adopting as public streets thoroughfares that were hitherto private, a process that proceeded throughout the nineteenth century. The early rationale is important especially as the board used it as a basis for ignoring the previous advice of their Clerk that they had no power to adopt any highway until the private owners had put it in good repair. The Local Board of Health, according to the *Berkshire Chronicle* (29 November 1856), took the view that since the residents of the six streets in question contributed to 'the general expenditure' they ought not to be expected to pay for improvements in their neighbourhood. Once again, there can be seen an expansion of the notion of the public domain, and a shift in the line between the public and the private. Similarly, the more frequent use of compulsory purchase powers after 1858 in order to improve not only Middle Row but also Abbey Wall and London Street is evidence of a change in the attitude of councillors to their proper role in the government of the town. Towards the end of the period under discussion here, in 1865, the council decided to purchase almshouses in St Mary's Butts in order to widen the road. At about the same time it authorized the Surveyor to make a thorough inspection of the town and to identify 'any removable causes of disease' which the LBH had power to deal with. This was action far removed from the earlier practice of suppressing only those nuisances which, because of their serious-ness, pressed themselves on the attention of the authorities. In 1863 the Clerk to the LBH was instructed to prepare by-laws under the legislation of 1848 and 1858 to ensure 'observance of proper regulations on the erection of new buildings throughout the Borough'. Thus, although the council had not yet faced up to the necessity of major investment on underground sewerage works it was prepared not only to act to remedy obvious evils above ground but also to ensure that future development was controlled in such a way as to prevent the creation of sanitary problems. The borough was, by small and fitful steps, becoming a planning authority.

Protecting the Borough

The delegated power given to the Watch Committee ensured that, unlike other committees, it operated almost as a separate authority, always chaired by the Mayor, but still subject to the same economic and fiscal pressure which pushed the council into economy measures that sometimes verged on the pennypinching. As in the earlier period, the greater part of the expenditure from the borough rate fund was taken up by the police, and of that, the vast majority was spent on wages. In 1853 Councillor George Palmer used the figures as part of one of his frequent appeals for council action against the evils of drink, while at the same meeting a memorial was received from the police seeking a rise in wages because 'the police force of Reading are receiving the lowest wages of any in the Kingdom'. The dominance of police expenditure is striking but a little misleading. In 1853, of a total borough expenditure of £4,780, £2,300 was spent on 'the detection and punishment of crime', and although this figure amounts to some 48 per cent of the total, it must be remembered that council expenditure under the Public Health Acts and charged to the general district rate is not included. Still, police services were particularly labour-intensive and, if the Watch Committee sought to contain expenditure, holding down wages and manpower were the most reliable ways of achieving that object. As Wykes puts it in his short history of the Reading Borough Police, 'Reading had never been particularly generous to its police and the Chief Constable was continually harrying the Watch Committee into recommending pay scales more in line with those of other boroughs' (Wykes, 1968, p. 8). In a report to the council in November 1853, moreover, the manpower levels of the Reading Police were compared with those of police forces in fourteen other boroughs. These revealed that only two of the fourteen had police-to-population ratios less favourable than in Reading, where the figure was one constable per thousand population. Wykes may be right to point out (ibid., p. 8) that 'Reading posed no special problems of lawlessness', but while it may be plausible to argue that police establishments were bound to be higher in major ports and industrial cities such as Hull, Liverpool and Manchester, it is difficult to think that Bath (with 1 constable to every 636 people) and Cambridge (1 to 843) were notably less peaceable towns than Reading. Also, by the end of the century, the strength of the force had risen to only 62, still only 1 policeman for every 970 people.

Despite its spare staffing levels, the police force was never criticized by Her Majesty's Inspectors of Constabulary for failings in efficiency and effectiveness in the day-to-day policing of the town. In 1857, however, as part of his report to the Mayor, the inspector, Captain Willis, said that the lock-up cells at the police station, then situated at No. 2 The Forbury, were 'quite unfit for the detention of prisoners' and recommended various improvements there. The council's reaction to this report provides an excellent example of a common characteristic of Reading's civic decision-making at this time – a tendency to postpone expenditure until it became impossible to avoid and a determination to limit spending to the minimum necessary. The council was in receipt of a police grant from central government amounting to 25 per cent of the cost of pay and clothing, but payment of the money was dependent upon the award by the Home Secretary of a certificate of efficiency, the issue of which was in 1857 put in question by the criticisms of the cell accommodation. In August the Watch Committee recommended that the council build a new police station, together with lock-up cells and magistrates courts under one roof because a positive response to the inspector's criticisms was the only way to guarantee continuance of the grant. Because of delays in finding a site, a proposal to do more than the absolute minimum necessary to secure the grant and an abortive attempt to combine the new police buildings with an extension to the Corn Exchange in Friar Street, the new station, at High Bridge House, London Street, was not built until 1862. Even then, the conflict between the public and the private arose once again when the owner of what was regarded as the only suitable site, Councillor

William Blandy, said he would not sell it unless the proposals of the special subcommittee set up to consider the matter were passed by a large majority. Fortunately, the council voted by thirteen votes to four in favour of the plan.

This question of the borough council's response to external pressures also raised again the issue of central control and local self-government. Here the dual role of councillors as members of the corporation and of the Local Board of Health was making them more and more sensitive to the issue of central intervention in local affairs. The Local Board of Health was subject to various kinds of supervision by the General Board of Health, the Home Office and, in the matter of loan sanctions, the Treasury. At about this time, despite the temporary victory of localism in the abolition in 1858 of the General Board of Health, the idea of the independence of municipalities, actively proselytized by Joshua Toulmin Smith and his Anti-Centralization Society, was under severe pressure from the public health movement and the recurrent outbreaks of epidemic disease, especially Asiatic cholera. But there were in most councils members whose municipal memory went back beyond 1848 and they viewed with special distaste all efforts by the centre to exert control over the localities. In 1857, for example, commenting on the need to spend money to qualify for grant, the redoubtable Alderman Brown said that 'it was much to be regretted that Parliament, in passing measures urging on public improvements, did not at the same time decrease the difficulty and expense of carrying them out'. Here, early in Reading's modern municipal history, is the familiar lament about government laying duties on local authorities but expecting them to meet the expenses from the rates.

In police matters, during the period now under discussion, the corporation frequently defended the borough's independence, both against central interference in the running of the force and against proposals to amalgamate it with the county constabulary. Perhaps the most striking example was the council's response to the Police Bill 1856, when fears were expressed that the Watch Committee would become only 'a shadow of authority' and when the council was reminded that 'the right of self-government was an Englishman's privilege and birthright' and asked, in relation to the police grant that would accompany the extension of the Home Secretary's powers over borough police authorities, whether they were 'prepared to sell that birthright for an uncertain pittance'. Some members, however, saw some virtue in 'a little of that which was miscalled centralisation' and argued that the introduction of some general rules 'would be very useful for the Borough of Reading'. But the 1850s were the last years in which flights of oratory in defence of local self-government were common currency in Reading's civic debates. Thereafter, as increasing expenditure and increasing statutory obligations were accepted by councils, with varying amounts of reluctance and enthusiasm, English politicians, at the centre and in the localities, dropped the prefix 'self' from their vocabulary. The accepted term became 'local government' with the implication of partnership with the centre at best, subordination at worst. Little more was heard of local *independence.*

The establishment of Reading Fire Brigade may be dated from 1862, although two fire engines had been placed under the supervision of the Watch Committee and the operational control of the Superintendent of Police as early as 1844. In 1862 a report of the Watch Committee said that there was a need for a more efficient fire engine and a new 'Crystal Palace' type fire escape, and in August 1862 a full report said that 'although the police were trained in the use of the fire engines . . . experience has proved that they are not the proper persons to whom the actual working of the engines at a fire should be entrusted' because at such a time they were usually needed 'for other purposes more connected with the police service'. It was recognized that the regulations made in 1843-4, to have three trained men paid as firemen only when called out, needed to be brought up to date, and the committee recommended that more firemen be immediately appointed. The Berkshire Volunteer Rifles, a militia regiment based at the barracks on the Oxford Road just west of the borough boundary, had offered to act as a volunteer fire brigade under the direction of the Watch Committee. At this stage, however, the council decided to appoint a subcommittee to frame the regulations for the operation of a fire brigade. The result of the committee's deliberations was the appointment of five permanent staff – a head engineer, two first-class engineers and two second-class engineers – who would maintain the fire equipment by testing it once a month and who would man the two fire engines, supported by rifle corps volunteers under control of their own officers. A list of fire plugs would be prepared by the borough police and the keys for them kept with the fire engines at all times. The regulations for the engineers, who would be paid a retainer plus fees for attendance at fires and other emergencies, would be drawn up by the Watch Committee who would continue to supervise the fire brigade although it was part of the police only in the sense that it acted under the ultimate supervision of the Superintendent of Police. On numerous occasions during the next twenty years the council had to deal with offers of further assistance from privately organized fire brigades. In 1870 such an offer was turned down on the grounds that it would cause confusion because the town already had a brigade, but in 1881 the offer was accepted as long as the volunteers accepted the supervision of the police. The Fire Brigade became a totally independent department of the corporation in 1893.

Markets, Gas and Water

In the years before the rapid expansion of Huntley & Palmer as the major local industrial employer, Reading was essentially a market town and agricultural centre. Its geographical position, both before and after the coming of first the canals and then the railway (and, much later, major roads and motorways) guaranteed its status as such. Under its pre-reform charters the corporation of the borough was entitled to receive a corn toll, paid in kind, on all transactions carried on at the town's Corn Exchange. That right was carried forward, perhaps a little anachronistically, to the new corporation under the Municipal Corporations Act, and in 1851 it raised a short but bitter controversy about how a modern local authority should operate in relation to a trading activity by then more commercialized and capitalized than it had been when the original corn toll was introduced. Again the issue was one between public and private enterprise.

In December 1851 the Mayor, William Silver Darter, told the corporation that because of the agricultural depression then being experienced he was opposed to any increase in the level of the corn tolls. As a result, the council set up a subcommittee to consider the whole question of the declining revenue accruing to the corporation from the tolls. Clearly the emergence of this issue on council was only part of a general concern about the marketing facilities offered by the town. By August 1852 the *Berkshire Chronicle* was editorializing about the decline of 'this once leading market' and stressing the need for a new market with stalls to rent as 'a first-rate emporium for business'. In October a meeting took place at the George Hotel of 'buyers and sellers of corn attending the Reading Corn Market', which recommended that the practice of levying tolls, which was 'vexatious . . . to both the seller and the buyer and an impediment to the free transaction of business', be ended. It went on to call for the erection of a new Corn Exchange, thus raising, as George Palmer pointed out, the possibility of conflict of interest between farmers and ratepayers, the corporation not being in a position to levy a rate for the purpose, especially if it simultaneously lost the revenue from the corn toll. A committee, led by the highly visible Thomas Rogers, already Clerk to the Local Board of Health, was appointed to negotiate with the corporation.

Two issues were raised by the pressure applied to the corporation by the corn toll abolitionists, one constitutional and one socio-political. On the constitutional side, the question was whether the corporation had any right to commute the tolls into money by, for example, charging fees to market users or, as the most implacable opponents of the measure, Councillors Walford and Worgan claimed, to abolish the tolls altogether. The related socio-political question was whether it was proper for the corporation to indulge in 'an uncertain speculation' by setting up not only a new Corn Exchange but also a general market. The argument of the abolitionists was that this was an enterprise best left to private companies and in October 1852 Rogers, in a letter to Town Clerk Blandy, raised the memory of the Improvement Bill controversy by reminding the council of the 'objections so strongly urged in 1846 to the Council entering upon undertakings of a commercial or speculative character and embarking therein either the property of the ratepayers or subjecting them to taxation in respect thereof'. Rogers, on behalf of 'Gentlemen Interested in the Corn Market', proposed that the council should support the application of a private company for parliamentary powers to establish a general market and Corn Exchange. The Act would include provisions to abolish the corn tolls and to pay a royalty to the corporation in compensation for the loss of revenue. On the advice of the Borough Recorder, however, the corporation decided to apply for its own Act and in 1853 the Reading Corporation Markets Acts was passed, embodying all the changes sought by the abolitionists and the

'Gentlemen Interested' but empowering the council to operate the markets directly.

The controversy over the market was brief but, to quote the *Berkshire Chronicle* (23 April 1853) it became so 'bitter . . . [that] the project was in extreme jeopardy'. Pamphlets were published by Walford and Worgan on one side and by Darter and Blandy on the other. A public meeting was held, the opinion of which was disputed, with Councillor Brain protesting that the Bill, which in its original form was thrown out by Parliament although it was unopposed, was 'very different from what might have been expected after what transpired at the meeting'.

The new market was opened on 23 June 1856 and it represented a major addition to the trading activities of the council and, therefore, a further change in the nature of government in Reading. During the rest of the nineteenth century the council frequently considered, and just as frequently deferred, proposals to extend the market. Also, as will be discussed in a later chapter, it was this role of the corporation in the commercial life of the town that produced, in 1885 from Mayor Arthur Hill, one of the most extraordinary acts of municipal philanthropy in Reading's history. But, for the purpose of the present discussion, its significance lies in the fact that a council composed predominantly of traders saw it as part of the corporation's duty to provide, from public funds if necessary, premises in which trade could be carried on. It is perhaps evidence that the council had the public mood right that the costs of the promotion of the private Act of Parliament were met by public subscription, the corporation having no powers to incur the expenditure. Again, Reading's elected members may not have been unique in their attitude to the promotion of trade. Gill (1952, p. 320) reports that in mid-nineteenth-century Birmingham, where most innovations were suggested by officers and contractors to a council determined to do as little as possible, 'the one task which they took up spontaneously . . . was the formation of markets'.

Although the borough had powers under the Public Health Act to acquire by purchase the companies supplying gas and water for public purposes, it preferred, until the Local Board of Health bought out the waterworks as a necessary preliminary to the major drainage scheme of 1870, to use its governmental influence to control the prices it was charged rather than to move towards the direct provision of the services. As was discussed earlier, the maximum price charged to consumers of water was prescribed in the private legislation extending the powers of the Reading Waterworks Company in 1851, a provision that was included at the behest of the council which did not wish to build its own works at that time. For the next fifteen years relations between the council and the water supply company were generally uneventful, no doubt partly because members of the council were shareholders and directors of the company. Only once, in 1860, did the council refuse, presumably as a negotiating tactic, to pay what it described as an 'exorbitant' bill for the supply of water to the abattoirs and the Forbury Pleasure Grounds, but this constituted a small part of the contractual relationship between the council and the company.

In 1867, when, as will be seen in the next section of this chapter, the Local Board of Health found itself under irresistible pressure to do something about main drainage and sewerage, a report from the Borough Surveyor and the board's consulting engineer put the subject of municipalization of the waterworks firmly on the agenda. The tone of the report is a little diffident, reflecting perhaps the sensitiveness of the developing relationship between professional advisers and local decision-makers, but its import was clear. The authors said that although 'we do not think it is incumbent upon us to advise you . . . it is most desirable that sewerage and water supply should be under one direction'.

In 1868, as it became clear that major drainage works would be undertaken very soon, the Reading Waterworks Company published a notice of its application for new legislation to extend its works. The response of the Local Board of Health, harking back to the arguments employed twenty years before, was to resolve that 'in view of the possible necessity of the Local Board of Health acquiring the works of the Reading Waterworks Company for the sanitary requirements of the Borough', the Clerk should approach the company to ensure that any new legislation gave them sufficient power to transfer ownership to the public authority. After some disagreements about the respective powers of the company and the board, the waterworks were acquired by the LBH in 1868, thus greatly increasing both the indebtedness of the authority and its capacity comprehensively to plan the sanitary future of the borough.

The borough's relations with the two gas companies were less easy and they provide evidence of the council's readiness to employ its public corporate power in what it perceived to be in the interests of the town and its people, both as ratepayers and residents. The first thing to be noted is that from the beginning of the contractual relationship with the Local Board of Health there was no real competition between the companies. As early as 1850, both J. J. Blandy for the Reading Gas Light Company and Edward Vines for the Reading Union Gas Company, in evidence to the Lee inquiry, agreed that amalgamation of the companies would be desirable. Amalgamation took place in 1861 after a price dispute in which, for the second time in five years, the council threatened to seek parliamentary powers to build their own works. Both disputes were concerned with the price charged to the council for gas for public lighting. In the first dispute, the companies, colluding together in a way which brought wholly justified allegations of monopoly power, sought to make continued supply dependent upon conditions which amounted to passing on to the Local Board of Health some of their capital costs. In particular, the companies sought to insist that the LBH should pay for laying all new gas mains further than 75 yards from existing ones. The Committee of the Whole Board set up to deal with the gas contractors said that it was convinced that 'a combination had been formed between the two companies having the two-fold object of dictating the conditions of the contract on securing a largely increased price for lighting'.

But in 1855, and again in 1861, it became clear that in a new era of extended government, the possible power of the public monopoly, with its legislative basis and its access both to rate-borne revenue and to preferential loans, was enough to overcome the apparent commercial power of a supplier monopoly. For, on both occasions, the Local Board of Health compelled the companies to come to terms by the simple tactic of publishing its intention to build its own gas works to supply its own needs. This, of course, would still have left the companies to supply private consumers, but their lighting contracts constituted a major part of their business, especially after 1858 when the council divided the borough into two districts, one to be lighted by each company at a common price.

On the occasion of the second dispute, the council received a petition from ratepayers opposing the application to Parliament on the grounds that 'the manufacture and sale of gas is purely a commercial speculation and public money ought not to be devoted to an object where so much risk is involved', clear evidence that the *laissez-faire* philosophy that opposed any kind of municipal trading had considerable life left in it, as it did throughout the nineteenth century. It is notable also that the language employed by opponents of municipal trading, or indeed of municipal capital expenditure, varied little whether the service concerned was sewerage, water supply, gas or markets. Nevertheless, even where a council did not take over the provision of public utilities, its capacity to dictate the terms of trade constituted an extension to public as against private power.

The Drainage of the Borough

That the council was sensitive about its failure to do anything convincing about the main sewerage of the town until it found itself with no alternative may be inferred from the sharpness of the Local Board of Health reply to evidence given in 1866 to the House of Commons Select Committee on the Thames Navigation Bill. Mr Robert Rawlinson, a civil engineer, had told the committee that 'schemes of drainage have been submitted to the Local Board of Reading and to their disgrace . . . they have been treated with the greatest contempt'. The council, in a reply that can only be called disingenuous, said that the 1858 scheme (to which attention is given later) 'was ultimately not proceeded with because of a difference of opinions as to the merits of the scheme . . . [and] the absence of any reliable evidence as to a safe and judicious method of disposing of the sewage'. For while there may have been those who had doubts about the technical feasibility of the 1858 scheme, its most vociferous opponents were the last standard bearers of the economizing movement of the 1840s.

Enough has already been said about the evidence that supported the need for a comprehensive drainage and sewerage system. In the fifteen years between 1851 and 1866, however, the council and ratepayer opinion continually addressed the issue and continually postponed doing anything about it. The records, however, do not support the view that the rejection of Borough Surveyor John Marshall's scheme in 1858 was solely because of doubts about the technical merits of the scheme. It is significant, first of all, that it took seven years, after the LBH had accepted the view of one of its committees that many of the 'nuisances' could not be dealt with 'until a better system of drainage has been carried out', for a comprehensive plan to be drawn up. Furthermore, in the intervening years the council had done some preparatory and investigatory work, in particular by authorizing a complete map survey of the town, but when it came to incurring the expenditure necessary actually to do anything the local government of Reading repeatedly came up against Fraser's 'basic questions about the legitimate use of power'. The issue was also affected by the ingenuity with which the value of localism as against centralization was employed by opponents of municipal expenditure and expansion. There was also, among the most extreme economizers, an attempt to expunge from the record any reference to the link between dirt and disease.

It is generally recognized that the four epidemics of Asiatic cholera that struck England between 1830 and 1865 helped to tip the balance of the argument about the limits of government in favour of interventionism and compulsion. In Reading there was an outbreak of cholera in 1854, following its appearance in the north of England the previous year. The board considered on 29 September 1853 a report recommending 'active measures of a precautionary character' such as flushing the streets, emptying cesspools, and so on. The report, however, emphasized the need for more fundamental measures. 'The necessity of an efficient system of drainage', it said, 'is being daily forced on [our] minds by constantly recurring evidences.' Without 'an efficient drainage', it went on, 'the utmost exertions of [the] Board . . . can produce only temporary and partial good', a point amply borne out by the failure of the precautionary measures of 1853 to prevent a cholera outbreak the following year. When the report was considered by the council, an amendment was moved by two of the extreme 'economizers', James Phillips and Henry James, 'that those parts of the report relating to the drainage of the town be omitted'. Although the amendment was withdrawn without coming to a vote, its proposition is evidence of the absence of consensus on either the necessity or the propriety of municipal action in this field, and the fact that it was withdrawn only 'after considerable discussion' suggests that its mover and seconder were not alone in their view.

The years between the establishment of the Local Board of Health and the rejection of Marshall's 1858 drainage scheme were characterized in Reading by frequent references to the issue of centralization and the financial burdens on ratepayers, both of which were skilfully employed by opponents of major capital expenditure. In 1854, for example, an attempt to commission a general scheme of drainage failed to get on to the drawing board, much less off it, because of a dispute about the relationship between the LBH and the General Board of Health and the contractual position of a consultant engineer in relation to the public authority. On receipt of the map survey of the borough, which the council had decided was an essential preliminary to the execution of drainage works, a Committee of the Whole Board decided by eight votes to five not to proceed to any drainage scheme, ostensibly because it expected that national legislation would soon alter the circumstances surrounding general drainage. The Home Secretary, Lord Palmerston, however, wrote to the LBH recommending that the works 'be proceeded with without delay' and the board so decided by a majority of four. There then followed an exchange of memorials, with the ratepayers using precisely the same words as those employed by the economizers on the council and the board stressing the importance of locally determined policy as against central compulsion. Two points should be made about the board's action in publishing its detailed memorial in favour of local action. First, it is evidence of a growing appreciation of the need to convince ratepayers and residents of the good intentions of the board. Second, its content was more generally directed to the issue of localism and centralization than particularly to the drainage of the town. In the event, this first attempt to produce a comprehensive scheme foundered upon the rock of centralization, as viewed by the engineer, Thomas Blackwell, who was invited by the board to design a scheme. He refused the commission because of the need to have the scheme approved by the General Board of Health who were 'understood to entertain peculiar notions quite at variance with engineering experience'. Also, he told the LBH, 'to obtain the concurrence of the General Board I must in effect become their officer and not yours'. The board proceeded no further with plans for main drainage until it authorized its own surveyor, John Marshall, to draw up a scheme in 1857.

Marshall's scheme was developed after a report from the Surveyor's Committee of the LBH to the effect that the question of sewerage was 'perpetually forced' upon them. There was opposition to authorizing the surveyor to prepare a plan with estimates, and the report was adopted only with the proviso that his expenses did not exceed £100. Marshall's scheme was costed at £9,000, a capital sum that would have required a 2d rate over thirty years, and the board decided to circulate it for comment. The plan was an issue in the municipal elections of 1858, in which two candidates who would ultimately vote against proceeding with the scheme were elected in contests which arose, according to the *Berkshire Chronicle* (30 October 1858), from 'dissatisfaction felt by many of the ratepayers with the public expenditure of the Borough, especially as connected with the Local Board of Health'. That dissatisfaction also found expression through the Ratepayers' Protection Society which opposed the drainage scheme on grounds of 'the general salubrity of the town' and which argued that 'the benefit . . . would not be commensurate with the enormous outlay required'.

The final debate on the scheme took place on 2 February 1859, the occasion when Alderman Brown talked about the 'impiety' of sewerage works and another opponent of the plan described sewerage schemes as 'in almost every instance a sanitary, and in all, a commercial failure'. The reference here is to the hostility of many members to any scheme the costs of which in the words of the *Berkshire Chronicle* (26 February 1859), editorializing after the decision not to implement the Marshall scheme, 'would necessarily be so large that, without a pecuniary return to mitigate the burden', the ratepayers would oppose it. The only possible financial return, and one which was far from certain, was the utilization of sewage for agricultural purposes. Objections to spending money were, however, clothed in the disguise of spurious technical criticisms. 'Sanitary science', Councillor Boorne argued, 'was yet in its infancy, and [the Board] ought to take warnings in the experience of others and not allow experiments to be tried upon them at their cost.' It is difficult to see in this debate the purely technical disagreements described in 1866 when the council sought to defend itself against condemnation in the House of Commons. Despite the efforts of George Palmer to persuade the council to submit the plan to the Home Secretary (the General Board of Health having by this time lapsed), for 'the sanction, approval or disapproval of a competent authority', the council rejected the scheme by twelve votes to eleven. The division list is revealing. Voting with the majority were both of the 'anti-sewerage' candidates elected in November 1858 (Councillors Hewett and Butler) and a third newcomer (Councillor Clark) elected at a by-election in Church Ward in January 1859 in which both candidates had opposed the drainage scheme. It is clear, then, that the defeat of the scheme was due more to objections to its cost than to doubts about its practicability or technical merit. By the narrowest of margins the council had exercised its local power not to act. But behind this decision, determined as it was by short-term ratepayer pressure exercised both by petition and through the electoral process, can be seen the weakening over time of anti-sewerage opinion. Several opponents of earlier schemes, including Aldermen Darter and Exall, were in favour of Marshall's scheme. The majority against it was composed of old-established economizers crucially strengthened by new members elected on a wave of ratepayer opposition to public expenditure. However, by not acting in 1859, the council effectively deprived itself of discretion and choice. Main drainage came to Reading when external pressure created an 'emergency' in the face of which the council had no alternative but to act.

In 1866 Reading Council found itself pushed into action by two developments, one private and one public, over which it had no control, and it is impossible not to note a mood of desperation in its actions and reactions. The corporation was on the run, making policy in a rush, trying to cope with an 'emergency' the nature of which it had recognized twenty years before. The chronology is simple. In December 1865 Henry Simonds, who had voted against the 1858 scheme, gave notice of a motion to refer the whole question of sewerage and drainage to a Committee of the Whole Council. In January 1866 the promoters of a private company issued notices of their intention to apply to Parliament for a Thames Purification Bill to enable them to build a sewage works near Reading. In March a committee of the LBH was appointed to investigate methods employed in other towns for the disposal of sewage. In May the council decided to petition Parliament against the Thames Navigation Bill, a measure to empower the Thames Conservators to issue notices to prevent any local authority from discharging sewage into the Thames and its tributaries.

While the external political and administrative pressures mounted, Reading Corporation was becoming convinced that the irrigation method of sewage disposal, first proposed in Reading by

John Billing in 1846, would have to be employed. In this, the council was in agreement with a developing national consensus, influentially expressed in a royal commission report in 1865 which had said that 'the right way to dispose of town sewage is to apply it continuously to the land, and that it is only by such application that the pollution of rivers can be avoided'. The committee appointed in March 1866 visited Croydon, Norwood, Worthing, Carlisle and Worksop and reported strongly in favour of the establishment of a sewage farm.

The decision in 1867 to acquire land outside the borough for the establishment of a sewage farm, together with the decision, already considered, to take over the waterworks, marks a major landmark in the government of Reading. The capacity of the corporation to affect the quality of life of the town was greatly enhanced. The municipal debt was greatly increased, a development that caused considerable controversy and, eventually, a comprehensive and innovatory recasting of the town's financial arrangements. The purchase of Manor Farm in Lower Whitley to accommodate the sewage farm emphasized once again the obsolescence of the municipal boundaries and formed a major part of the case for boundary extensions in 1887. The administrative needs of the corporation, already growing before 1870, increased and led quickly to plans for internal reorganization and the provision of new offices and a new Town Hall. Most of these developments are the subjects of the next chapter. This one concludes with a brief examination of the effects of increased government responsibilities in the conduct of the public business between 1850 and 1870.

The Conduct of the Public Business

The twenty years following the expansion of municipal activities stimulated by the application to Reading of the Public Health Act 1848 saw a continuous shifting and redefinition of the line between the public and the private. The period of redefinition began with the Municipal Corporations Act but the process quickened as the conception of the role of government changed from an emphasis on maintaining order and peace to a concentration on improvement and the prevention of disease. Such a change necessitated a greater use of public money, a more insistent call on the ratepayers to support the costs of government and, inevitably, the gradual development of a new definition of the stewardship of public resources.

Throughout the period, there were examples of conflicts of interest, favouritism and jobbery, but it is important to note that this was a time of change, a time when one view of municipal responsibility was in decline and another beginning to assert itself. In 1851 an attempt to nominate 'two intensely independent and anti-jobbing candidates' in Abbey Ward failed and two sitting members were returned unopposed. However, in 1852 accusations of favouritism were made against the corporation in regard to the appointment of policemen, with the *Berkshire Chronicle* (28 August 1852) commenting on the selection 'of untried men, often from personal recommendation and interest' and calling on the Watch Committee to increase salaries in order to recruit experienced men from the Metropolitan Police and so remove 'the charge of favouritism and patronage'. In the same month the corporation had to appoint a committee to investigate the question of nominations to scholarships at St John's College, Oxford, for which it was responsible as trustees of the Reading Free Grammar School. It had found itself in a dispute with the Charity Commissioners over the nomination to a scholarship of the son of a member of the council.

Of greater significance than these examples of favouritism and what might be called low-level corruption is the fact that on several occasions the auditors of both the corporation and the Local Board of Health refused to sign the accounts. At this time and for a long time after the accounts of the borough council, both as the corporation and as the Local Board, were audited by an elected auditor and by a mayor's auditor, and for the period under discussion one of these posts was held by George Lovejoy, a bookseller and printer of London Street. Until a few weeks before his death in 1883, Lovejoy campaigned for better public accountability by the publication of properly audited accounts showing, as he and his co-auditor argued in refusing to sign the LBH accounts in 1864, 'full information as to how the money comes in, and how the money goes out'. In 1857, 1858 and 1864 there were disputes about the accounts. Lovejoy claimed in 1857 the right not only to declare the borough accounts to be technically correct (which they were) but also to pass judgement upon whether certain expenditures were legitimate. To some extent, Lovejoy's argument was before its time, though he supported it by reference to the discretionary power of the Poor Law Board auditor to decide what expenses were legitimate for the Guardians. Town Clerk Blandy, standing very much on a pre-modern conception of corporate municipal autonomy, replied that such powers, in the case of the corporation, rested with the Finance Committee. Again, in 1858 the council met Lovejoy's objections to a £10,000 expenditure on the market when the Markets Act 1853 specified a maximum of £7,000, by resolving 'upon legal authority [presumably that of Blandy] that the excess beyond £7,000 . . . is lawfully chargeable to the Borough Funds'. Perhaps most serious of all was the refusal of both auditors to the LBH to sign the accounts in 1864 because the board had entered into contracts with its own members for the supply of goods and that this was contrary to the Public Health Acts. They demanded 'that these illegal practices shall cease'. Although no immediate remedial action was taken, the publicity given to these protests by the auditors helped in the creation of a climate of opinion that would, between 1868 and 1885, transform and professionalize the conduct of the affairs of the corporation.

The period after the establishment of the Local Board of Health also saw the beginnings of professionalism in the public service. In 1856 the LBH decided that its surveyor should be a full-time official. John Marshall was appointed to the post and the board declined to consent to the corporation's request that he also be appointed Borough Surveyor on the grounds that his duties to the LBH were 'sufficient to occupy his whole time'. The combination of the two posts was delayed until William Woodman, appointed Borough Surveyor in the same year that Marshall became Surveyor to the LBH, assumed the latter post in 1866. Elected members were only hesitantly coming to terms with the functions of professionals who would, inevitably, take over not only functions hitherto performed under contract but also some hitherto undertaken by councillors themselves. Their judgement of the amount of work to be done varied with their view of what the public authority ought properly to undertake. When Marshall resigned in 1859, not long after the decision not to proceed with his drainage scheme, the LBH, now in one of its periodic phases of municipal economy, decided to reorganize its officer structure by combining the post of Surveyor with that of Collector of Rates. At the same time, it sought and received the consent of the borough Watch Committee to the appointment of the Superintendent of Police as Inspector of

Nuisances and Inspector of Lodging Houses. Not surprisingly, his police functions took precedence and his other duties were to some extent titular. But the intention of the board was the saving of money rather than the efficient performance of the duties of the various officers. However, these joint appointments did help to blur the remaining distinctions between corporation and board.

It was not until 1868 that the council examined comprehensively the conduct of its business, although some effort was made in 1866, on the death of J. J. Blandy, to define the responsibilities of the Town Clerk. In response to a memorial from the ratepayers urging the appointment of a 'non-professional man', which implied someone who would not charge professional legal rates to the council, the corporation decided that the Town Clerk must be a solicitor but that instead of being paid by professional charges he should be appointed 'at a fixed salary which shall include all remuneration for discharging the entire duties of the office whether ordinary, legal, parliamentary or otherwise'. At the same time, however, a motion which would have had the effect of making the Town Clerk a full-time official as well as a salaried one was voted down. Thomas Rogers was appointed Town Clerk and Clerk to the LBH at a salary of £600 per annum. The following year the council changed its position and resolved in response to a request for an increase in salary, not to change the basis of remuneration but 'to consider any special transaction . . . with a view to their being made the object of special remuneration'. This decision would become a controversial one, further grist to George Lovejoy's mill, and important in the reorganization of the council's management and decision-making process which is considered in the next chapter.

3

'Democracy and Proper Drains'

Free speech, free passes, class distinction,
Democracy and proper drains
     John Betjeman, *In Westminster Abbey*

It was as individuals that officials influenced policy and set
standards of administration. . . . Councils must often have
got the officials they deserved.
     E. P. Hennock, *Fit and Proper Persons*, 1973, p. 9

I do not look upon sewage as filth to be got rid of but as
valuable manure which it is a sin to waste.
     William Donaldson, *On the Present and Future Work of
Engineers in Reference to Public Health*, 1878, p. 2

The influence of the drainage question on the government of
Reading continued into the 1870s. The day-to-day controversy had
abated by the middle of the decade and had ended almost entirely
when the reordering of the borough's finances after the passage of
the Reading Corporation Act 1881 led to a substantial reduction in
the general district rate. It is possible, however, to trace the effects
of both the politics and the finance of the acquisition of land for
sewage disposal on the developing structure of Reading's governmental system in the years running up to the attainment of county
borough status under the Local Government Act 1888.

In the four years between 1868 and 1872, to the evident
confusion of a council struggling to come to terms with a new era in
local government and local public expenditure, the powers of the
corporation were enlarged and made more complex by three pieces
of legislation, two private and one public. In 1868, as we have seen,
the Local Board of Health secured an Act that empowered it to
acquire the Reading Waterworks; in 1870 the Reading Local Board

Waterworks, Sewerage, Drainage and Improvement Act gave the council the powers to put into effect the major sewerage scheme drawn up because the Thames Conservators had, in the words of the Act's preamble, 'required the Local Board to discontinue the flow . . . of sewage . . . into the River Kennet'; and in 1872, the Public Health Act, as a response to the report of the Royal Sanitary Commission, had greatly extended the public health powers of the corporation by designating it the Urban Sanitary Authority for the borough. All of these statutes, as well as enhancing the corporation's powers, increased its borrowing limits (subject, of course, to central government approval of the actual loans). By 1875 the indebtedness of the corporation was considerable, and a report from the Finance Committee presented to the council on 5 May 1875 showed that its borrowing powers had been used to an extent which left the borough with little further scope for loan-financed capital expenditure (see Table 3.1). The report also showed that the costs of the drainage scheme at Manor Farm, Lower Whitley, amounted to almost half of that part of the indebtedness of the corporation that was attributable to loans raised under the Public Health Acts and the Local Act 1870. Thus the effect of the sewerage scheme on the financial position of the borough was considerable, especially since the cost of servicing the loans was charged to the rates. Between 1868 and 1875 the amount collected from the rates rose by 250 per cent, and the rate poundage went up from $5\frac{1}{2}$d to 3s $1\frac{1}{2}$d. The general district rate, levied for public health purposes, rose from 1s 6d to 2s 8d between 1873 and 1875.

Table 3.1 *Reading Corporation Debt, 1875*

Statute	Extent of borrowing power	Loans	Borrowing power used (%)	Loans repaid (%)
Public Health Acts	£255,466	£208,062	81·4	10·2
Waterworks Act	£44,000	£27,500	62·5	8·4
Local Act 1870	£60,000	£50,000	83·3	3·1
Total	£359,466	£285,562	79·4	8·8

The Manor Farm sewage disposal scheme was Reading's first major capital investment project. It affected not only the accounts of the borough, and its developing financial and accounting policies, but also the internal organization of the authority. The scheme was a controversial one, consistently opposed and criticized well into the 1870s by the *Berkshire Chronicle* because of its expense, its alleged technical failings, and its affects on the personal fortunes of local notables who were, one way and another, involved with the scheme. In particular, the resignation of Thomas Rogers as Town Clerk in January 1873, an event which the *Chronicle* (4 January 1873) welcomed by remarking that 'the Corporation will gain in dignity what it loses in picturesqueness', was provoked by allegations that he had wrongly advised the council on the extent of its powers under the Municipal Corporations Act on the one hand and under the Public Health Acts on the other. But this issue, which related specifically to the costs of the new municipal offices, was the culmination of a period in which the council was undergoing a painful transition from a minimalist to a multipurpose local authority.

As was suggested at the end of the previous chapter, the need to do something about the drainage of the borough became so urgent that the corporation had to make policy in a rush. The result was that the council found itself uncertain as to the actual extent of its powers, especially in the aftermath of the general jurisdictional changes imposed by the public legislation of 1872. In particular, the corporation had to seek counsel's opinion, and ultimately an order from the Local Government Board, on the compatibility of its local legislation (in particular the 1870 Act) with the general legislation. Also, it was discovered in 1873 that the powers of the corporation to deepen the River Kennet, as part of the drainage scheme, granted by the 1870 Act, were insufficient to ensure the full execution of the plans drawn up by the corporation's engineers. The *Chronicle* was disposed to blame all of these difficulties on Rogers and it looked forward to the appointment of a Town Clerk 'who is really as well as nominally the servant of the Corporation'.

The *Chronicle* carried on its vendetta against Rogers long after he ceased to be Town Clerk, and although its criticisms have to be seen in the light of its strongly Conservative politics shining on an individual who had successfully resisted in 1866 an attempt to make the holding of the office of Town Clerk incompatible with his long-standing position as Liberal Parliamentary Agent for the town, it is likely that the suggestions that the council had acted largely on Rogers's advice were well-founded. His influence arose not only from his long association with the corporation but also from the fact that throughout the 1860s and into the period now under discussion the council was dominated by members of the party of which he was agent. Certainly the corporation debate on a motion of tribute to Rogers for his services to the council was more acrimonious than would now be expected, with Councillor Richard Attenborough declaring that on political grounds he would have liked to see Rogers continue as Town Clerk indefinitely: 'Certainly nothing would have been more advantageous to the political party to which Mr. Rogers does not belong.'

Attenborough's animosity to Rogers was not merely that of a leading Conservative towards the leading Liberal. A large tract of land owned by Attenborough was required for the sewage farm scheme and from 1870 until the issue was finally resolved in open court in 1873, he was in dispute with the corporation over the amount of his compensation. The *Chronicle* continued to assert, long after the matter was settled, that the dispute arose from the incompetence and partiality of Rogers and to claim that if the Town Clerk had not so grossly mismanaged the negotiations with Attenborough, the eventual cost to the borough would have been much less than the £44,000 that was eventually paid.

The borough's difficulties between 1868 and 1873 arose, at least in part, from the inevitable uncertainties created by a rapidly changing conception of local government. The statutory basis of the corporation's activities was being extended and the technical complexity of the tasks it had to perform greatly increased. The resolution of the engineering, legal and, eventually, financial problems associated with the drainage of the borough impelled the corporation to provide itself with an increasing amount of professional advice, first by frequent recourse to outside consultants and advisers and then by the direct employment of its own qualified staff. The sheer volume of the work that the corporation now had to do precipitated a series of internal reorganizations, a need for new public buildings, the development of a new professionalism and a new conception of the relationship between the professional and the political leadership, and the adoption in Reading of an approach to municipal finance pioneered by civic leaders in much larger cities.

The influence of Thomas Rogers on the administrative shape of the borough council extended beyond the period of his tenure of office as Town Clerk. He became Town Clerk, as we have seen, on the death of J. J. Blandy in 1866 and in 1869 he persuaded the council that for certain specified legal duties he should be paid professional fees over and above his salary of £600 per annum. It was the controversy surrounding this decision, together with the feeling among at least the Conservative members of the corporation that Rogers had become too powerful that ensured that when Rogers finally resigned in 1873, ostensibly on health grounds but with complaints of 'incessant harassment', the corporation would examine the nature and duties of the office of Town Clerk. The process of decision-making which led to the appointment of Robert Coster Dryland as Rogers's successor reveals that there was little disposition on the council simply to carry on as before.

The last three or four years of Rogers's Town Clerkship were dominated by the Manor Farm Sewerage Scheme and the private Acts of Parliament, especially that of 1870, that were necessary to ensure its execution. It was in connection with the local Acts, the acquisition of land for the sewerage scheme and the negotiation of compensation for the owners that Rogers in 1870-1 received special payments which became a source of acrimonious dispute in the council and of some controversy in the town. In 1871 the *Berkshire Chronicle* extended its attacks on Rogers by publishing two pamphlets attacking unaudited accounts in general and the payments of fees to Rogers in respect of his work on two 'unopposed bills', in particular. The tone of the pamphlets, even allowing for the exaggeration that arises from political antipathy, reveals something of the effect that Rogers's tenure had on conceptions of the Town Clerkship and of the proper administration of the borough. In *A Little Book* . . . (*Berkshire Chronicle*, 1871a), which had the punning subtitle 'A Little Preface to a Large Bill', the anonymous author wrote:

The same Finance Committee which last year gave Mr. Rogers a thousand guineas for his services in respect of an unopposed Bill, has this year paid him twenty-seven hundred and nine pounds, thirteen shillings and ten pence for his services in respect of an unopposed Bill. Last year, the Committee required no voucher; not even a list of items to support the Thousand Guinea claim. This year they have got, we believe, a list of items, but not a single voucher in support of these items.

And in *Another Little Book* (*Berkshire Chronicle*, 1871b), quoting from a speech in support of a motion, passed unanimously by the council, 'to enquire into the manner in which the Public Offices in the Borough are administered, with special reference to the Office of Town Clerk', the author writes:

> I wish to give no offence to the gentleman who holds the office of Clerk to this Board, yet at the same time *I feel that I am a tool in his hands*. (Emphasis in original)

The 1871 inquiry, to which the motion quoted in the *Berkshire Chronicle* pamphlet refers, was precipitated by what seems to have been a tactical resignation by Rogers in protest against the refusal of the council, both as the body corporate and as the Board of Health, to reorganize its departments and official appointments to cope with the increased volume of work generated by new legislation and by the execution of the sewerage and drainage works. The report of the inquiry resulted in a strengthening of Rogers's position in that although his salary was reduced to £300 per annum out of which he had to find the remuneration for any assistants he employed on council work, the position was restored that had obtained prior to 1868, whereby he was entitled to charge professional rates for most of the legal work he performed on behalf of the corporation, rather than only for specified duties under the 1871 agreement. Before it was adopted, however, various amendments to defer consideration and to employ a 'non-professional' (that is, non-lawyer) as Clerk to the Local Board of Health were lost by thirteen votes to eight. This latter amendment was evidence of the disquiet felt by the Conservative minority on the council about the legal charges associated with the rapid increase in the capital works and associated land acquisitions of the council as Board of Health and of their wish to diminish the involvement and therefore the influence of Rogers.

As part of the reorganization of the administration of the council (other features of which are considered later) Rogers was induced to stay on as Town Clerk and Clerk to the Local Board of Health under the new arrangements, but the council had a further opportunity to consider the matter when Rogers finally departed in January 1873. The council set up a special committee on the Town Clerkship, and the decision-making process relating to the appointment of Robert Coster Dryland as Rogers's successor showed that the corporation was in some disarray in its efforts to resolve the now publicly controversial issue of what the Town Clerk should do and how he should be paid, quite apart from the question of finding someone to fill the office. As the matter was considered by the council, by the special committee, and, no doubt, by informal groups of influential members, the borough had three choices. It could continue to pay a substantial salary to a Town Clerk who would not be full time and who could, therefore, continue both to charge for some specific services and to engage in private practice in the town. It could pay what was effectively a nominal retainer to a Town Clerk who would then levy properly taxed legal charges. Or it could decide that the time had come to employ a full-time salaried Town Clerk.

The council at first decided to pay the new Town Clerk a salary of £400 per annum 'to discharge all duties, legal and otherwise', but the special committee that was instructed to draft specific resolutions and the form of an advertisement was advised to seek the legal opinion of the Borough Recorder. That opinion was in favour of the appointment, as part-time Town Clerk on a minimal salary, of a qualified lawyer who would be paid professional fees for legal work done on the council's behalf. The *Berkshire Chronicle* editorialized in favour of the appointment of a full-time Clerk, but was willing to try the experiment of a salary of £400 and an entitlement to engage in private practice. In the event, the salary was fixed at £100 per annum to discharge the duties of both Town Clerk and Clerk to the Local Board of Health. Significantly, however, in a clear response to the continuing controversy over unaudited accounts, the council also decided that the professional fees charged should be 'taxed in such a manner as the Council . . . may require'. Later in the year, the Finance Committee of the council decided that legal bills in respect of the council's duties as the Urban Sanitary Authority should be taxed by the Clerk of the Peace for Berkshire and those of the council in its municipal capacity by a Common Law or Chancery Taxing Master, as appropriate. There can be no doubt that this significant step towards public accountability of the corporation was stimulated by the controversy over the manner in which Rogers had discharged his duties. It should also be noted that the accountability upon which democracy depends is sometimes expensive. The minutes of the Finance Committee for 1 June 1877 reveal at least one occasion when the reduction in charges demanded by the taxing master was exceeded by the cost of taxing them.

The *Berkshire Chronicle*, never missing an opportunity to attack Rogers, was withering about the council's inconsistency: 'The Corporation', it editorialized on 25 January 1873, 'has had so little practice lately in managing its own affairs that it may well be excused if it hesitates and bungles at first.' But although the *Chronicle*, because of a concern for the public good that was clearly motivated by its own political stance, was in favour of the appointment of a full-time Clerk, as had already happened in some of the larger boroughs, a political consensus in favour of such an appointment did not develop in Reading until Dryland's resigna- tion in 1877. In the 1873 debate, it was not only the long- established Liberals like Darter (who revealed, somewhat ingenuously, that the change in the basis of remuneration in 1871 had been necessary to persuade Rogers to stay on) who opposed a full-time appointment but also the newer, younger members who were part of a generation of improvers and extenders of the range of public provision. George William Colebrook, who, in the next decade, would be the prime mover in the first major extension of the borough, spoke in favour of a part-time Town Clerk, not because such an appointment would be economical but because the presence of a full-time salaried chief official might inhibit the activities of the corporation:

We are living in a growing town. . . . The Town Clerk will have considerable influence in extending or impeding the growth or improvement of the town. I can easily conceive that if the Caversham Bridge scheme [i.e. securing the 1868 Act to reconstruct the bridge jointly with Oxfordshire] had been submitted by a Town Clerk who had a fixed salary he would have said it cannot be done.

Clearly the concept of public duty, of the obligation of salaried officials to facilitate the wishes of the elected authority, had not yet developed to the point where it was accepted that professional advice and commitment could be guaranteed on other than a fee-for-service basis.

Dryland resigned as Town Clerk in August 1877, noting in his letter to the Mayor that 'the amount of time required of me, and other circumstances combined, had caused me to look the matter in the face'. The 'other circumstances' were, according to Alderman Darter, that 'he had not been treated as one gentleman should be treated by another'. Certainly issues related to fees had continued to arise, with the council, on one occasion, deferring payment of the Town Clerk's bills. But it is impossible not to conclude that the real problem was that the work of the council, and the controversy that was inevitably raised by the costs of urban improvement and modernization, combined to make the office of chief adviser to the corporation incompatible with a division of loyalty between public service and private practice. As Alderman George Palmer observed, the criticism which Dryland referred to as 'annoyances' from members of the council 'was one of the things to which a man who held a public position must submit'. The conflict between the public and the private which was so much a part of the struggle between the improvers and the economizers before 1868 still had some influence on politicians' perceptions of the nature of the government of the town.

The decision of the council to appoint a non-lawyer as Dryland's successor, though controversial at the time, looks in retrospect like a natural conclusion to the disputes, acrimony, charges and countercharges of the preceding ten years. Certainly the view expressed by Councillor J. T. Morris, Chairman of the Finance Committee, that the appointment of Henry Day, who had been Deputy Town Clerk for four years, as Reading's first full-time salaried Town Clerk would settle the issue 'for many years to come' proved to be remarkably accurate. Day, whose initial salary in 1877 was fixed at £500 per annum, served for twenty-six years. His appointment was unanimously endorsed by the council, although there was some controversy over the necessary resolution to rescind the 1873 decision that the Town Clerk be a lawyer. It was very unusual for a Town Clerk not to be trained in the law and it would be mistaken to see Reading's decision as an early anticipation of the series of recommendations in the twentieth century, culminating in the Bains Report of 1971, that the Clerk's role was more appropriately seen as that of co-ordinator and leader of the professional staff than that of permanent counsel to the corporation. The reasons were much more concerned with the recriminations over fees and the professional comportment of Day's two predecessors. As the *Chronicle* put it (6 October 1877):

> This is an experiment, and at all events not likely to prove so costly as many of the experiments which Municipal Corporations try. . . . What its positive advantages are there will be ample opportunities for judging.

The appointment was a great success, and the influence and leadership of Day during a crucial period in the development of the borough was on several occasions publicly recognized by the council. Still, when Day retired in 1903 his successor was a lawyer and Day retains the unique distinction of having been the only modern Town Clerk of Reading who was not a lawyer.

The concern about the form and content of the corporation accounts which led, in the 1850s and 1860s, to the series of refusals by the auditors to sign them was sharpened both by the rapid increase in expenditure and debt of the borough and by the public row over the specific issue of the payment of the Town Clerk. As early as 1869, a Special Accounts Committee had noted that 'in its twofold capacity of the Council and the Local Board of Health . . . the business of the Corporation has assumed very large proportions'. It was, therefore, essential that it be conducted 'on sound principles'. On the face of it, this conclusion pointed clearly in the direction of the appointment of an accountant, especially in view of the rapid disappearance, noted by the committee, of any meaningful distinction between activity under the Local Government Acts and activity under the Public Health Acts. 'The result undoubtedly is that the financial transactions of the Local Board are becoming very complicated and extensive.' However, with the aversion to quick action that had by then become characteristic of the corporation, the committee recommended that the appointment of a Borough Accountant be postponed until the drainage of the borough had been completed. The recommendation in the report that it was necessary to build new offices for the corporation provided a further reason for delay, and the only changes made as a result of the recommendations were that the accounts of the corporation and of the Local Board of Health were to be kept at separate local banks, with a member of the appropriate bank appointed treasurer to each of the corporate bodies. The day-to-day financial administration was left in the hands of the Town Clerk and Clerk to the Local Board of Health.

The corporation next turned to its internal management in 1871 when the Committee on the Official Appointments of the Borough, as well as consolidating the position of Thomas Rogers as Town Clerk, recommended that the council appoint a Deputy Town Clerk who would discharge the duties of accountant: to assist the Treasurer (a position still held external to the corporation) in keeping the books, preparing estimates and reconciling the balance sheets for presentation to the auditors. The Deputy Town Clerk would work under the direction of the Finance Committee, but the continuing reluctance of the Council to expand its staff or to provide itself with an administration specialized enough to deal effectively with a growth and complexity of business that was clearly recognized may be seen in two decisions associated with the 1871 report. First, the implementation of the recommendations was postponed pending the passage of the Rating and Valuation Bill which, had it not been withdrawn, might have affected the position of the council and the Local Board of Health, though quite how this would have altered the clear need for better management of the financial affairs of the local authority is not clear. Second, by placing the responsibility for the day-to-day accounting of the corporation directly under the control of the Town Clerk the council showed both an antagonism to administrative innovation and, perhaps, an insensitivity to the reservations which many councillors and ratepayers had about the growing power of the holder of the office. The recommendations were passed by a majority on a vote that followed party lines and after the defeat of amendments moved by a leading Conservative, J. T. Morris, which were clearly intended to indicate the need to assert the authority of the council over a Town Clerk whose influence had become, for some, a cause of concern.

Given that the position of Treasurer was largely an honorary one, the accountancy work of the corporation was done, for many years until the decision in 1878 to set up a Borough Accountant's Department, by a local practitioner, Robert Bradley, working from his own office. By 1878, when a Committee of the Whole Council, assisted by a special subcommittee, examined again the borough's accounting arrangements, the new public offices recommended in 1869 were occupied and, as the debt and rate figures quoted above indicate, the capital works associated with Manor Farm had complicated and increased the financial business of the authority even beyond what had been anticipated ten or five years before. In addition, other public works and the possible extension of corporation activity into other areas all indicated a need to bring the accountancy of the borough 'in house'. Nevertheless, and out of a sense of the need for economy at a time when the Reading Ratepayers' Association was particularly active, the committee recommended that although it was essential that a Borough Accountant be appointed, that all relevant books and papers be kept at the municipal buildings and that Bradley, if willing, should be given the post, 'he should not be required to devote his whole time to the service of the Corporation'. Bradley was appointed at a salary of £150 per annum, and he was given two assistants at salaries of £140 and £100.

During the 1870s and the early 1880s, as the corporation moved reluctantly towards a more professional control of its internal accounting and financial management, it showed little disposition to improve its public image by ensuring wide publication of its accounts. Indeed in 1873 the council, much to the displeasure (presumably both financial and political) of the *Berkshire Chronicle*, decided to discontinue the practice of publishing its accounts as advertisements in the local newspapers, deciding instead to print them in pamphlet form and announce by advertisement their availability to any ratepayer who wished to acquire a copy. Throughout this period, George Lovejoy and others, including the Reading Ratepayers' Association, continued to press for a wider availability of a broader range of financial information. The Finance Committee, however, showed no enthusiasm either for a general change of practice or for providing information in specific cases. In 1882, for example, it decided to deny a request from a ratepayer to inspect and take copies of details of the borough accounts not included in the printed abstracts. In 1883 the Mayor, Blackall Simonds, in opposing a motion tabled by the mayor's auditor, Councillor Arthur Hill, to improve the quality and quantity of financial information made easily available to the public, argued that the extra expense would not be justified because ratepayers could get hold of any information they required (Cook,

1970, p. 205). Hill, whose expertise in financial matters had been demonstrated when the borough's finances were completely recast under the terms of the 1881 Act (which is considered below), argued that 'it was by no means an unreasonable desire on the part of the people outside that they should get a little more full information'. This object was achieved in 1884 when a new form of accounts, largely designed by Hill, was adopted.

Hill's influence on the reform of the corporation's finances is difficult to exaggerate, for it is unlikely that the impetus for change could have been generated within an authority which had so recently set up an accountant's department, and that headed by an officer who was part-time. Hill, a manufacturer of rubber goods in the town, was elected to the council in 1876 on the promise of 'a jealous regard for the practice of every economy . . . consistent with our true interests', a manifesto which was evidence of a move away from the 'economy at any price' attitudes of the 1850s and 1860s. As Cook (1970, p. 172) points out, Hill brought 'special financial skills' to the council, and he did so at a time when the corporation was already considering ways of refinancing the municipal debt in order to reduce the rate burden and to provide some scope to deal with several pressing financial demands. Among the most insistent of the latter were the need to do something about the ramshackle financial condition of Reading School (which is considered in Chapter 5) and the imminent commitment of public money to ensure the completion of the new municipal buildings, the costs of which could not be met, as had been intended, from public voluntary subscription.

Early in 1879 the corporation wrote to the Local Government Board with a proposal 'for lightening the burdens of the ratepayers'. That burden arose, as we have seen, from a hugely increased municipal debt, a very large portion of which was attributable to the costs of the sewerage scheme. By this time, the general district rate stood at 5s 4d in the pound, of which almost half (2s 6d) went on interest on the sewerage loans. The corporation argued, as local government had sometimes argued before and would argue increasingly in the future, that since this burden had arisen because of the compulsion of national legislation, the government, through the agency of the Local Government Board, should be prepared to assist the borough in the economical discharge of its duties. The borough's proposal was for a straightforward refinancing deal: it wished to borrow, preferably from the Public Works Loans Commissioners, enough to repay existing loans and mortgages, most of which had been obtained from private financial institutions and, by such consolidation and the extension of the repayment period to a minimum of fifty years, so reduce interest payments. This would allow a significant lowering of the rate.

The Local Government Board refused to entertain the proposal, suggesting instead, with the obscurantism that often characterizes the central supervision of local authorities, that the borough raise extra money by selling some of its land. But, of course, the major part of the corporation's land-holdings was accounted for by property acquired for the sewage irrigation scheme. After further communications, the Local Government Board softened its position to the extent of saying that it would recommend an application for reborrowing, but that it would not recommend that the Public Loans Commissioners should advance the money. The result was that the corporation sought advice on its legal powers to borrow on the security of the Manor Farm land. In February 1879 the Town Clerk reported that the power to raise money on sewage farm land existed, but that it had not been used by the corporations of nine other towns which he had contacted. Counsel's opinion, however, confirmed that it could be done 'on terms . . . entirely advantageous to the Council and the Town'. By May the council had negotiated a loan of up to £60,000 from the Scarisbrook Trustees which enabled the Finance Committee to recommend a reduction of 5d in the rate poundage.

The rate reduction was delayed until 1880 by difficulties over the title to the land, and by that time the influence of Arthur Hill was being felt on the council. In 1880 the City of Nottingham had been empowered to issue Corporation Stock to raise money for capital projects, and Hill took the lead in persuading Reading to be one of the first boroughs to follow suit. In October 1880 the council received from the recently renamed Finance and General Purposes Committee a report on the borough's financial position which indicated that the recently negotiated loan was regarded as a stopgap measure in anticipation of 'a comprehensive rearrangement of the financial position', a result that could be achieved only by the promotion of a new Act of Parliament. The Reading Corporation Act 1881, which extended the council's powers in many directions, particularly in the fields of planning and the enforcement of public health and other regulations, conferred on the corporation a power to issue Corporation Stock, through the Bank of England, up to an amount specified by the council, and to use the proceeds for the liquidation of existing debts. In 1882 the corporation raised £500,000 on an issue which was oversubscribed. The use of the money to repay existing debts facilitated, in 1883, a further reduction of 6d in the rates.

The speed and absence of controversy with which the Reading Corporation Act reached the statute book is indicative of the nature of the preoccupations of public opinion and civic leaders in the 1870s and 1880s. In 1872 the Borough Funds Act had made the commitment of ratepayers' money to the promotion of a local Act of Parliament subject to the passage of an enabling resolution at two consecutive meetings of the borough council by a clear majority of the members. If this was achieved, the proposal then had to be endorsed by a properly summoned meeting of ratepayers or, failing such endorsement, by a poll of the ratepayers. These provisions were resented by corporations as an infringement of their municipal independence, and Reading Borough Council, both unilaterally and through the Association of Municipal Corporations, frequently lobbied for their repeal. The intent of the Act was to curb municipal extravagance as expressed by corporations which relied on their representative and elective basis as a legitimation of any and every decision they might take. It also provided a statutory procedure by which ratepayer pressure could be exerted on elected members: it was a plebiscitary condition imposed upon local representative government.

In the ten years following the passage of the Borough Funds Act, as well as memorializing against it, Reading Corporation found itself, on two occasions, compelled to use its provisions. In 1873, when it was realized that the powers granted by the Local Act 1870 were insufficient to enable the corporation to complete the deepening of the Kennet that, according to its engineer, was essential to the success of the drainage scheme, the council failed to muster a sufficient majority to take the matter any further. The *Berkshire Chronicle* attributed this to a desire to prevent the public discussion of the scheme that would have taken place at the ratepayers' meeting and whether for this reason, or simply because of a feeling that the expense of the scheme would have ensured its defeat in a poll, the corporation had demonstrated the effectiveness of the Act in curbing municipal expenditure. The contrast in 1880-1 could hardly have been sharper. Not only were the necessary council resolutions overwhelmingly passed, but also the motion in favour of the application to Parliament was carried at the ratepayers' meeting by a very large majority, thus obviating any demand for a poll. The object of the 1881 Bill was to lighten the immediate burdens on the ratepayers, while the proposal of 1873 would surely have added to them. Even when the corporation secured the support of the voters, as it was to do in 1886 for the extension of the borough boundaries (see Chapter 4) after the proposal had been voted down by the ratepayers' meeting, the provisions of the Borough Funds Act made it more difficult for municipal innovators to secure the statutory cover their plans required. As Cook (1970, p. 202) notes, it was 'not surprising that many members found the provisions of the Borough Funds Act irksome'. However, in attempting to secure their repeal, the corporation was acting against 'the whole spirit of nineteenth century local government . . . the principle that ratepayers *should* have ultimate control'.

These changes to the way the business of the local authority was conducted were accomplished hesitantly, largely because of the inherent incompatibility between the prevailing attitudes of local politicians and the inexorable and externally determined redefinition of the nature of local government. Reading Borough Council, at the time when it was forced into the commitment of a large amount of capital to the sewerage scheme, was still dominated by members whose view of local government had been formed in the 1840s and 1850s. Although the power of the extreme *laissez-faire* economizers had all but disappeared, the council was not yet under the influence of men who believed that the proper function of the corporation was to articulate and express popular pride in the success and achievements of the town. To this extent the council, had it been left to set its own priorities, might have continued a little longer to espouse a minimalist view of the proper sphere of local initiative. As the external environment changed, however, so also did the opinions of local political leaders. In Reading this change was expressed, as it was throughout the country, in municipal architecture, in the erection of public buildings that were both essential to the conduct of municipal business and symbolic of the acceptance of the leading role of the corporation in promoting the development and protecting the welfare of the town and its inhabitants.

For British local government, the late 1860s and the 1870s were years of profound change. The climate of politics was fundamentally changed by the passage in 1867 of the Second Reform Act. This major extension of the limits of participation in the democratic process was followed, as had been its predecessor in 1832, by a torrent of social legislation much of which relied on local authorities for its implementation. The Education Act 1870 began the era of compulsory, publicly funded education (see Chapter 5) and the Public Health Acts of 1872 and 1875, together with major changes in housing law, placed new obligations on councils already stretched by the piecemeal social legislation of the preceding twenty years. One response to this change was the acceptance of the need for new staff and new administrative arrangements. Another was the acceptance of the need to provide premises in which the work of authorities could efficiently be conducted. In short, even where a reluctance to spend remained, both as a legacy of the past and as a reaction to insistent ratepayer pressure, the obligations imposed by legislation created pressure to do well locally that which was prescribed centrally.

In Reading the need for new public offices 'in which the whole business of the Corporate Body may be conducted' was recognized by the Special Accounts Committee Report of 1869. The report, perhaps demonstrating an awareness of the changing climate of politics and government, also commented on 'the transition state of much of the public business' and specific proposals for new municipal buildings were not made until 1871. The Joint Committee Report on the Official Appointments of the Borough recommended that the council provide itself with new offices, though it could not agree upon whether to proceed immediately or to rent premises in the meantime. The now familiar case for the efficiency of centralized headquarters was made by the Borough Surveyor who said that he knew 'of no town equal in size to Reading and with such important works in hand without proper accommodation for its officers: at present, the offices . . . are anything but creditable to the town'. Despite a dispute about how the money for the building was to be raised, and against a recommendation from the Local Government Board that the council should give priority to the completion of the sewerage works over the erection of new public buildings, the council resolved on 22 September 1873, by eleven votes to two, to go ahead with the construction of the buildings which became the Town Hall. The building was designed by Alfred Waterhouse, the architect of Manchester Town Hall, and the foundation stone, which surmounted a box containing 'coin of the realm, newspapers and records', was laid by Mayor Alex Beale on 8 October 1874. The first meeting of the corporation in the new Council Chamber took place on 6 June 1876 followed by a banquet attended by the Lord Mayor of London.

This first range of new buildings was purely functional, necessitated by the expansion in the business of the corporation, but within a short period pressure mounted for the provision of buildings of a more recreational and cultural character. In February 1877 the town was offered, by the executors of his will, a museum collection of Mr Horatio Bland, a collector who had lived at Burghfield, just to the south-west of Reading. The council decided that the Mayor should 'ascertain the opinion of the inhabitants of the Borough'. The council was clearly reluctant to commit the ratepayers to any further capital expenditure, in view of the facts that the new public buildings had just been completed, the costs of Manor Farm were becoming clear, and the activities of the Reading Ratepayers' Association, whose chairman, James King, had been elected to the council, had succeeded in making members very sensitive on the matter of the existing municipal debt. On 17 May Thomas Rogers, now a private citizen but still an influential one, proposed at a public meeting that the corporation be asked to adopt the provisions of the Public Libraries Act 1855. The proposal was carried and the necessary resolution was put through council at its meeting on 7 June 1877. At the same meeting it was reported that 'A Committee of Gentlemen', including Rogers and William Isaac Palmer, had proposed the erection of a new public hall, a free library, Reading Room and Museum, and rooms for the Schools of Science and Art. By including the Schools of Science and Art, the project would attract a grant from the Education Department and it was proposed that the rest of the cost be raised by public subscription. The promoters of the scheme, showing an awareness that Reading's influence extended beyond its boundaries, saw the proposal to build a public hall 'not only as a Town Hall for the

Borough of Reading, but also as a Concert Hall for all County and general public purposes thus supplying a want which has been long felt by the large and rapidly increasing population of which Reading is the centre'. The proposed museum would house the Bland Collection, and the Committee of Gentlemen, judging accurately the state of local opinion and to emphasize the need for public subscription, said:

> It has not been thought right (in view of the heavy taxation which has been imposed . . . [for] a complete system of drainage and sewerage . . .) to resort to the local rates for the funds for the completion of these works.

The council gave the plan its blessing and agreed to purchase the land required for the project.

The land purchase was not, however, the end of the corporation's financial commitment to the venture. In January 1879, nine months after the council had finally agreed to the plans, the Committee of Gentlemen came back to report that although they had raised just under £22,000, the lowest tender, even after revisions to incorporate the Schools for Science and Art in the same building contract as the hall, library and museum, was nearly £44,000. They requested that the council should contribute £10,000 but 'not without the sanction of a Public Meeting of the Ratepayers'. The meeting was held on 4 February and the proposal to contribute £10,000 was carried on a show of hands. A poll was demanded by Councillor Blackall Simonds and the proposal was approved by 1,675 votes to 336. The foundation stone was laid 'with Masonic rites' by the Earl of Carnarvon on 3 November 1879 and the new buildings were opened on 31 May 1882 after the corporation had passed a motion that 'the expense of any opening ceremonial is not to be paid out of the rates of the Borough'. It was decided that there should be a luncheon for which tickets would be on sale to other than invited guests.

Despite the public's lack of enthusiasm for supporting the project by subscription (in contrast with their support for a contribution from public funds), the announcement that the town was to have a museum brought the corporation a steady stream of offers of exhibits. These offers were faithfully recorded in the council minutes and they give the impression of attics and cupboards being cleared of white elephants that had become an embarrassment to their owners. A moose's head, a collection of butterflies and, in 1881, a crocodile, were accepted by a council obviously unwilling to seem ungrateful to its ratepayers. The offer of the crocodile, by a donor who wished to 'deposit' it in the museum 'because I gave a kind of promise . . . that I would not give it away but it is . . . very unlikely that I should again require it for my own purposes, but if I should again require it, would give timely notice', was clearly too much for some members. A motion was moved to restrict donations until a committee had been appointed 'to determine the general character of the museum'. The motion was, however, defeated.

By the early 1880s, then, the nature of corporation business had greatly changed, and the change was emphasized by the completion of a range of public buildings that served as the administrative and cultural centre of the town until the completion of the new civic offices and of the Hexagon multipurpose assembly hall over ninety years later. It is easy to underestimate the quality of the change in the scope and nature of the government of the town, from a corporation served by a small number of professional officers, most of whom were part-time, to a multipurpose authority able, in 1888, to put up a convincing case for exemption from the provisions of the Local Government Act and establishment as a county borough providing single-tier, comprehensive local government. The expansion in the staff and departmental structure of the corporation was accompanied by an increasing sophistication in its committee system and a rapid increase in its powers, both to provide services directly and to supervise, as the licensing or regulatory agency, services provided by private companies. This chapter concludes with a brief account of these changes and an examination of the determination with which the corporation approached the preservation of the town's municipal independence and its capacity to influence and direct the twentieth-century development to the borough.

So far as the committee system of the council is concerned, the most significant changes were in the direction of a consolidation of power and influence in the hands of committees not charged with the provision or regulation of specific services. In the 1870s there begin to appear in the minutes references to meetings of a committee (or conference) of committee chairmen. In 1875, for example, as part of a growing concern with the accounts of the corporation, a Committee of Chairmen of Committees, acting on behalf of a Committee of the Whole Council, examined a 'tabular statement' which it had requested on the numbers and wages of the non-manual staff of the authority and made recommendations which covered departments supervised by several committees. Similarly in 1880 a Conference of Chairmen discussed the details of the proposed legislation to consolidate the borough's debt and to extend the environmental and other powers of the corporation. In 1879 the Finance Committee was renamed the Finance and General Purposes Committee and had added to its financial duties the function of being 'the consulting committee of the Town Clerk with power to authorise him to obtain legal advice' and in 1884, in response to a motion in council to restrict highways expenditure in the year 1883-4 to £6,000, a Committee of the Whole Council recommended that half-yearly estimates of the spending committees, after approval by the appropriate committee, be submitted to the Finance and General Purposes Committee before they were approved by the council for rate-fixing purposes. Finally, in the period running up to the extension of the borough boundaries in 1887, the Borough Extension and Improvement Committee, acted as a co-ordinating committee over a wide range of local policy areas.

All these innovations show the corporation responding to a rapid increase in its business and a rapid expansion in its capacity to affect the life of the town. Throughout this period, the council continued in contractual relationships with the Reading Gas Company and was ready to use its influence as the company's biggest customer to affect both the price and quality of the gas supplied. In 1877 in response to the proposals of a private company to provide a tramway system in the town, the council, recognizing the benefit for the ratepayers of the right to oblige the company to maintain the major part of the roadways along which their lines were laid, to standards specified by the Borough Surveyor, agreed to the principle of the provision of a tramway system. In responding to this innovation, the council instructed the Town Clerk to investigate the experience and practices of other boroughs. Its treatment of his report was significant in two ways. In procedural terms it showed that the elected political leadership was strong enough to do other than accept the advice of officers, for although 'the advice from various towns was strongly expressed against the construction of tramways otherwise than by the local authority' and 'the general opinion that Tramways ought to be made by Corporations and leased to Companies', the council decided against seeking powers to construct its own system. Substantively it decided to support the application of the Reading Tramway Company to the Board of Trade for a provisional order to allow it to provide a system, while reserving the power to regulate speed and the distance between stops, and to license the drivers. It also reserved the right to buy the company out within twenty-one years. The Tramway Undertaking was acquired by the corporation in 1901 and electric power replaced the horse-drawn trams in July 1903.

The corporation also showed its preference for regulation and licensing over direct provision and public ownership when it considered in 1882 the question of electric lighting. Six companies had published notices of intent to seek provisional orders for the generation and supply of electricity in the borough, and although the Finance and General Purposes Committee reported that 'the only satisfactory course' was for the corporation itself to apply for a licence, the full council was more cautious, largely because of uncertainty over the question of whether the issue to the borough of a provisional order would oblige it to supply power throughout its jurisdiction. In the event, and again after a report from the Town Clerk on practices elsewhere, the corporation decided to support the licensing of a private company 'upon conditions to be imposed for the protection of the public'. The Reading Electricity Supply Company had its provisional order confirmed by Parliament in 1893 and it passed into the ownership of the corporation forty years later in 1933.

The entry of the corporation into the field of licensing and regulating new utility companies served to emphasize its importance and influence in the life of the town. These extensions to the powers of the council, and so of its impact on the locality, were in addition to the many statutory obligations laid upon it by the social legislation of the 1870s and those it acquired by the Reading Corporation Act 1881. Most of these new duties were concerned with the environmental health of the town and with its physical planning. Of major significance was the requirement in the Public Health Act 1872 that the borough appoint a Medical Officer of

Health (MOH). As Cook points out (1970, pp. 209-12), the influence of the first holder of the post on the public health policies of the town was formidable. Dr Shea was in a position that was then unique: he was a professional officer and an employee of the corporation but he held the only appointment that the borough was specifically obliged by law to make. Therefore he derived an additional degree of influence, as did his colleagues throughout the country, from the statutory foundation of his office. Shea's impact on the government of Reading was immediate. He recommended in 1873 that the council should have a Sanitary Committee, that in accordance with Home Office advice he should report monthly to a Committee of the Whole Council, quarterly to the council itself and annually for publication. These reports, as well as documenting the health and vital statistics of the borough, provided a channel of influence for the MOH and a specification for the regulatory and enforcement powers of the corporation. Shea's capacity to retain the confidence of the council, to press it towards action even during its periodic fits of extreme penny-pinching, and to achieve a major improvement in the public health and physical condition of the town were recognized in the tributes to him on his death in 1887. Mayor William Berkeley Monck referred to his 'great firmness and determination in insisting on necessary reforms' and his ability 'to carry out schemes which must have been distasteful to many, with the least possible amount of friction or ill-feeling'. It was at the insistent urging of Dr Shea that the corporation was persuaded to enter the housing field by using its powers of enforcement under the Artisans and Labourers Dwelling Act 1868. But in an early example of the local government officer's sensitivity to the mind of his council, he made it clear that by proceeding against individual owners of unfit houses, the expense of the borough would be strictly limited. He was alive to the fact that Reading, like many other boroughs responding to the permissive housing legislation of the last quarter of the nineteenth century, would be unlikely to entertain any proposal to exercise the extensive compulsory purchase and redevelopment powers of the Artisans' Dwellings Act 1875. In the direct provision of services, Dr Shea pressed the corporation towards the construction of a temporary infectious diseases hospital, which was built in Bridge Street after other sites had been rejected as unsuitable as a result of ratepayer opposition. A permanent hospital was not provided until the construction of the Park Fever Hospital after the acquisition of Prospect Park in the early years of the twentieth century.

It is clear then that the impact of the corporation on the physical aspect of the town and upon the services provided for the people was greatly increased in the two decades before the extension of the borough and the attainment of county borough status. The streets of the town were progressively improved and brought under the control of the council, major improvement projects were undertaken, such as the widening of St Mary's Butts and the demolition of the row houses that made the area extremely congested and insanitary. But there were also disappointments. Hopes for a new Corn Exchange and general market were unfulfilled despite a spectacular act of philanthropy by Major Arthur Hill in 1885. On 5 February 1885 Hill informed the council that he had bought, for £10,260 (the equivalent land value, a century later, would be about £1 million), a block of property 'extending from Broad Street to Friar Street' which he was prepared, at any time within two years (a period which he subsequently extended to 1890), to sell to the corporation at the same price. This was the second time that Hill had acted in this way, and on the previous occasion (in relation to land adjacent to the municipal buildings) he had explained his actions thus: 'I know we cannot, as a corporate body, proceed without delay [and I believe] that it is generally felt that the land ought to be available for the use of the Town.'

The sewage farm continued to lose money, and the investment was justified more by the non-financial return of improvements in the health of the town. Improvements to the water supply, the deficiencies of which had been dramatically illustrated in December 1874 when a fire at the Great Western Railway works raged out of control because of a shortage of supply which had caused the water to be cut off each night, were eventually achieved by the construction of a new rising main to a new reservoir in Bath Road, but its efficiency was reduced by a number of 'burstings' of the main in the 1880s. The council was still seeking, with the same consulting engineer who had advised it between 1868 and 1873, a more reliable and purer source of supply after the borough extension in 1887.

Finally, as will become clear in Chapter 5, the council's interest and involvement in what would become the most expensive local government service of all was increasing. Under the Education Act

1870, and upon a motion moved in council by George Palmer, a School Board, elected separately from the council, was established in Reading. The corporation was already involved in the provision of education through its trusteeship of the Reading Free Grammar School, and during this period the nature, staffing and economics of the school became both problematical and controversial. The council's relationship with the School Board was such as to reduce the significance of the separateness of the two bodies. The board raised its revenue by precepting on the corporation which then had responsibility for collecting the School Board rate. Thus, despite its lack of direct control, the corporation was continually aware of the effect on the total burden of local taxation of the steeply rising cost of education, as reflected in the School Board precept, in the 1870s and 1880s. Although the corporation did not become the local education authority until 1903, the School Board quickly became a closely related part of the government of the town.

Until the passage of the Local Government Act 1972, the most serious threat to Reading's local autonomy and municipal independence was contained in the Local Government Bill, introduced in the Commons by Charles Ritchie, President of the Local Government Board, in 1888, with the central objective of bringing democratic government to the counties. If that had been the only purpose of the Bill, Town Clerk Day pointed out in a report to a Committee of the Whole Council on 12 April 1888, 'the Borough of Reading would have had no grievance whatever'. What was at first proposed by the government, however, was to make all but the ten largest boroughs (those with populations of more than 150,000) integral parts of the counties of which they were geographically, but had never been politically, a part. For a borough that had so recently secured major boundary extensions (see Chapter 4), it would have been a cruel irony to lose, within a year, the municipal independence that had made it desirable for the extension to take place. Through the Association of Municipal Corporations, through its Member of Parliament and in concert with other threatened boroughs, Reading lobbied against the Bill as it stood and for the town's exemption from those provisions which it found objectionable. In the end, Ritchie capitulated to the insistent pressure of borough MPs and the population threshold for what became known as county borough status was reduced to 50,000. The amendment to achieve such a change was moved by Sir Henry James, MP for

Bury, to whom Town Clerk Day wrote on 5 May 1888 to point out
that this change would still not ensure the safety of Reading's
independence if the population level were taken as that recorded in
the most recent census. That had been in 1881, a long time in the
life of a growing town, and before the extension of the boundaries.
Although Sir Henry took the point and moved an amendment to
make the qualification a population of 50,000 at the time of the
passage of the Act, Reading was still not home and dry. Another
amendment, to be moved by W. S. Caine, MP for Barrow-in-
Furness, a borough with a declining population, would have made
the qualification the figure in the Quarterly Return of the Registrar-
General dated 31 January 1888. But these figures referred to
boundaries *before* the passage of the Reading Corporation Act 1887.
Reading would have been the only borough in the country to
qualify under James's amendment but not under Caine's. After
extension, the town's population was approaching 60,000 but, as
Day pointed out in a letter dated 5 June 1888 to C. T. Murdoch,
MP for Reading, 'in the middle of 1887 [the date to which the
Registrar-General's return referred] the whole of the Reading Poor
Law Union was not within the Municipal Borough and the
population then . . . would probably have been something over
49,000 but not 50,000'. Reading's case was clearly a strong one and
it would have been ludicrous if a quickly expanding town had lost
its independence while a declining one retained it. Under pressure
from Murdoch and Sir Henry James the government conceded that
county borough status be granted to those boroughs having a
population of 50,000 in 1881 and to 'certain other boroughs . . .
which could give satisfactory proof that they now have 50,000
inhabitants'. The borough's municipal independence was safe.

The securing of county borough status was much more than
symbolic. It was calculated in 1888 that independence of the county
was worth about £5,000 a year to the corporation in government
grants-in-aid, money which would otherwise have gone to the
newly established Berkshire County Council with no guarantee that
it would have been spent in Reading. More importantly, the
continuation of the corporation as a multipurpose authority
provided the institutional base for the development of local politics
and local services that is considered in subsequent chapters.

4

'Earth Hunger'

The Town Council have an earth hunger. . . . What Bulgaria is to Russia, Earley is to Reading.
> Berkshire Chronicle, 16 October and 30 October 1886

Caversham has the resources of a village and the requirements of a town.
> Alderman Felix Brodribb Parfitt, 1908

The Suburbs are for a considerable portion of the Borough's contours almost indistinguishable from the town of Reading.
> G. A. R. Fitzgerald, counsel for the corporation, before the House of Commons Select Committee on Police and Sanitary Regulations, 27 April 1887

The Extension of the Borough Boundaries in 1887

At the time that Reading Council found it essential to commit itself first to the acquisition of the waterworks and then to the execution of the major sewerage scheme, the Royal Sanitary Commission of 1869 was in the midst of its investigations. This inquiry, pressed on the government by the Social Science Association and other scientific institutions, examined the sanitary state of the nation after twenty years of permissive legislation during which there had been several outbreaks of epidemic disease, including cholera, whose effects had been felt most strongly in the rapidly growing industrial towns. The legislative outcome of the Royal Sanitary Commission Report was the passage of two major Public Health Acts, one in 1872 and one in 1875, the combined effect of which was to move from the permissive basis of local government pioneered in the 1848 Act to a system of obligation and compulsion. Institutionally the Public Health Act 1872 is the more significant, for it created sanitary authorities throughout the country. In Reading, as in other municipal boroughs, the corporation, whether or not it was already the Local Board of Health, became the urban sanitary authority. In most county areas outside the boroughs the Poor Law Guardians were designated the rural sanitary authority (RSA) and empowered to levy a rate for sanitary purposes.

These institutional changes produced a pattern of authorities in the Reading area (ignoring for the present purposes the 'suburbs' north of the Thames in Caversham which, being across the river and in another geographical county, were regarded as naturally separate) where the borough was contiguous with two rural sanitary authorities – Wokingham on the east and south and Bradfield on the south and west – and where for Poor Law purposes Reading was administered by a Board of Guardians whose sanitary responsibilities extended only to that part of their jurisdiction not within the borough boundaries.

The urban fringe of Reading was growing quite rapidly, particularly in Earley, that part of the Poor Law Union of Wokingham that clung to the borough's eastern boundary. Development had been particularly rapid on the northern side of the London Road east of Cemetery Junction and on both sides of the Wokingham Road between the junction of the Three Tuns Inn at Earley Crossroads. In the area known as New Town, bounded by the borough's eastern limit, the River Kennet, Suttons' nursery ground and the London Road, artisans' dwellings, mainly to house the fast-growing Huntley & Palmer workforce, had been constructed from the 1850s. Drainage had been provided by the builders, principally George Palmer, but the sewage outfall was, until the borough was extended in 1887, into the Kennet, despite the efforts of the Thames Conservators to impose upon the Wokingham RSA the same kinds of restrictions that, in the case of Reading, had created the sewage 'emergency' of 1868.

Despite the fact that Reading Corporation would, in 1886, be accused by the *Berkshire Chronicle* of 'earth hunger' and, in a flight of rhetorical fancy to which the modern local press would hardly aspire, of being Russia to Wokingham's Bulgaria, the first step in a process of territorial reorganization that lasted more than ten years was taken by the Medical Officer of Health (MOH) of the Wokingham RSA. Dr Shea, who was also MOH for Reading, wrote to the corporation in November 1876 supporting the request of the RSA that the sewers of Earley be connected to the borough's drainage system. At a council meeting on 7 December Councillor John Morris, seconded by Councillor Sir Peter Spokes, moved that any such connection should be conditional on an extension of the borough boundaries in Earley, Whitley and Southcote. This motion, which amounted to a territorial claim on land in the jurisdictions of all three Poor Law Unions, was withdrawn by leave of the council pending a report from a Committee of the Whole Council to which Wokingham's request had been referred.

Dr Shea's letter to the council reflects his position as MOH to both authorities. In particular, he argued that 'an undrained suburb is always a standing menace to the town to which it is joined'. When the issue was considered by the council in January 1877, Morris and Spokes moved the establishment of a committee to consider boundary extensions but the motion was defeated. A report from the Town Clerk made it clear that while the council could enter an agreement with the RSA, any extension to the borough for either municipal or sanitary purposes would require legislation. The council decided, however, not to enter any agreement until enough land had been laid out at Manor Farm to deal with the borough's own sewage.

Between 1879 and 1883 three further approaches were made to the council by Wokingham RSA. On the second and third occasions, there was a noticeable hardening of Reading's view and on 1 March 1883, having defeated a motion to meet for the purpose of discussing either extensions to the borough or an arrangement to deal with Earley's sewage, the council agreed to grant an interview to representatives of the Wokingham RSA. At the same time, however, it reaffirmed that no arrangement was possible that did not bring into the borough the areas to be drained. The response, reported to the council a month later, was a resolution passed by Wokingham RSA that 'it had no power to entertain the question of extending the Borough boundaries'.

At this time, not long after the Reading Corporation Act 1881 had completely reordered the borough's finances in a way which had enabled the corporation substantially to reduce the level of the rate, members began to believe that there was an opportunity not only for the extension of the borough boundary but also for a rapid expansion in the activities of the council. This was the era of municipal enterprise. Joseph Chamberlain in Birmingham, W. G. Forwood in Liverpool, civic leaders in many of the great towns, especially in the north of England, were in the van of the movement to modernize and revitalize urban England. In Reading the first signs of such a movement had been the erection of the Town Hall, Museum and Library in the late 1870s and early 1880s and there was a mood of activism and a drive to extend the influence and impact of civic government. Industrial and commercial growth had emphasized the obsolescence of the boundaries and the success of the public health reform movement had convinced all but the most determined diehards that the proper engine of reform was a multipurpose borough council.

On 20 February 1884 the council carried unanimously a motion moved by Councillor George William Colebrook and seconded by Councillor William Berkeley Monck to refer to a Committee of the Whole Council 'to consider whether the time has not arrived when steps should be taken with a view to the enlargement of . . . the boundaries of the Borough, the development of the General Market and the provision of an adequate Corn Exchange, the initiation of a comprehensive scheme for the improvement of St. Mary's Butts and other public improvements'. The committee was also instructed to report on 'the advisability of applying to Parliament for additional powers'. The council was aware, to use a phrase that was to be employed by the Town Clerk, Henry Day, in evidence to the House of Commons Select Committee on Police and Sanitary Regulations that considered the Extension Bill in 1887, that the fringes of the borough 'consisted of people having their employment, business and interest in Reading'.

The terms of reference for the committee amounted to a considerable shopping list for the borough. The central objective, however, was to extend the boundaries of the town, with other measures included, as is often the case with local authority private legislation, because of the convenience of lumping together in one Bill all of the major and minor things for which the council needed statutory cover. As will be seen later, some of these additions, tacked on to a Bill the main purpose of which was territorial and jurisdictional, were either withdrawn by the council or struck out by the parliamentary committee which considered the measure. However, on territory, the borough's ambitions were to a large extent satisfied.

The fact that the motion was moved by G. W. Colebrook is the first indication of the major and leading part that this former Mayor

(1880-1) would take in the expansion of the borough, an expansion which, because of its effect on the population level of the town, would be a crucial factor in ensuring that Reading's municipal independence from Berkshire would be maintained in 1888. Colebrook's contribution, which came at a time when elected political leadership was at its most confident and before it was eclipsed by growing professionalism, was continuous from 1884 until the Reading Corporation Act became law in September 1887. In March 1884 he drew his own line on a map of the area, proposing a new boundary that he hoped would form the basis of the council's application to Parliament. This suggestion was referred to the Borough Surveyor, Albert Parry, to prepare detailed maps and statistics, but it was not without significance that it was members and not officers who, in the early stages, were making the running. In the event, the Borough Surveyor said of Colebrook's line, 'It is not the one that I would recommend', and he went on to argue the need to push the boundary out further than Colebrook had proposed. Parry said that it was desirable to take in not only the developed and developing urban/suburban fringe but also 'a fair drainage area . . . and . . . such eligible lands and properties in the vicinity of the present boundary as would immediately become building estates in the event of a very limited area being decided upon'.

The Borough Surveyor's report, as well as marrying the planning to the jurisdictional demands of the town, constitutes the first official recognition of one of Reading's perennial problems: the definition of the natural boundary of the town. Given the topography of this part of the Thames Valley, the only natural boundary is the River Thames and, as the continual concern over the state of the bridges and the early consultations on the extension of the tramway service to Caversham suggest, even that became less firm as technological advance proceeded. (As the one member of the Council who opposed the application of 1887, Isaiah Birt Nicholson, presciently noted in October 1886, 'Ultimately we shall have to take in Caversham'.) On the east, south and west there were no clearly defined limits to the area that might be urbanized, no range of hills, no dramatic escarpment, no major river or fault line, no boundary that was not defined by man or, as in the case of railway lines and, much later, motorways, technologically determined. Reading, then, was a prey to suburbanization – the extension of the social and economic entity of the town into areas not governed by it and in which the population, though drawing services from the borough, made no direct tax contribution to their costs. In 1884, at the beginning of public transport but before its impact on patterns of life and work could be anticipated, the council was convinced by the surveyor that a line could be drawn that would satisfy the present governmental and future developmental needs of the town. Subject only to minor modifications, the surveyor's line formed the basis of the corporation's application to Parliament.

The Committee of the Whole Council to which the Colebrook-Monck resolution was referred recommended in August 1884 the appointment of a Borough Extension and Improvements Committee of which Colebrook became chairman. In this capacity, and working closely with Arthur Hill, who served as Mayor throughout the period now under discussion (four terms, 1883-7, exceeded only by the five terms served by William McIlroy during the Second World War), he presided over the extension campaign, monitored its parliamentary progress, participated directly in negotiations with opponents, 'sold' the proposal to the ratepayers after a public meeting required under the terms of the Borough Funds Act 1872 had voted the whole scheme down, and gave evidence on behalf of the corporation to the House of Commons Select Committee considering the Bill.

As in any extension or annexation campaign, the opposition to the borough's proposals was more serious in what came to be called the 'added areas' than in the town itself. Private legislation of the type necessary to implement the council's proposals was always more likely to succeed if it was not strongly opposed. In particular the House of Commons was likely to look very carefully at opposition from other local authorities and at the extent to which the applicant for boundary extensions had sought to secure the co-operation of its neighbours. The possibility of achieving agreement, however, was influenced by the fiscal and jurisdictional consequences of the institutional arrangements made by the Public Health Act 1872. The Poor Law Guardians of Wokingham, Bradfield and Reading, as well as administering the Poor Laws and levying a Poor Law rate, were also the sanitary authorities for their areas, levying a rate for public health purposes. Because the rates were and are fundamentally a tax on real property any boundary change was also a tax base change. In the case of suburban annexation, which was what Reading embarked upon in 1884, the local authority in what would be the 'added areas' of the expanded town was faced with the loss of some of its most recently built and therefore highest rated property. In the jurisdictional world of the 1880s, this had a consequential effect on the rural sanitary authority which would lose territory: it would remain statutorily obliged to provide sanitation for the area remaining to it but it would lack some of its most productive areas in terms of rate revenue. For the individual, too, there was the ever-present possibility that annexation would lead to an increase in rates. In short, even a strong case for boundary rationalization would be likely to meet strong, perhaps implacable, opposition. In the face of such opposition, Parliament might be less receptive to a borough's case, as is shown in a letter to the Town Clerk from the borough's parliamentary agents (Sherwood & Co.) in June 1885. Commenting on the failure of extension Bills promoted by the boroughs of Sunderland and Wakefield, Sherwoods noted 'the tendency of the House of Commons Committee is rather hostile . . . to borough extension Bills if opposed by the Districts proposed to be included'. The period between the establishment of the Borough Extensions and Improvements Committee in 1884 and the promotion of the Bill in 1886 was occupied in seeking to defuse the opposition from the surrounding areas.

It was clear from the outset that, in Parliament, the views of public authorities would carry more weight than any private opposition to the corporation's Bill. Any increase in the territory and tax base of Reading was a permanent decrease in those of the other district or districts. Private objections, by contrast, would be more likely to be based on individual grievance and short-term hardship, and in any case negotiation with private objectors could not anticipate the publication of the Bill since their standing to oppose arose from the commencement of parliamentary proceedings. Where other local authorities were concerned, the formal submission to Parliament would be postponed until the corporation had exhausted all possibilities of achieving agreement. It is significant that the Borough Extensions and Improvements Committee decided in June 1885, after receipt of Sherwoods' letter referred to above, that a Bill ought not to be promoted in the 1885-6 session of Parliament.

Paradoxically, since it was the drainage needs of that part of their jurisdiction that abutted on Reading which stimulated the moves towards boundary changes, the most determined opponents of the corporation's plans were the Poor Law Guardians of Wokingham, acting also in their capacity as the rural sanitary authority. The position of the Wokingham Guardians was complex and perhaps a little confused. They clearly wanted to connect Earley to Reading's sewerage system because they remained, after more than ten years, unable to comply with the regulations of the Thames Conservators. They continually refused to consider the extension of the borough as a means to achieve this object. They resolved in 1886 'to take the opinion of a competent engineer' with a view to producing their own scheme of drainage for Earley, where public meetings of residents had come out in favour of incorporation in Reading. They appeared, at first, to object to any extension of the borough's authority but ended up by conceding the corporation's case for boundary changes in Earley so long as no provision was included in the Extension Bill to alter the Poor Law arrangements as they affected their area. In this way the Earley tax base was retained for Poor Law purposes, but at the price of adding a further confusion of jurisdiction which would eventually have to be resolved by action of the Poor Law authorities at national level.

The compromise between Reading and Wokingham that is suggested by the concession on the Poor Law boundaries is important in understanding the determination of the borough both to achieve an extension of the boundaries and to go to Parliament with an unopposed Bill. To achieve both of these objects, the borough had to make some sacrifices, but since after extension Reading would, even more than before, be the predominant local authority in the area, it had good reason to believe that the effects of compromise would be temporary.

The medium- to long-term objective of the corporation, under the guidance of Colebrook, Town Clerk Henry Day and the Borough Extensions and Improvements Committee was well expressed in the brief of the corporation as promoters of the Bill:

The Bill . . . provides for making the area for municipal, sanitary, educational and Poor Law purposes coincident, the main intention being the consolidation and simplification of

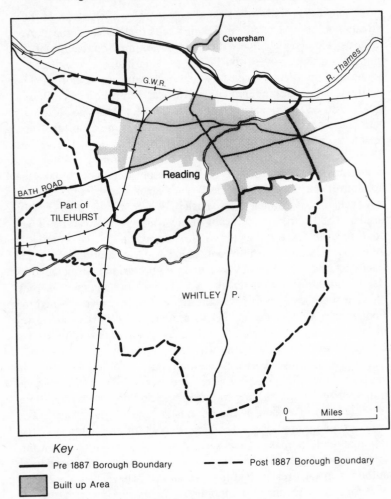

Figure 4.1 *Boundary Extensions, 1887*

jurisdiction and administration throughout the entire area and
the avoidance of a multiplication of local Authorities.

Reading was by this time a multipurpose authority. It was on the
eve of the county borough status which would make it an all-
purpose one. Its Bill, as well as providing for an extension to the
municipal boundaries, proposed to take into ownership the

Reading Cemetery Company and the Reading Cattle Market Company. It had seriously considered and rather reluctantly rejected a proposal to acquire the Gas Company. But the major obstacle in the way of complete 'avoidance of a multiplication of local authorities' was the separate statutory existence of two kinds of single-purpose elected local authority, the School Boards and the Poor Law Guardians. The existence of these institutions made the pre-legislative negotiations more complex and, because the Guardians were also the rural sanitary authorities, compelled the corporation to be skilful in its presentation of the issues and sensitive to the need for and timing of any concessions.

The case of the School Boards was much simpler than that of the Poor Law administration. The reasons for this were both local and national. Locally the corporation had been instrumental in the establishment of a School Board in Reading, the School Board boundaries coincided exactly with those of the borough, and the School Board had existed only since 1871. Also, there was a degree of cross-membership between council and School Board and the board, rather than being a rating authority, precepted for its revenue on the corporation which raised the necessary funds as a part of the borough rate. It was, therefore, to some extent integrated with the administration of the town. In the event, the only consequences of boundary changes in the case of educational administration were the transfer to the Reading School Board of the full ownership of a school in Earley already jointly owned with the Earley School Board, and of a school in Tilehurst.

The administration of the Poor Law and the associated status of the Poor Law Guardians as the rural sanitary authority was very much more complex, as was suggested above. In addition, the Poor Law arrangements predated the modern existence of the borough and were supervised by a national body, the Local Government Board, in which the influence of the old Poor Law Board which it had replaced in 1872 was still dominant. These complications worked both for and against the interests of the borough and had a direct influence on the tactics of the corporation in the pre-legislative negotiations.

In one sense, in arguing for a consolidation and rationalization of boundaries, the corporation was pushing at an open door. In another, the Local Government Board controlled passage through it. When the Reading Corporation Bill was presented to Parliament in 1887, reports on it were prepared by both the Home Office and the Local Government Board. The latter, which in the present context was the more important, while sympathetic to the objectives of the corporation was anxious that alterations to Poor Law jurisdiction should remain in its own hands rather than be changed piecemeal by private legislation. Its report said that such alterations, if 'it can be shown that they are desirable' would be made 'by means of orders of the Local Government Board. . . . Before issuing orders . . . the Board would cause a local enquiry to be held in the district, at which all parties interested would have the opportunity of attending and being heard without incurring the costs of a parliamentary opposition'.

Reading's problems, at the start of its negotiations, were confined to the area to be incorporated from Wokingham. In the case of the Reading Poor Law Union, the Guardians approached Reading's territorial ambitions in a more co-operative frame of mind than did their neighbours in Wokingham. They suggested to the corporation that, rather than leave the Guardians, as the rural sanitary authority, with a 'rump' area to administer for sanitary purposes, the boundaries should be extended to include the whole of the Poor Law Union area within the borough. Similarly, the Bradfield Guardians, in reply to the corporation's proposals as they affected Tilehurst, said that 'although we should lose a good deal of rateable value, we shall do our best to assist you'.

Later in the negotiations, very shortly before the Bill was to be considered in committee, the corporation, in order to be able to go to Parliament with an unopposed Bill, agreed to drop the Poor Law provisions as they applied to Wokingham, thus departing from the principle that the boundaries be coterminous for municipal and Poor Law purposes. Both Bradfield and Reading Guardians were enraged. On behalf of the corporation, the Town Clerk argued that in the Bradfield case, the borough had, as the price of co-operation, reduced the area of land in Tilehurst it proposed to include in the borough but that in the case of Earley it had decided that 'the new boundaries proposed by the Corporation will be strictly adhered to'. So far as Reading was concerned, Colebrook, in a meeting with the Chairman of the Reading Guardians, argued, in effect, that the Reading Poor Law Union had no *locus standi* in the matter of the corporation's proposals as they affected Earley and that their agreement ought not to be affected by the dropping of the Poor

Law aspects of the scheme as it applied to the Wokingham Union. Colebrook said that the Guardians should 'give [him] . . . credit for the step they took . . . knowing that poor law matters could be afterwards settled'. He also noted that 'opposition to the Bill by Wokingham would have cost £3,000-£4,000', and that there were precedents where Poor Law boundaries had been altered after extensions had been granted for municipal purposes. It may be a tribute to Colebrook's command of his subject, or to his willingness to negotiate on the basis of strength of argument rather than verifiable fact that, according to the Chairman of Reading Guardians, the corporation received the Local Government Board report, with its references to action through the general law, only after Colebrook's meeting with him. In the event, the Chairman of the Guardians, Reuben Bracher, gave evidence to the Select Committee in support of the Bill and the clauses relating to Poor Law jurisdiction in Bradfield and Reading were struck out, without much opposition from the corporation's counsel, thus placing all three unions on the same footing.

In the case of the property-owners who objected to the Bill (including Alderman George William Palmer, who resigned from the Borough Extensions and Improvements Committee after petitioning against the rating implications for his property in Earley) negotiations were successful in obtaining the withdrawal of all fifteen petitions from a total of eleven landowners including several members of the corporation. According to counsel for the corporation, the properties affected would be subject to 'a long and very elaborate clause', negotiated by Henry Day and the committee, which provided for 'preferential rating in the added part of the Borough'. This meant, quite simply, that for varying periods depending on the state of drainage and the time that would elapse before the services in the new areas were brought up to the standards already provided in the old borough, rates would be charged at reduced levels. In reply to a question in the Select Committee asking why the levels and periods of partial de-rating varied among the added areas, Day said that the committee 'had already been told that the arrangement . . . was the subject to agreement between the parties first'. The corporation's willingness to do such deals was well judged, for the Chairman of the Select Committee commended the council for the fact that agreements did not have to be 'fought out before the Committee', as in the case of the Bury Corporation Bill two years before.

As was noted when considering the Reading Corporation Act 1881, the Borough Funds Act 1872 obliged a council to test public opinion in the town before committing money to the promotion of a private Bill in Parliament. In the case of the 1887 Bill to extend the borough, the statutory public meeting, chaired and addressed by Mayor Arthur Hill with Town Clerk Day describing and defending the detailed intentions of the council, was held on 24 November 1886. According to the *Berkshire Chronicle* (27 November 1886), the crowded meeting was 'on the whole, hostile to the Reading Corporation Bill'. At the conclusion of the meeting a resolution to proceed with the Bill was lost by a large majority and a poll of the ratepayers was demanded. The poll took place on 20 December and in the interim the corporation, to quote the *Berkshire Chronicle* (25 December 1886) 'interested themselves in educating the people'. On 11 December there was held an all-day meeting of the council at which the Mayor tried to reassure ratepayers that, except immediately after expansion, there would be no significant increase in the rates. Before the poll took place, the proceedings of the council meeting at which the Bill was considered were sent by the council to every house in the borough. As Colebrook said in evidence to the Select Committee, the council was under no obligation to do this and it is probable that this action influenced the outcome of the poll. The result was a majority of 1,885 votes in favour of the Bill on a turnout of 48 per cent, which the *Berkshire Chronicle* described as 'very low'. It is interesting to speculate on the likely turnout in such a poll in Christmas week a century later.

The Extension of the Borough Boundaries in 1911

The extension of the borough boundaries in 1887 affected the eastern, southern and western limits of the town. The northern limit, as was implied earlier, was the nineteenth-century borough's only 'natural' boundary, the River Thames as the ancient line dividing the counties of Berkshire and Oxfordshire. The one member of the council who had opposed the parliamentary application of 1887 had done so partly because of the failure to recognize that Caversham, which was 'merely a village' in 1881 (Reading Corporation, 1908, p. 13, para. 35), was fast becoming a residential suburb of Reading. But it is clear that, although only Councillor Nicholson publicly argued the case for the incorporation of Caversham, leading members of the corporation had considered and privately rejected extension north of the river. In his evidence prepared first for the local inquiry of 1909 and revised for committees of the Commons and Lords which, in 1910 and 1911, considered the Local Government Board's Bill to confirm its provisional order extending Reading's boundaries, George William Palmer said:

> The question of including Caversham . . . was discussed in 1887 but the Corporation desired . . . that the extension should be unopposed and as it was known that the inhabitants of Caversham did not favour the idea . . . it was decided to leave it out of the scheme.

This recollection was confirmed by other witnesses appearing before the parliamentary committees on the Bill, including the Mayor, Alderman John Wessley Martin, who, like Palmer, had been a member of the council at the time of the 1887 extension.

Institutionally it might have been a little easier for Reading to secure the agreement of Caversham in 1887 than it turned out to be in the period leading up to the extension of 1911. For although there is no doubt that the matter would have been complicated by the need not only to cross the river but also to go into another geographical county, opposition to the borough would have been weaker because of the absence, until 1888, of democratically elected local authorities (other than Poor Law Guardians) outside the boroughs. Reading would have been opposed by Henley Poor Law Guardians in whose area Caversham was situated, and perhaps by the Quarter Sessions of the County of Oxford. However, the probable attitude of the latter may, perhaps, be inferred from the almost total lack of interest demonstrated by the Berkshire Quarter Sessions in Reading's ambitions in Earley, Whitley and Tilehurst. Town Clerk Henry Day told the House of Commons Committee considering the Extension Bill 1887 that he had had from the county authorities 'no communication except that the Chairman of the Quarter Sessions applied to me for a copy of the Bill some months ago and I handed it to him'. In the time that elapsed between Reading's two expansion campaigns, however, county government had been reformed. Elected councils on the pattern introduced in the boroughs in 1835 had been created in the counties in 1888 and district councils had been set up in 1894. Around Reading, as well as creating the Berkshire County Council and the Oxfordshire County Council, these reforms had the effect of constituting the two rural sanitary authorities in Wokingham and Bradfield as rural district councils (RDCs) and of the establishment of Caversham Urban District Council (UDC). Thus when Reading sought to take in Caversham in 1908 the popular opposition perceived in 1887 had found an institutional focus in the district council. Also the democratic basis of the new county councils offered another channel through which local antagonism to Reading could, with some legitimacy, be expressed. Indeed, in the county council elections of 1910, Reading's boundary proposals were the sole issue put before the electors of Caversham. By that time, however, the incorporation question was all but settled.

The basis for Reading's territorial ambitions in 1908, when the first formal steps towards extension were taken, differed markedly from that of 1887. Only in Tilehurst, where the idea of incorporation was generally supported by the public and the local authorities, was drainage an important reason for amalgamation. The eastern part of the parish of Tilehurst had been brought into the borough in 1887 but thereafter development had continued outside the new borough boundary. The population in 1891 of the area proposed to be brought into the borough had been 2,275. It had risen to 2,545 in 1901 and to an estimated 3,000 in 1908. The corporation's brief described this population as 'an outgrowth of the Borough, a large proportion of the residents being employed or otherwise connected with the Borough'. Also, as with the corporation's attitude to Earley in 1887, the brief indicated Reading's willingness to deal with Tilehurst's sewage, 'but only subject to the condition that the parish becomes part of the borough for all purposes'. In making such a statement, the corporation was aware that the Local Government Board had already concluded that there was no convincing justification for Tilehurst's executing its own scheme of main drainage, which would have entailed the construction not only of new sewers but also of a new sewage works, while the borough had the capacity to deal with Tilehurst's sewage at Manor Farm. Also, as Martin told the House of Commons Committee on Private Bills, there was an environmental and policy implication, quite apart from considerations of the most effective way of dealing with sewage and the undesirability of an unnecessary increase in the number of sewerage works. The borough had, in 1907, acquired a length of river frontage on the south bank of the Thames opposite The Warren and up-river of Caversham Bridge. This had been laid out as the Thames Side Promenade in order that it could be 'secured for the benefit . . . of future generations, with a view to keeping off the jerry builder'. Bradfield RDC's plan for a separate sewage works, to be built at Scours Lane between the Great Western Railway line and the river, would have put that policy at risk and, as Martin told the committee, 'when the Corporation heard there was a possibility of . . . putting a new sewage works there we opposed it tooth and nail'. Here, then, was an environmental and recreational justification for extension, to add to the administrative and public health arguments.

The case for bringing in Caversham was rather different, relying almost entirely on the argument that there was a community of interest between Caversham and Reading which rendered anomalous and anachronistic the continued status of the former as a separate district council area governed for police, highway and education purposes from Oxford. At the beginning of the incorporation campaign, Caversham's position was weakened by the fact that there was evidence that opinion there was not wholly opposed to joining Reading. In 1898 Reading Borough Council had refused to entertain a proposal from the Caversham Local Board of Health to dispose of Caversham's sewage at Manor Farm and the proposal seems not to have been resubmitted, the authorities in Caversham having subsequently made their own drainage arrangements, although there is some evidence that these were under some strain from the increased population of the district at the start of the extension campaign. In 1899 a well-attended public meeting in Caversham resolved in favour of the construction of a new vehicular bridge over the Thames at Caversham. The chairman of the meeting sent a detailed report, in the form of a letter to the Town Clerk of Reading, in the hope of persuading the borough to enter an agreement with Oxfordshire County Council to improve or rebuild Caversham Bridge, for which they were already jointly responsible. The motion in favour of building a new bridge had been seconded by Alderman G. W. Palmer MP who had said, according to the letter from Dryland Haslam, chairman of the meeting, to the Town Clerk, 'that Reading had always taken a kindly and fatherly interest in the growing suburb of Caversham, and already did its best to supply the district with gas and water'. Palmer was both a member of the Reading Borough Council and MP for the borough and it could not have been lost on him, nor on the other advocates of a new bridge, that their object was more likely to be achieved if both sides of the river were under the same local jurisdiction. Until then, as Martin would tell the House of Commons Committee on Private Bills, a bridge would be simply 'a means of depleting Reading's population and rateable value'. The need for a bridge both to emphasize and facilitate the developing community of interest between Caversham and Reading was an issue that the parties to the extension controversy constantly referred to, and the consequences for the rates levied by Caversham UDC if that council decided to build a bridge were an important reason, in 1911, for the final acceptance of amalgamation.

In 1901, when R. E. Rawstorne was appointed Clerk to Caversham UDC, the appointment was on condition that he would have 'no claim for compensation . . . on abolition of the office'. This condition was pointed out in the Reading brief to the Local Government Board and, in evidence both to the local inquiry and to the parliamentary committees, it was emphasized that the only possible cause of the abolition of the office of Clerk was the abolition of the authority itself by virtue of its incorporation in, or amalgamation with, another local authority. Reading's argument was a convincing one, for it was indeed difficult if not impossible to imagine any other occasion for the abolition of the position of Clerk, so it must be assumed that Caversham anticipated that at some time it would become part of the Borough of Reading.

In October 1904, at a meeting of Caversham UDC, Councillors Frank Cooksey and H. C. Dryland (son of the late Town Clerk of Reading, Robert Coster Dryland) moved a resolution to the effect that the council should send a delegation to Reading Borough Council to discuss incorporation. There is no evidence in contemporary reports that this resolution, moved and seconded by members whose homes were in Caversham but whose businesses were in Reading, was anything other than a straightforward expression of the view that the time had come to recognize that Caversham should be politically, as well as socially and economically, part of Reading. In 1909, however, Dryland was to claim that the motion had been a ploy to put pressure on Oxfordshire County Council to put up money for a new bridge at Lower Caversham, 'by letting them think that the District Council was in favour of incorporation with Reading'. By 1909, when he became Chairman of Caversham UDC, Dryland was a vehement opponent of incorporation, but the apparent inconsistency of his view over a relatively short period allowed the promoters of Reading's extension to cast doubt on the firmness and genuineness of his opinions. Also he was one of the first of Caversham's civic leaders to bow to the inevitable after the Local Government Board issued its draft provisional order in favour of the borough's proposals. In June 1909 he wrote to Thomas Chivers, one of Caversham's members on the Oxfordshire County Council and a consistent supporter of incorporation, that he now accepted incorporation as unavoidable but that the time between the publication of the Provisional Order and its confirmation should be used to improve the terms offered to Caversham: 'I shall continue to resist the proposals of Reading Corporation but my main efforts will be directed to selling my pigs in the best market.' His success would depend on the importance attached by the corporation to the desirability of going to the final, parliamentary stages of the extension campaign with a package agreed with the major local opponents. In this, the 1911 extension differed little from that of 1887.

Procedurally, however, there was a substantial difference between the two extension campaigns. In 1887 the corporation's objectives could be achieved only by the promotion of a private Act of Parliament subject, as was described earlier, to the public meeting and ratepayers' poll procedures specified by the Borough Funds Act 1872. In 1908 when the second expansion proposal came to the council, the Town Clerk, W. S. Clutterbuck, advised the members that the borough could now choose between two methods. The private Act procedure was still available but, quite apart from the requirement to test public opinion at meetings and ballot box, it raised the possibility that the council would be obliged by Parliament to include in its Bill compensatory payments to owners and public authorities affected by its proposals. The corporation, in common with many other boroughs which, at this time, were responding to suburbanization by proposing the annexation of surrounding areas, preferred the alternative method. This was to apply to the Local Government Board for a Provisional Order granting the extension subject to confirmation by Parliament. This procedure had a number of advantages for the corporation. First, it was likely to be less expensive because a key stage in the process, the local public inquiry, would be called by the Local Government Board whose inspector would be paid by central government, the council's costs being limited to the fees of its parliamentary agents and the counsel instructed by them. Second, the parliamentary stages of the process would be in the form of a Provisional Order Confirmation Bill promoted and supported by the Government, through the President of the Local Government Board, as a piece of public legislation. As subsequent events were to show, such a procedure provided opportunities for the expression of general opposition to piecemeal alterations to the political and fiscal bases of the local government system, but it made the eventual confirmation of the Local Government Board's provisional order virtually certain. Third, the provisional order procedure allowed the council to keep control of the process of expansion. By the early years of the twentieth century, the notion of civic leadership was well developed to the point where both leading members and senior officers interpreted it in a way which viewed representation as essentially Burkean. In other words, members and their advisers were legitimized by election and therefore there was no need for any plebiscitary or participatory democracy. The corporation knew what was best for the town and, if it was wrong, the town could say so through the ballot box at election time. This was a view clearly expressed by the Mayor of Reading before the committee examining the Confirmation Bill in answer to questions from counsel for Caversham UDC contrasting his client's decision to poll the ratepayers with Reading's choice of the provisional order procedure which avoided the requirements of the Borough Funds Act. Martin said that he did not accept that Reading had been less democratic than Caversham and he defended his view by referring to the fact that since the borough's proposals had been published there had been three municipal elections in which the ratepayers could have expressed their views about expansion, the major local issue of the day, by voting against those who supported the corporation's plans.

Once the corporation had decided to proceed by application to the Local Government Board for a provisional order, the extension campaign followed a course not dissimilar to that of the previous campaign between 1884 and 1887. For although the formal procedure differed, there was still a premium on going to Parliament with an unopposed Confirmation Bill. Pressure towards such an outcome was, moreover, increased by the provisional order procedure which, in effect, set out the terms upon which the Local Government Board thought that agreement might be reached. The earlier in the process that local agreement could be reached, the better: so the corporation's negotiations with the public authorities began as soon as the issue of dealing with Tilehurst's sewage was raised in 1907. Negotiations were, however, more complex than in the 1880s for reasons which were both geographical and political. The corporation decided to seek extensions in Tilehurst, Caversham and Mapledurham (a proposal to take the whole of Whiteknights Park into the borough, which would have affected Wokingham RDC, was not proceeded with) and this entailed negotiations with Bradfield RDC, Caversham UDC and Goring RDC, the last two being in Oxfordshire. The geographical implication of going across the river, justified by the fact that Caversham was clearly developing as a residential suburb of Reading, complicated the politics of amalgamation campaign, for it brought into the argument not one but two county councils. This was to be of particular significance in the later stages of the process, when Reading's claims on Berkshire and Oxfordshire were seen as part of the tension between the counties and the county boroughs which, by the early years of the twentieth century, was the most salient characteristic of the working of the local government system. It was this adversary relationship that motivated Town Clerk Clutterbuck to undertake a determined and successful effort to whip up borough support in Parliament to ensure the eventual passage of the Confirmation Bill.

In the earlier stages, however, the search for local agreement occupied centre stage. The negotiations with Tilehurst and Bradfield were relatively uncontentious, marred only by an allegation of bad faith levelled at the borough by the parish council because of a misunderstanding of the obligations laid upon Reading by the 1887 Act in regard to the drainage of Tilehurst. In 1908, the issue having been raised by the problem of Tilehurst's sewage, the Rev. H. R. Cooper, Rector of Tilehurst, commented upon the 'distinctly . . . urban and suburban character' of the village and said that 'the body controlling it should have urban powers'. Since, at that time, the western part of the parish of Tilehurst was entirely rural, such an object could be achieved by taking the built-up part of the parish into Reading. Similarly the Chairman of Tilehurst Parish Council said that although he was not wholly in favour of incorporation, 'the Parish, taken as a whole, would be favourable to it'. He went on to say that he was 'prepared to submit to it, for a sewage scheme is an absolute necessity', a view that was given added point by an outbreak of diphtheria in Tilehurst which was attributed to the inadequacy of the drainage arrangements.

Quite apart from the drainage needs of Tilehurst, the physical expansion of Reading was making a nonsense of the boundaries set in 1887. Also the corporation had made considerable capital investments in Tilehurst which, as a member of the Tilehurst Parish Council pointed out in 1908, made the borough liable to pay rates to Bradfield RDC. Since 1887 the corporation had acquired Prospect Park, built the Park Fever Hospital and enlarged its waterworks, all in the Tilehurst area, outside the borough boundaries.

Both the drainage argument and that relating to community of interest militated against the incorporation of the whole of the parish of Tilehurst because, as Alderman Martin said when finally proposing to the council that it proceed with an application to the Local Government Board, 'there is a certain portion of Tilehurst which is purely rural and agricultural'. Martin, as Chairman first of the Finance and General Purposes Committee and then, from July 1910, of the Borough Extension Committee, was fully aware of the desirability of achieving agreement and he was experienced enough as a local politician to know when concession was prudent. Thus, when the application to the Local Government Board was recommended to council on 19 September 1908, its reference to Tilehurst was to 'either the whole of Tilehurst or as much as agreed with Bradfield Rural District Council'. this form of words implied that opinion in Tilehurst followed the lines of development and was reflected in the wishes of two levels of public authority. Tilehurst Parish Council was generally in favour of incorporation, largely on public health grounds, while Bradfield, which would lose a considerable amount of rateable value as a result of Reading's expansion, was likely to be opposed. The corporation's tactics, therefore, were to restrict its claim to that part of Tilehurst where there was both public and official support for incorporation. By so doing, it was possible to ensure that the borough's proposals would not be opposed by either Tilehurst Parish Council or by Bradfield RDC.

In the preliminary stages of the corporation's extension campaign, the borough's interest in securing agreement considerably strengthened the bargaining position of the local authorities in what would be the added areas. For the borough, as promoter of the extension plan, the trick to be turned was to judge when, in a disputed issue, the Local Government Board and Parliament would come down on Reading's side. In the case of Caversham, as will be seen, the borough took the view that the obduracy and non-co-operation of the urban district council would be to Reading's advantage, and its policy was therefore to combine firmness in its territorial claims with openness and approachability in its local pursuit of them. In Tilehurst the corporation was faced with a favourable, if fragile, public opinion and a public authority determined to get the best deal, both in terms of the implementation of a sewerage scheme and the negotiation of advantageous terms for differential rating. The first obstacle to be removed was the opposition of Bradfield and this was achieved by restricting the application, in effect, to the built-up area immediately contiguous to the existing borough boundary. The second was to achieve agreement on preferential rating. Here, as in 1887, the negotiating positions of the protagonists were affected both by their judgements of the likely outcome and by the imminence of the public stages of the extension process, which would begin at the end of January 1909 with the Local Government Board public inquiry.

In November 1908 Reading's opening bid was that the added area in Tilehurst should be subject to only two-thirds of the borough rate for twelve years after incorporation. This was reported to Tilehurst Parish Council on 12 December when Councillor Sarjeant accused 'the deputation from Tilehurst' of 'running into the arms of Reading' and said that 'had they not done so Reading would have offered them half-rating for twenty years'. That meeting was adjourned for two weeks during which time the question of differential rating was considered in committee and, no doubt, discussed informally with Reading. On Boxing Day, the Committee of the Whole recommended acceptance of Reading's proposals as long as the period of preferential rating was extended to twenty-one years. A week later at a parish meeting, the chairman of the parish council took a coolly realistic view of Tilehurst's position when he said that 'there was a consensus of opinion that incorporation will come' and that Tilehurst should seek the best terms. The relative strengths of the negotiators were well perceived when Mr Ball continued: 'I believe that the Finance Committee of Reading Corporation will give us every consideration. If we oppose incorporation and incorporation comes about we will have to accept whatever terms Reading offers.' By thirty-eight votes to one the meeting voted in favour of incorporation 'on satisfactory terms' and set these terms at three-fifths of the borough rate until Reading supplied Tilehurst with water and thereafter two-thirds, not exceeding 4s 4d, until fifteen years after incorporation.

The date of the public inquiry was fixed for 27 January 1909 and it was announced soon after the Tilehurst parish meeting. It then became part of Reading's negotiating strategy to reach an agreement with Tilehurst so that it could go to the inquiry facing a battle only with Caversham, with which it had found it impossible to negotiate. The *Berkshire Chronicle* of 23 January announced that agreement had been reached on the basis of three-fifths rating for seven years and two-thirds for the next eight, and on the understanding that a drainage scheme would be started immediately after incorporation.

To all intents and purposes, the agreement on preferential rating settled the issue between corporation and Tilehurst. It ensured that Reading's proposals would not be opposed at the public inquiry by Tilehurst Parish Council or by Bradfield RDC. But the provisional order procedure provided opponents of an extension plan with a series of opportunities to object to and petition against it. After the public inquiry, the Local Government Board received the report of its inspector and would then decide whether to issue a provisional order. If a provisional order was issued, opponents could petition Parliament and could expect to be heard in committee in both the Commons and the Lords. In the case of Tilehurst, Reading Corporation was faced, between the end of the public inquiry and the introduction in Parliament of the Confirmation Bill, with two further hesitations on the part of the public authorities in the added area. The first concerned Reading's statutory obligations to dispose of Tilehurst's sewage and it arose out of a 'revelation' at the public

above George Lovejoy (1808-83), campaigner for audited Corporation accounts.

right Lorenzo Quelch, Socialist Councillor and Alderman.

Reading Corporation in 1879, Mayor H. P. Blandy presiding.

Dr Stoke and boys, Reading School, 1877.

John Rabson succeeds William Henry Short in 1927, accompanied by Town Clerk C. S. Johnson.

Municipal enterprise in Reading, the first electric tram, July 1903.

The last electric tram, Mayor W. E. C. McIlroy driving, May 1939.

George William Colebrook, Mayor 1880.

Arthur Hill, Mayor 1883-6.

John Wessley Martin, Mayor 1892 and 1910-11.

Edith Mary Sutton, Reading's first woman Mayor 1933.

MISS CAVERSHAM : " How dare you say I'm not clean.   Take that ! "
    Councillor Rabson gets into hot water by saying that Caversham was a menace to the health of Reading.

A graphic view of Caversham's hostility to Reading. *Berkshire Chronicle*, 3 October, 1908.

Cartoonist's view of Caversham's obduracy after the issue in 1910 of the Provisional Order extending the borough boundaries (John Burns was President of the Local Government Board). *Berkshire Chronicle*, 7 May, 1910.

inquiry into Bradfield's proposed new sewerage works that under the Extension Act 1887, Reading was already obliged to connect the sewers of Tilehurst to its own system of disposal and treatment. Councillor Sarjeant, the leading Tilehurst anti-incorporationist, accused Reading of deviousness and bad faith; it was alleged that Reading had kept Tilehurst in the dark about the existence of the relevant clause in the 1887 Act in order to achieve agreement to the extension plan. The Tilehurst Parish Council passed by three votes to two a resolution in favour of Bradfield's scheme (which had already been turned down for loan sanction by the Local Government Board) and called for the immediate connection of Tilehurst to Reading's drainage system.

In fact, as Martin told the corporation, the clause in the 1887 Act relating to the drainage of Tilehurst had been inserted to protect the borough and it empowered the corporation to impose conditions on the reception of sewage from outside its boundaries. This view was finally accepted by Tilehurst. The whole issue had been something of a storm in a teacup. Sarjeant's views, as the chairman of the parish council conceded, 'were not representative of Tilehurst' and the *Berkshire Chronicle*'s columnist 'Q.T.' was probably right to say (11 September 1909) that it was 'an anti-incorporation move plain and simple . . . one more weapon in the armoury that is to be used in the anti-incorporation fight'. Reading, for its part, was resolute, recognizing the strength of its position not only as the dominant local authority but also as the winner of the first round of the fight. Having got its provisional order, Reading could take a hard line. 'Whatever Tilehurst Parish Council may think,' said Alderman Martin, 'whatever Tilehurst Parish Council may do, it is quite clear that the Town Council will refuse [to deal with the sewage] unless Tilehurst becomes a part of the Borough of Reading.'

The second hitch concerning Tilehurst came in the summer of 1910 when four members of the Tilehurst Parish Council refused to sign the agreement with Reading on sewerage and preferential rating that would have ensured that neither Tilehurst nor Bradfield would petition against the Confirmation Bill which was introduced in late June and was due to receive its Second Reading in July. It is unlikely that this refusal, had it been persisted in, would have affected the course of the extension campaign, for there was evidence that the view taken by the four was unrepresentative of public opinion which, on public health grounds, remained in favour of Tilehurst's joining Reading. The hitch, however, came at a particularly sensitive time for the borough. The issue of the territorial ambitions of the boroughs and the consequent effect on county government, as will be discussed later, was about to be joined in the Commons, and Town Clerk Clutterbuck was actively canvassing parliamentary support for the Confirmation Bill. Council members needed to know the strength of any local opposition. On 21 June 1910 Councillor E. P. Collier, Chairman of the Education Committee and a prominent supporter of incorporation, wrote privately to Clutterbuck:

> I went up to Tilehurst and saw Mr Wheeler [the proprietor of the Kew Kiln Brickworks, Tilehurst] this afternoon and he says that he does not believe the Parish Council will go the length of opposing, that they will *talk* as long as they can. . . . His view is that a Parish Meeting . . . would squash [opposition] as all those interested in the sewerage question would be out for incorporation.

Collier's letter is interesting for a number of reasons. First, his informant got it right and the recalcitrant councillors eventually signed the agreement. Second, it is evidence of the closeness of the co-operation that existed between members and officers over the extension issue. The Town Clerk was in continuous correspondence with leading members of the council and the interchange of information between them was evidence of a relationship of confidence. Third, Collier's action in regard to the apparent change of mind in Tilehurst supports the statement made by Martin to one of the parliamentary committees refuting the assertion 'that on this question of the extension of the Borough the Town Council have been dominated by their officials, that the scheme was initiated by the officials, and that but for the officials it would have died of inanition'. Both in its genesis and in the activity of councillors in its development, the evidence supports Martin's view that allegations of officer dominance were 'sheer nonsense'.

The strength of Reading's case for incorporating Caversham arose in large measure from the effect that the corporation, as a most-purpose authority, was having on the development of the area. That effect, extending as it did to such diverse areas of public provision as gas, water, electricity, highways, public transport, education, fire protection, police, public health and, in the sense that the poor rate was by this time collected with other local government rates, welfare, was a powerful counterweight to the theoretical, historical and psychological difficulty of crossing the river and annexing territory from another county. For although there was a tone of self-confidence in the brief of the corporation to the Local Government Board, there was also an awareness that the difficulty of incorporating land from Oxfordshire would have to be faced and argued, to an extent quite separately from the case for amalgamation based on affinity, dependency and the rationalization of local government boundaries.

In the corporation's brief to its counsel before the public inquiry, the issue was dealt with by referring to other borough extensions: 'A precedent for a borough going outside its geographical county on extension will be found in the case of Birmingham; and a precedent for a borough crossing a river to absorb [part of] another county exists in the City of Oxford where the corporation took in a part of Berkshire.' This response to Caversham's argument for the maintenance of the historic boundary is evidence of the work done behind the scenes by Town Clerk Clutterbuck. As will be seen later, Clutterbuck was in regular touch with E. V. (later Sir Ernest) Hiley, Town Clerk of Birmingham, whose authority had a major extension Bill before Parliament at the same time as Reading's. Also, in 1909, there was an exchange of correspondence between Clutterbuck and the Town Clerk of Oxford, in which the latter gave a detailed account of the Oxford extension across the Thames and into Berkshire in 1889.

At base, Reading's case was that Caversham was no longer a village but an 'outgrowth', a residential suburb of Reading. Much of Caversham received its water supply from Reading and those parts of the urban district that had gas and electricity were served by companies which, though not yet municipally owned, carried on business under regulation and control exercised by the corporation. Reading's tramway service had been electrified in 1903 and ran to the southern end of Caversham Bridge, its extension into Caversham having been prevented because the urban district council had refused in 1899 to spend the money necessary to widen its streets. In consequence, a large number of Caversham residents, as was shown by a census conducted by the borough as part of the incorporation campaign, daily walked across the Clappers Foot-bridge and back, using the trams to get to and from work. In 1908, moreover, the Town Clerk conducted a house-to-house survey of 2,063 Caversham householders of whom almost half were employed or in business in Reading. This was also true of half of the members of Caversham UDC.

Since 1903 the borough had been an education authority and by 1909 the anomalous position of Caversham was apparent in a number of ways, all of which were brought out in the evidence of Councillor E. P. Collier to the local public inquiry and subse-quently to the parliamentary committees considering the Confirmation Bill. First, there were sixty-nine Caversham children at Swansea Road School, the nearest Reading school to the southern end of Caversham Bridge. Second, twenty-two school-teachers employed by Reading Education Committee lived in Caversham. Third, Reading had raised the school leaving age to fourteen, while in Oxfordshire it remained at thirteen. Thus Caversham children at Reading schools could leave a year earlier than their classmates and, according to Collier, 'families . . . did go over to Caversham . . . to send a boy into employment at thirteen'. Even allowing for a degree of exaggeration of the incidence of such moves, the clearly anomalous position of having two education regimes in the same urban area was a strong point in Reading's favour. Finally, education provision was quite simply of a much higher standard in Reading than in Caversham, a fact that had financial as well as educational implications. At the time of Reading's application to the Local Government Board, the education rate in Reading was 2s $0^1$4d while in Caversham it was $9^1$2d and, as Collier said in his evidence, 'it was solely the difference in the education rate which prevented Caversham rates from being in excess of the total of the Reading rates'. This was a bull point for Reading, for it was a way of undermining the opposition from Caversham based upon a fear of higher rates. All in all, the effects on education, a service to which national government gave a high priority, of the separation of Caversham from Reading, added strength to Reading's case.

Finally, in the protective services, Reading could argue the advantages that would accrue to Caversham after incorporation. On policing, as with education, it was argued that both service and efficiency levels would improve if policy and administration came from Reading rather than Oxford. As the borough's reply to the Caversham UDC petition against its proposals drily observed: 'The petitioners appear to have overlooked the fact that as regards . . . education and police . . . the district is administered by a body whose offices are situate about twenty-eight miles away.' Captain Henderson, Reading's Chief Constable, pointed out that, quite apart from the fact that the police station was about to move from High Bridge House to Valpy Street and would therefore be much closer to Caversham, the borough police could cover Caversham at least as effectively as could the county force and be more accessible. On fire cover, although Reading had said that it could not guarantee to protect Caversham while the district remained outside the borough to the same level as it did the town itself, 'neighbouring districts [knew] full well that in the case of a serious fire they could rely' on the Reading Fire Brigade. That reliance, because of the level of fire cover provided by Caversham UDC, was entirely one way, and Reading saw this as another point in favour of incorporation.

In public health, Reading argued that the Park Fever Hospital had been so designed as to facilitate expansion to serve a greater population, while Caversham UDC had no local provision for infectious diseases, the only other isolation hospital being in Henley. It was also alleged, so controversially that Councillor John Rabson, Chairman of the Public Health Committee, had to explain himself both publicly and in private letters to the Town Clerk (one of which was scribbled on the back of a Labour Party election leaflet), that standards of public health were so much higher in the borough that practice in Caversham constituted a threat to Reading. In particular, Rabson had referred to meat inspection by saying that 'all efforts which Reading made to keep its food supply pure . . . were negatived by the opportunities given in these . . . districts that were practically part of Reading', and he cited examples of meat that failed to conform to Reading's standards being taken to be slaughtered and sold in Caversham. Caversham's reply was couched in more general terms related to the reports of the Medical Officer of Health, and it is difficult not to conclude that, despite the public outcry in Caversham, Reading had the better of the argument.

When all these arguments were put together, Reading's case was a strong one and one which depended on the capacity of the county borough to see public provision in the round. Caversham would fight against incorporation on many specific grounds but, in the end, it found it very difficult to refute the conclusion of Reading's Alderman Parfitt that 'Caversham has the resources of a village and the requirements of a town'.

Reading's tactics in the incorporation campaign were, in many ways, determined by the attitude taken by Caversham UDC as its main opponent. The corporation was under no illusions at the start of the expansion process about the implacability of the district council's opposition. None the less it was essential, in the preparation of the borough's case, to go through the motions of seeking consultations, negotiations, information and agreement. Caversham, however, pressed its opposition to the point of total non-co-operation with the corporation, refusing to meet the Finance and General Purposes Committee or to provide the corporation with the information of a purely factual kind that it requested during the period when the original brief was in preparation. Caversham adhered to this policy throughout, even after Dryland had decided to 'sell his pigs in the best market'. As late as April 1910, a year after the publication of the provisional order, although still before the second reading of the Confirmation Bill, Caversham refused to provide, for the inspection of the Borough Surveyor, plans of a road scheme for which the district council had applied to the Local Government Board for loan sanction. Rawstorne, Clerk to Caversham UDC, wrote to Clutterbuck on 6 April 1910 advising Reading 'to obtain from the Local Government Board any information and particulars' the council required. Similarly in November 1910, when all that remained of the process was the Commons committee stage of the Confirmation Bill already given a second reading, and its considerations by the Lords (both of which were, in the event, delayed by the second general election of 1910), Caversham UDC refused to attend a meeting with Reading Borough Council to discuss terms because 'as this Council are still as strongly opposed as ever . . . they are of the opinion that no useful purpose would be served'. Caversham did not enter negotiations until the spring of 1911, just before the House of Lords committee stage, by which time, in the words of J. St Laurence Stallwood, an anti-incorporationist Caversham district and Oxfordshire county councillor, 'Caversham could not afford to win'. Stallwood's remark was a perceptive one, and one which indicated the strength of Reading's arguments. For as well as emphasizing the affinity between Caversham and Reading, the corporation had succeeded in demonstrating how much lower were the standards of public services across the river. This had stimulated the district council into a series of proposals for capital expenditure on waterworks, road improvements, the fire brigade, provision of an infectious diseases hospital, even extension of its boundaries into Mapledurham, and it was clear that Caversham's rates advantage over Reading was either artificial or temporary or both. Thus as the incorporation question put improvements on the agenda for Caversham, it also strengthened the case for Caversham becoming part of a larger local government area and so able to draw on greater expertise, more resources and higher borrowing power. By rushing to spend, particularly in 1909 and 1910, Caversham UDC, rather paradoxically perhaps, strengthened Reading's case by trying to weaken it.

Throughout the extension campaign, Reading sought to demonstrate openness, approachability and, except in the matter of its determination to take in the whole of the Caversham UDC area, flexibility. At no time did the corporation retaliate in response to Caversham's refusal to co-operate. The corporation accepted without demur the conditions specified by Caversham for observers from Reading to scrutinize the ratepayers' poll called by the district council and acceded readily to a request that the consultant engineer to the district council be allowed to inspect the borough's sewage farm and works at Manor Farm. To emphasize its wish to consult with Caversham and also, no doubt, to emphasize the contrast between Caversham UDC's obduracy and its own wish to proceed by agreement, the corporation decided in May 1909, after Caversham's refusal to negotiate, to invite representatives of a committee of Caversham property-owners and residents in favour of incorporation to discuss the possible terms for preferential rating.

The corporation's case for taking in Mapledurham and Caversham Park was, in the context of its time, less strong than that for incorporating Caversham itself. It could be argued that on development grounds and on the basis of the water supply area, it would be prudent for the corporation to go beyond the urban district council area, but the case could hardly be presented with the emphasis on natural affinity and community of interest that had been so successfully deployed in the case of Caversham. Besides, there was vociferous opposition on Reading Council to the proposals to bring in Mapledurham, as well as the complication introduced by the need to deal with yet another authority, Goring RDC. Councillor Frame not only opposed the incorporation of Mapledurham by motion in council, but also corresponded privately on the matter with one of Caversham's county councillors,

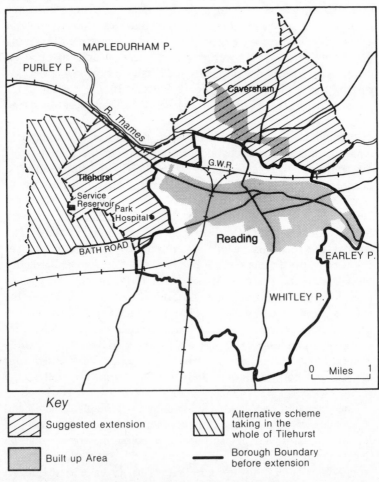

Figure 4.2   *Boundary Extensions, 1911*

the Reverend R. H. Hart-Davis, who was in favour of the Caversham proposals but not those for the adjacent rural areas. The position of Mapledurham was, in fact, very similar to that of the rural part of Tilehurst and the corporation dropped the proposals for Mapledurham before the public inquiry took place.

The provisional order issued by the Local Government Board approved the extensions proposed by the borough subject to two conditions. First, Reading would be required to build a new vehicular bridge at Lower Caversham within five years of incorporation; and, second, Caversham would be subject to preferential rating for a longer period than the ten years proposed by Reading. These conditions were readily accepted by Alderman Martin who was aware that the borough's most important objective, the extension of its boundaries, would now be met. Moreover, he was clear that the issue of the provisional order greatly strengthened the borough's hand for, as he put it:

> If the Caversham Council refuse to negotiate it will be for Reading to inform the Local Government Board of the terms they are willing to offer. If Caversham are prepared to be obstinate, they will no doubt have to pay for it.

As we have seen, Caversham's obstinacy was maintained until 1911 when there took place a series of negotiations, not dissimilar to the earlier ones involving Tilehurst, the result of which was an agreement that Caversham's rates would be abated by 9d in the pound for fifteen years in return for the withdrawal by Caversham Urban District Council and Oxfordshire County Council of their opposition to the Confirmation Bill in the House of Lords. This was Reading's final concession, raising the abatement by 1d as the price of easing the final passage of the Confirmation Bill.

The parliamentary consideration of the extension of Reading's boundaries was notable for a number of reasons. First, the Confirmation Bill was opposed at second reading by members briefed both by Caversham and by Oxfordshire and by county members alarmed at the general effects on county government of the territorial ambitions of boroughs throughout the country. Martin was not unduly concerned. 'I am not surprised at the opposition', he wrote to Clutterbuck on 8 July 1910, only a few days before the second reading debate in the Commons, 'consider-

ing how *irresponsible* MPs have been got at.' The motion against
second reading was moved by Sir Alfred Cripps, the Unionist
Member for Wycombe, and it cannot be said that his speech, on 13
July, was very well informed. In condemning what Lord Valentia,
the MP for Oxford and Chairman of Oxfordshire County Council
had earlier described as the 'predatory policy' of Reading, Cripps
gave the population of Reading as 'something like a quarter of a
million' when it was actually about 80,000. Cripps's exaggeration
was pointed out later in the debate by John Burns, the President of
the Local Government Board, who as sponsoring minister was
determined that the Bill should have its second reading and be
referred to the Select Committee on Private Bills which, in
accordance with normal procedure, would then report to the House
on the conditions upon which it should be passed.

The unusual step of opposing second reading was, in fact, a part
of the campaign to ensure that county councils would be
compensated for the loss of rateable value, an issue which, on the
authority of the Prime Minister, had already been referred to a
Joint Committee of the two Houses of Parliament. The Bill got its
second reading without a division, and the Select Committee was
instructed to insert a clause to implement in the cases of Berkshire
and Oxfordshire the decision of the Joint Committee. It was on this
basis that Reading, in the spring of 1911, reached agreement with
the two county councils.

Although it was never likely that the Confirmation Bill would
fail, Reading, through the tireless efforts of the Town Clerk, took
no chances. Concern about the future of the counties had been
raised, in particular, by the major territorial ambitions of
Birmingham whose extension into Worcestershire, Warwickshire
and Staffordshire was under consideration at the same time as the
Reading Bill. E. V. Hiley, the Town Clerk of Birmingham, wrote
to Clutterbuck on 14 June 1910 proposing joint action with Bath
City Council, which was also seeking boundary extensions at the
time. The result was a campaign to enlist the support of boroughs
and their MPs from all over the country. On the specific issue of
financial compensation, Reading's parliamentary agents circularized
all Town Clerks on the need to oppose the claims of the counties.
Clutterbuck himself contacted a large number of Town Clerks (for
example, those of Bristol, Cheltenham, Dartford, King's Lynn,
Gloucester) asking them, successfully in most cases, to ensure that

their borough MPs were present in the event of a vote being called on the Reading Bill, as it had been on the Birmingham Bill shortly before. Telegrams went out from the Town Hall in the days before the second reading debate and telegrams in reply flooded into Clutterbuck's office. Almost unanimously the Town Clerks promised support, though some were doubtful about the attitude of the MPs concerned.

Reading's own MP, Sir Rufus Isaacs, was in a difficult position. As Solicitor-General he had on 11 June 1910 excused himself from giving evidence before the Select Committee which would consider the Confirmation Bill 'in view of my official position and the possibilities of my having to deal with this Bill as a Law Officer advising the Local Government Board' (Isaacs-Clutterbuck, 11 June 1910). He did, however, act as a constituency MP in keeping Clutterbuck informed of moves in Westminster and Whitehall. He had also on 23 July 1909 sent a telegram to the Mayor saying that he had satisfied himself that there was 'no truth in the report that the Local Government Board has changed its mind respecting issue of Provisional Order'. He intervened in the second reading debate both to correct the grosser errors of the opponents and to emphasize that it was 'most unusual to discuss a private Bill of this character in its intricacies' at second reading. On the evening of the second reading debate, he entertained the Mayor and the Town Clerk to dinner at the House of Commons, taking care to inform them that although they might choose to wear formal clothes, 'I myself shall not dress'.

The Confirmation Bill was finally passed by the House of Lords in July 1911, with certain changes from the text of both the provisional order and the Bill as it had emerged from the Commons. Most significantly, the provision obliging the corporation to build a new vehicular bridge was replaced by a provision to widen or reconstruct the existing Caversham Bridge and to construct a new footbridge. (In the event, a second vehicular bridge was not completed until the opening of Reading Bridge in 1923 and the new Caversham Bridge was opened in 1926.) The agreement on differential rating was inserted in the Bill and the petition of the only substantial property-owner to oppose extension, Mr Crawshay of Caversham Park, succeeded and his estate remained outside the borough. In view of the later history of the Caversham Park Estate which, as the site of the major modern residential suburb of

Caversham Park Village, came into Reading in 1977, it is interesting, and perhaps a little ironic, that the strongest argument deployed against its inclusion in the extension of 1911 was that it would never be developed.

Extension Proposals: 1947 and 1965

In 1945 the wartime Coalition government published a White Paper (Cmd 6579) entitled *Local Government in England and Wales During the Period of Reconstruction*. Its conclusions had been anticipated the previous year when Parliament was told that changes were necessary in the status, boundaries and areas of local authorities, but in the context of the existing system of counties and county boroughs. The Local Government (Boundary Commission) Act 1945 gave legislative effect to the proposal to set up a Local Government Boundary Commission (LGBC) and, as the commission began the reviews which it was intended would eventually cover the whole country, Reading, in common with many other boroughs, began to consider the case it could make for extensions to the boundaries set in 1911.

In May 1946 the Town Clerk reported to the Parliamentary Committee of the council on the arguments in favour of preparing a detailed application for extension. It was clear enough that Reading fell within the priority classification of the commission, which entailed giving preference in its reviews to issues of the status and boundaries of upper-tier authorities – the counties and the county boroughs – rather than to those involving only county districts. The corporation had to decide whether to proceed in the light of the main factors which the commission indicated that it would consider: community of interest, development and anticipated development, economic and industrial characteristics, financial resources and financial need, physical features, administrative record, and the wishes of the inhabitants.

The Boundary Commission procedure offered boroughs that wanted to expand the first new opportunity to make their case since the passage in 1926 of an Act which limited the provisional order method to unopposed boundary extensions, all others to be promoted by private Bill. This change, introduced to regulate and mitigate the acrimonious disputes between county boroughs on the one hand, and counties and county districts on the other, over territory and tax base, had greatly decelerated the process of change in the local government system. It had reduced the incidence of open and official hostility between councils but, in a period of rapid demographic change, this inevitably resulted in an equally rapid obsolescence of boundaries established between 1888 and 1926. The extent of this obsolescence was revealed in 1940 by the report of the Barlow Commission on the Distribution of the Industrial Population. In Reading the effects were seen in the expansion of urban development into areas on the fringe of the 1911 boundary, in Tilehurst, Earley, Woodley and Caversham. It was unlikely that the council would hesitate to state its case.

The application to extend in 1946 was quite unlike the two previous campaigns in 1887 and 1911. On both of these occasions, as we have seen, the council had shown itself to be a self-starter, the initiatives taken by members and by the officers whom they employed. The agenda was set in Reading and the tactics were developed in Reading, with councillors, Town Clerk, parliamentary agents and counsel reacting quickly and effectively to issues raised by opponents, by Parliament and by public opinion. In 1946-8, the council's role was largely reactive, tailoring its case to suit the policies and prejudices of a reforming government whose view of the local government system was intimately connected with its commitment to a new conception of the scope and importance of planning in all its forms. Thus, not only did the brief prepared by the corporation take as its guide the main factors indicated by the commission, but also it was couched in terms calculated to appeal to the preferences of the Ministry of Town and Country Planning, whose political head, Lewis Silkin, on a visit to Reading in June 1946, urged the borough council 'to make a comprehensive plan for the town' and stressed 'the need for joint planning of the whole area'. He described Reading as 'the centre of a region' and indicated that, to some extent, the future development of the town and its environs would be affected both by the implementation of the Greater London Plan and by the government's decision to overspill some of London's population into Berkshire. In short, the case to be made would be constrained both by the need to placate as far as possible the inevitable local opposition and by the need to demonstrate its compatibility with a developing planning orthodoxy.

The council's proposals for extension were published in 1947 and they represented the borough's most ambitious territorial claim. In area, the borough would have increased by well over two-and-a-half times, though the proposed increase in population was only 17·5 per cent and in rateable value 20 per cent. The heavy emphasis on territorial growth, growth which, as the proposals conceded, would have added to rather than eased the borough's immediate financial commitments, arose directly from the interpretation placed by the council's professional staff on two government pronouncements. First, Cmd 6579 had said that 'the time has come for a different approach to [linking town and country] and for a recognition of the fact that the interests of the country town and the surrounding countryside are not diverse but complementary'. Second, the guidelines of the boundary commission had emphasized that boundary reviews would look at both actual and anticipated development.

Thus, for the third time in sixty years, the borough sought to define its area in a way that would be conclusive. It did so by seeking to expand well beyond the existing line of development to take in Purley, Burghfield, Three Mile Cross, Earley, Woodley, Sonning, Binfield Heath and Mapledurham. The application failed when the government in 1948 abruptly abolished the boundary commission and because of this it is easy to forget that, of all Reading's attempts to solve the conundrum of fit between its social and economic reality and its political jurisdiction, this was the most convincing and, in some ways, the most prescient. The point is made by noting that all of the major suburban developments of the 1960s, 1970s and 1980s – in Calcot, Woodley, Lower Earley, Caversham Park, Purley, Tilehurst – which occurred outside the borough (with only Caversham Park coming in as a belated consequence of local government reorganization) were situated within what was known as the 'Purple Plan Area' of the 1947 proposals. Had the application succeeded, they would have been part of the Borough of Reading.

Despite the fact that it did not succeed, a number of factors should be noted about the 1947 extension plan. It is significant of the rapid growth of local government professionalism in the twentieth century that in 1947, in contrast to 1887 and 1911, the lead in the move to expand was clearly taken by the council's officers, with members reacting to and endorsing the recommendations and professional judgements of Town Clerk, Surveyor and other chief officers. When the council gave the authority to proceed with the preparation of a detailed proposal to the LGBC, Town Clerk Darlow wrote to all chief officers instructing them to prepare memoranda on how their departments' performance and future needs would assist in promoting the expansion cause. His memorandum was detailed and specific on the planning of the campaign and on the form and content of the document that would be the basis of the application. Also, it was the Town Clerk who attended public meetings in the proposed added areas to explain Reading's case, playing a role that, in the earlier campaigns, would have been performed by Councillor George William Colebrook and Alderman John Wessley Martin. The proposal, moreover, in reviewing the history of attempts to co-ordinate planning on both sides of the borough boundary, said that before the issue came to council, the officers had concluded 'that the area adjacent to the existing Borough boundary, and shown on the various maps by a purple line, should be considered for development of an urban character'. This was a different process of decision-making from the occasion in 1884 when Colebrook drew his line on the map and then sought the reactions of the Borough Surveyor.

As in previous extension moves, relations with the surrounding authorities, and in particular with the county councils, were important. And here, the clearer definition of the spheres of operation of the members and the officers was revealed late in 1946. After the borough's Parliamentary Committee had agreed to inform the LGBC of the corporation's intention to apply for an extension to its boundaries, preliminary discussions took place between Reading's planners and their colleagues in neighbouring authorities. These discussions were exploratory in two directions: Reading needed to know the strength of the opposition to its plans; and even without an extension to the borough, there was a need to investigate the joint planning possibilities for the area, particularly in view of Lewis Silkin's exhortation to all the planning authorities in the area to look comprehensively at the needs of the town. In November 1946, however, the Mayor of Reading, Alderman Phoebe Cusden, was quoted in the press as saying that these discussions had made 'substantial progress in the drawing-up of suggested new boundaries'. This elicited from the Vice-Chairman of Berkshire County Council a denial that any such discussions had taken place. The Mayor then issued a statement to the effect that she had 'inadvertently connected the two questions of planning and borough extension'.

A final point to be made about the 1947 application concerns those specific parts of the proposal dealing with Reading's need to expand in order to satisfy the existing as distinct from the anticipated needs of the urban area. For although the stimulus for the application came from central government pronouncements on the future of both planning and local government, Reading was experiencing locally a serious shortage of land. Councillor Baker, Chairman of the Housing Committee, had said in 1946 that the borough's target of building 3,400 houses in five years would be achieved only if it went outside its boundaries for sites. The pressure on the borough's housing provision would be increased by the slum clearance proposals in the town centre that were a necessary preliminary to the plans for a new civic centre. In education, too, the borough's development plan for primary and secondary schools, and the proposals for a technical college, increased the land requirements of the council and, given the need to build schools near existing centres of population within the borough, this added to the pressure to go outside for housing purposes.

The abolition of the LGBC was not quite the final act in the 1947-9 extension campaign. Even if Reading had succeeded in gaining territory, it might have done so only at the cost of losing its status as an all-purpose county borough, a fate that did not overtake the borough until 1974. The second report of the LGBC in 1947 had proposed that Reading should become a 'new county borough', losing its powers in town and country planning, major highways, police and fire cover to the county council. That idea died with the commission as did the hope of extension to the boundaries, but Reading's need for land persisted. In October 1949, two months after the LGBC had been wound up, the corporation resolved to promote a local Bill to extend the borough boundaries.

It is doubtful whether the corporation would have been successful in the promotion of a Bill that would have been fiercely contested by two county councils and four rural districts, one of which – Wokingham – had, like Caversham in 1908, refused to provide the borough with the information it requested during the preparation of the proposals for the LGBC. In the local area, however, the decision to proceed by private Bill was a valuable bargaining ploy in the search for development sites outside the borough. In December 1949 the point was put clearly by Alderman Bale: 'The Council has no desire at this time to promote an Extension Bill . . . except from the point of view of safeguarding the Housing programme.' In the two months between October and December 1949, agreement was reached with both Berkshire and Oxfordshire whereby the counties would release land to Reading for housing purposes and help to put pressure on the Ministry of Town and Country Planning to get development approval, while Reading would not proceed with its private Bill. The county councils could afford to be co-operative, for the release of sites to Reading for overspill housing neither fundamentally compromised

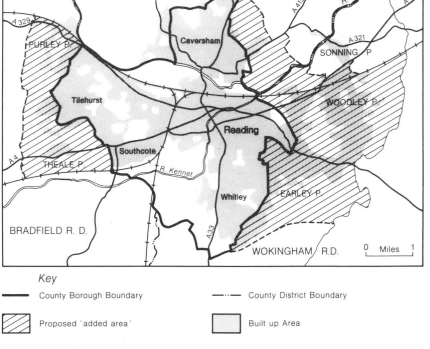

Key

━━━ County Borough Boundary   ─··─ County District Boundary

▨ Proposed 'added area'   ▢ Built up Area

Figure 4.3 *Boundary Proposals, 1965*

the rural character they attributed to their areas, nor resulted in loss of territory or tax base. On the contrary, the Reading housing developments would increase the revenue value of the land so released. None the less the need to build housing estates outside the borough was clear evidence that the boundaries were out of date. It was hard to defend a situation where council tenants in, for example, Woodley, paid rents to Reading and rates to Wokingham and Berkshire. But that anomaly still awaits a solution.

Reading's final attempt to secure a major extension to its boundaries may be dealt with briefly. The Local Government Act 1958 had set up a Local Government Commission to conduct boundary reviews throughout the country. In 1965 it announced that it intended to proceed with a review in the Reading area. The council's proposals to the commission, tailored as in 1947 to meet the guidelines published and drawn up in the light of the conclusions of reviews already complete, were based on the work done in 1947. They were, however, more modest, restricted to the 'blue line' on the 1947 plan, the area agreed by the Berkshire, Oxfordshire and Reading Joint Advisory Planning Committee as the desirable area for urban and suburban development. Under the proposal, the area of the borough would have not quite doubled but the population would have risen by 33·5 per cent to 164,691, twice as big an increase as that proposed in a much larger area in 1947. The difference arose from the council's response to the Local Government Commission, which did not emphasize, as the LGBC had done after the war, the need to consider town and country comprehensively. Thus the council saw no advantage in including the Green Belt within the borough's proposed new boundaries.

In the event, and despite the appointment of a strong delegation composed of two party leaders and six senior officers, including Town Clerk Darlow and Deputy Town Clerk Harry Tee, to meet the commission to press Reading's case, the proposal never got off the ground. The work of the Local Government Commission was suspended in early 1966 when the responsible minister, Richard Crossman, proposed the appointment of the Royal Commission on Local Government in England. From then on, the local government future of Reading, in both area and status, was out of the hands of the borough council, decided by the complex interplay of impartial inquiry, the search for national partisan advantage and the tortuous processes of parliamentary bargaining.

5

Education and the Politicians

The educational opportunities offered by the Council are
many and valuable. They will be fully effective only when the
lost belief in education returns.
> Reading Education Committee Report, 1909-10

The cynical [may] observe that the Development Plans of
Local Authorities are mere records of pious hopes which
provided a good deal of exercise for ingenious minds but
which can now acquire . . . dust in pigeon holes.
> Reading Education Committee Report, 1945-50

The reason for selecting children at the age of eleven is . . .
conditioned by the shortage of grammar school places and not
by lack of talent among the child population.
> Reading Labour Group, *Report . . . into the System of
> Selecting Children . . . for Secondary Education*, 1963

Reading Borough Council became an education authority in 1903.
The Education Act 1902 had abolished the separately constituted
and directly elected School Boards and had made county councils
and county borough councils responsible for the provision of
elementary and secondary education. This change had the effect of
integrating the education service with other aspects of local public
services provided by the borough council, leaving only the Poor
Law in the hands of a separate public authority. This institutional
rearrangement should be seen, in the case of a county borough like
Reading, more as a rationalization and consolidation than as an
innovation. The council had had an interest in educational matters
since the corporation was reformed in 1835, and in the years
between the establishment of the School Board in 1871 and the
transfer of its functions to the Education Committee in 1903 that
interest had been increased both by the continuing role of the

corporation as collector of the School Board rate and by the adoption by the council of various permissive statutes in the educational field. From 1898, for example, the corporation had an Educational and Technical Instruction Committee through which it provided support, mainly from excise taxes transferred to local authorities under an Act of 1890, for continuing education in the Schools of Science and Art, Reading University Extension College and various private and philanthropic societies and institutions.

Under the Municipal Corporations Act 1835, the corporation were trustees not only of the so-called Free Grammar School (founded in the fifteenth century by Henry VII and supported by various charitable bequests) but also of the Kendrick Charities set up to administer bequests to the town for the relief of the poor. By the 1860s the reputation of Reading School had declined to the point where the council, on the initiative of the Mayor, Henry John Simonds, a member of a local brewing family associated with the corporation throughout the nineteenth century, secured a new Act of Parliament reconstituting the school under a new scheme of management under which the trustees were named as the Mayor and aldermen *ex officiis*, the vicars of the three parishes, also *ex officiis*, and three further trustees appointed by the corporation. Under the new scheme, the trustees were able to buy for £4,000 a ten-acre site from the Redlands Estate Company and to build a new school, designed by Alfred Waterhouse, to replace the unsuitable and crowded premises in the centre of the town, which the school had formerly occupied.

The financial position of the school was, however, far from secure and it was for financial reasons rather than educational ones that the corporation got intimately involved in its affairs. Briefly stated, the income of the school from scholars' fees for tuition and boarding were insufficient to meet its needs. In particular, the 1867 Act had empowered the trustees to raise the money required to purchase the site for the new school and to erect the new buildings by raising mortgage loans on the security of the Portland Place Estate, owned by the John Kendricke Loan Charity of which they were also trustees. Loans to a total of £26,000 were secured from the Economic Life Assurance Company and from George Palmer, but in 1877 the trustees, finding themselves unable to meet the mortgage payments, decided to apply to the Charity Commissioners to raise the fees charged to scholars. Such an increase required the consent of the corporation which was withheld pending a conference between the council and the trustees of the school. The council's concern arose from three distinct sources. First, when the trustees had taken out the mortgages (£20,000 to Economic Life and £6,000 to George Palmer) in 1872, the corporation had acted as guarantor, and counsel's opinion suggested that in default of payment by the trustees, the corporation would be liable. Second, as the corporate body representative of the town's public opinion, the council was not favourably disposed to any increase in fees, or any change in the character of the school, which would be to the disadvantage of their constituents. Third, and more generally, this first of several financial crises in the history of Reading School came at a time when the corporation, because of the vast capital spending associated with the sewerage scheme and the consequent economizing pressures of the Ratepayers' Association, was intent on minimizing any call on the rate fund that might arise from a position in which, to quote the report of the trustees in 1877, 'the great difficulty with which the School has to contend is the unsatisfactory condition of its finances'. Part of the corporation's difficulty was that the courses of action implied by these concerns might well be mutually incompatible.

The corporation was caught between the pressures of economy and the consequences of the decision that Reading School should be a 'first grade school'. The trustees, a very clear majority of whom were members of the corporation, were reluctant to offend their constituents by raising the fees charged to the sons of the middle classes with whose interests they closely identified. At the same time, the council's economizing spirit made the trustees set their face against subsidizing the school from the borough rates. A proposal for differential fees, with Reading boys charged less than those from other places, was opposed by the headmaster, Dr Thomas Stokoe, on the grounds that it would amount to a change in the school's character which would make it uncompetitive with other public schools.

Stokoe's attitude emphasizes the underlying problem about Reading School and the position of the corporation in relation to it. At no time was the council very clear about the educational character it wanted the school to assume. For reasons of local and civic prestige, and perhaps because of a historical sentiment which sought to attribute to the school founded by Henry VII a continuity of existence which the facts would not support, civic leaders were attracted by the notion of having a public school in the town. At the same time, because they were civic leaders, and because of the role in the governing of the school given to the corporation by the 1867 Act, the council saw the school as a local institution which added to the range of opportunity for their constituents. The possible incompatibility of these views of the school was highlighted in a letter sent by the headmaster to the trustees in June 1877 in which he claimed to have been misled by the advertisement to which he had replied in 1870 into believing that he would be head of a public school which 'would emulate the example of Rugby and Harrow'. The 1870 prospectus of the school had referred to 'a thorough Middle Class education to be supplemented by a lower school for the benefit of the lower classes'. Stokoe argued that such a statement was inconsistent with the advertisement to which he had replied and that had that description appeared in the advertisement he would not have come forward. Soon after writing this letter, Stokoe resigned, having 'give[n] up all hope of . . . raising this school to a recognised and important position among the "first grade" or public schools'.

The 1877 controversy about the nature and future of Reading School produced both a leading article and a long correspondence in *The Times*. It also caused such controversy in the town that the Charity Commissioners, whose approval was necessary for changes in the fees charged to pupils and for the sale of assets to discharge the school's indebtedness, declined to be further involved until the trustees came up with a clear plan for the financial viability of the school. They took this action because of 'the contentious character which the case has now assumed'. That contentiousness arose not only from debates about the character of the school and the attempts of the corporation to arrive at a fee structure that discriminated in favour of boys resident in Reading, but also from the form which any rate fund contribution to the finances of the school might take. There was widespread opposition, as part of the generally economizing mood of the time, to any subsidy of the operating costs of the school. On 3 November 1877 the *Berkshire Chronicle*, in an objection to expenditure couched in terms which anticipated by almost a century socialist objections to grammar and direct grant schools, asked of those proposing a rate fund contribution: 'Do they mean that the denizens of Silver Street are to pay for the education of boys who live in the best houses in the town and neighbourhood?' However, by the terms of the 1867 Act, a corporation contribution might become unavoidable, a view confirmed by counsel's opinion in September 1877. Any instalment of the mortgages not paid by the trustees would fall to be paid by the corporation and according to counsel, they could not do 'anything . . . in their Corporate capacity for protecting the interests of the ratepayers'.

The outcome of the 1877 financial crisis was one that did nothing conclusive to settle either the nature of the school or its long-term financial viability. The trustees, after a conference with the corporation, decided that the school should continue as 'a first grade school with a large modern element', an obvious but potentially unstable compromise between the two views discussed above. The Portland Place Estate was sold to George Palmer, who then donated £500 to the school on condition that the trustees did the same with £1,000 of the proceeds from the sale. Thus the mortgage to Palmer was discharged and it was hoped that this, together with increased fee income and the proceeds both of the donations and of the balance of the sale price, would enable the school to diminish its indebtedness and meet repayments on the mortgage still outstanding to Economic Life. A new headmaster, William Walker, was, after several hesitations related to the ferocity of the local controversy about the school, persuaded to confirm his acceptance of the post. The school, having been closed after the departure of Stokoe, reopened in January 1878.

Without any continuing aid from the rates, Reading School was almost entirely dependent on a fee income that was clearly insufficient to meet its expenditure. As part of the rearrangement of the corporation's finances under the terms of the 1881 Act (see Chapter 3), the corporation was authorized to lend £18,000 to the Reading School Trustees to pay off the mortgage to Economic Life. This loan was repayable over seventy years in half-yearly instalments, but by 1886 the trustees had insufficient funds to meet the repayments. The corporation received no further payments between 1886 and the eventual take-over of the school by the council (as the local education authority) in 1908. Thus, as those who supported such a take-over, first unsuccessfully in 1905 and then successfully in 1908, argued, the ratepayers, because the corporation was not receiving any repayments, were contributing to the running costs of the school, but in a way that gave their elected representatives no direct influence on the expenditure.

It is difficult to resist the conclusion that between 1870 and 1902, when the level of educational provision, despite the continuing pressure for economy in public services, was constantly increased by the activities of the School Board, the development of education in the borough was ill-served by the increasingly anomalous position not only of Reading School, but also of the Kendrick Schools. The Kendrick Schools were established in 1875 to provide education for one hundred boys and one hundred girls and were financed by the conversion to educational purposes of certain non-educational charities. The trustees were to be appointed in part by the corporation and in part by the School Board and there were to be exhibitions and scholarships, awarded on merit, to prospective entrants to the schools. Accessibility to the Kendrick Schools was a controversial issue from the outset. When the Kendrick School scheme was under consideration, the council received a memorial from the Reading Working Men's Liberal Association objecting to the fact that the conversion of the charities would divert to the middle classes money 'left to a great extent for the benefit of the poor' and the *Berkshire Chronicle* agreed (16 January 1875) when it said of the Kendrick scheme: 'It is essentially a middle class school. The amount of fees payable establish this beyond question. . . . In our opinion the Kendrick School [sic] and the Grammar School are each a peg too high.'

While the corporation might congratulate itself, both on the reconstitution of Reading School and on the establishment of the Kendrick Schools, it had done so in a way which would complicate the development of the town's education policies recurrently for over a century. In particular, as will be described later, Reading School exerted an influence on educational administrators and policy-makers far in excess of that to which, on any objective assessment of its contribution to the education of the town's children, it might have been entitled. Also, in the years before the corporation itself became the education authority, its attempts to deal with the very weak financial condition of Reading School had to be undertaken in a way that was divorced from the general provision of education by the School Board. For much of the period, to quote a Board of Education Report on the inspection of the school in 1903, 'the School [was] practically farmed to the Head

Master', the corporation and the trustees having effectively given up any attempt to secure the future of the school. In 1887 there was an abortive negotiation to amalgamate the school with the Royal Merchant Navy School at New Cross in Kent after which a new headmaster, F. P. Barnard, was appointed. The financial arrangements, whereby three-fifths of the scholars' fees went to the head who was thereafter responsible for all aspects of the running of the school including the salaries of assistant masters, were such that, as the 1903 report noted, the headmaster 'could not have continued in office without private means'. This position was affected only marginally by the corporation's decisions in 1889 to relieve the school of liability for rates for three years and in 1890 to pay the headmaster a small stipend in addition to his share of the capitation fees. The extent of the headmaster's personal subsidy to the school may be inferred from the claim for compensation made in 1914 by the then headmaster, Dr Eppstein, for loss of office after the amalgamation of Kendrick Boys' School with Reading School. In his letter to the Education Committee, Eppstein suggested that he was by then £6,000 poorer than he had been when he came to Reading in 1894. No doubt the corporation was proud to have Reading School available to provide 'a thorough Middle Class education' to the sons of their constituents, but apart from not insisting on receipt of loan repayments, it did little to ensure its continuing viability. Even in the provision of scholarship funds, the corporation's contribution was derisory, and the inspectors in 1903 'consider[ed] it a matter of regret that part of the public funds granted by the Council was not applied to assist poor boys to enter the School'. Apart from the notional amount accounted for by not enforcing loan repayment after 1886, that sum was only £200 per annum and the entrance scholarships provided by the headmaster and his staff 'out of their own pockets' were quite inadequate to fill the gap. The corporation's withdrawal and the institutional detachment of the School Board led inevitably to a process by which a school that was nominally in the public sector assumed a private and separate character. It was that character which supporters of the school continuously defended after responsibility for education was assumed by the corporation in 1903.

During this period, while the corporation wrestled intermittently and unsuccessfully with the financial problems of Reading School, the range of educational provision in the town was expanding through the efforts of the School Board. The original council resolution to seek the establishment of a School Board was moved in council in 1870 by George Palmer and the first elections to the board took place on 20 March 1871. In terms of the comprehensive provision of local services, the importance of education in the government of Reading was greatly enhanced when the corporation became the local education authority in 1903, but it is important to note here the relationship in the School Board years, for there is a degree of continuity both in the policies and in the administrative and political arrangements as one institution succeeded the other. Moreover, it was the School Board which laid the educational foundations upon which the corporation had to build.

As was noted at the end of Chapter 3, the detachment from the corporation of the School Board, as a directly elected public authority, was diminished in its effects by a number of functional relationships. The most important of these was the method whereby the board raised its revenue. It did not directly levy a rate. Rather it determined its budget and then sent a precept or claim to the corporation which then raised the money as part of the borough rates. Thus, throughout the School Board period, the corporation was aware of the costs of education, though it had little opportunity directly to affect them. Some impression of these costs may be gained from the information given in the School Board Reports of the amounts received from the borough council. In 1875 the amount was £1,450, the equivalent of a rate of little more than $2\frac{1}{2}$d in the pound; by 1879 a rate of $5\frac{1}{2}$d brought in £3,000; in 1892 the rate was $10\frac{1}{4}$d which raised £12,500; and in the last year of the School Board, 1902, the precept was for £25,000, the equivalent of a rate of 1s $3\frac{3}{4}$d in the pound. As with all local government precepts, the corporation had no option but to pay up, though there is some evidence that payments were sometimes remitted late. In 1878, for example, the board complained that 'much inconvenience had arisen from delay in the payment of the amounts by the Rating Authority' and in 1881 it noted that all the money it had received in the financial year had been from previous precepts, the current year's still being unpaid.

A second functional relationship arose from the personnel of board and council. It should be noted first that, quite apart from the individuals involved, the membership of public bodies was drawn predominantly from the prosperous middle class and that there was therefore a community of interest, a shared attitude to the role of public authorities and to the proper role of government in the provision of services. To some extent, the influence of this factor was mitigated in the case of the School Boards, first by the encouragement of expenditure which arose from national policy and central government grants and second from an electoral system which made it easier for minority or rising groups to achieve representation. The Education Act 1870, in order to protect the interests of religious minorities, had introduced for School Board elections a system of plural voting, whereby each eligible elector had a number of votes equal to the number of places to be filled. The voter could, however, distribute these votes in any way he chose, including casting them all for a single candidate. As Cook (1970, p. 296) notes, this facilitated the earlier election of working-class, Socialist and Labour representatives to the School Board than to the corporation.

More specifically, the distance between board and council was reduced by cross-membership, by the election of individuals to both bodies. Cook (1970, pp. 182, 252) shows that throughout the School Board years there was no occasion when fewer than half the members of the corporation were also involved in education. It is true that these figures would not differentiate between such involvements as trusteeship of Reading School and elected membership of the School Board, but the membership lists of the latter reveal frequent presence of individuals prominent also in corporation affairs. Cook's figures also reflect the extent to which the board appointed members of the corporation to be school managers, a position which was often the first step on the road to membership of the board itself. Sometimes the direction was reversed, with appointment as a manager preceding both election to the board and election as a councillor. Edith Sutton, who in 1907 was to become the first woman elected to Reading Corporation (and the first woman borough councillor in the country), became a school manager in the 1890s, was elected to the School Board in 1901, and was co-opted to the Education Committee when it was set up in 1903.

Finally, just as the board and corporation drew on the same 'pool' of members, so they were affected by the same social political and economic pressures, some pushing them towards expenditure, others towards economy. The School Board was under the insistent pressure not only of national policy as promulgated by the Education Department and facilitated by its grants-in-aid, but also, more subtly, of its perception of its own performance in the light of national statistics. In such fields as level of school attendance, school space per pupil, examination passes and the balance of educational provision between the public and private sectors, the board's local predilection for economy came up against a national pressure towards improved provision. In the latter part of the period, moreover, the election of Socialist and Labour representatives to the board brought an additional local pressure in favour of increased local expenditure. The first Socialist member, J. W. Burness, was elected on the Social Democratic Federation label in 1893 and several others were elected in subsequent years. One of these G. H. Wilson, who was elected in 1895 and who served until he left Reading in 1899 said that he and his fellow Socialists 'had come there with a definite programme' and, as Cook (1970, p. 303) says, the pressure exerted by members whose view of the function of the board was more expansionist and more *dirigiste* than the institution had hitherto experienced 'played an important part in keeping the Board aware of the needs which it should be satisfying'. At the same time, resistance to 'extravagant' or 'unnecessary' expenditure remained strong, with board members sympathetic to an economizing approach to educational expenditure supported both by the local press and by the Ratepayers' Associations which, though not continuously strong, had periods of considerable influence in each of the three decades of the School Board's existence.

The main thrust of the School Board's activity was, of course, in the provision of elementary education and although much of its work attracted government grants, it had a greater degree of discretion than do modern education authorities. The school leaving age, for example, was regulated by by-law rather than by legislation, and the board was able to decide what, if any, fees to charge for elementary education. The clearest measures of the impact of the School Board on the life of the town were, of course, the increase in the number of schools and school places, and here, even although there were occasions when the board, like the corporation itself, resisted the need for new capital expenditure and failed to act even when the evidence suggested that it must, the picture presented in the years between 1871 and 1902 is of a steady increase in the level of education provision. By the time of the transfer of responsibility to the corporation the number of schools provided by the board had risen to thirteen, eleven of which had been built by the board itself, the remaining two having come into the borough as a result of the extension of the boundaries in 1887. One of these, Earley Combined School, had been jointly owned by the Reading and Earley School Boards and the other by Tilehust School Board, a body established in 1879 as an alternative to what, in retrospect, would have been the more rational arrangement recommended by the national Education Department, the designation of Tilehurst as a contributory district to the Reading School Board.

When measured by the number of places provided, the impact of the School Board becomes even clearer. In the first year of operation, 1872, the board provided 371 places out of a total (that is, including private, voluntary and church schools) of 5,255; when the corporation assumed responsibility, the comparative numbers had moved, as shown in the following table, to 9,552 out of a total of 14,010. Table 5.1 also indicates the performance of the School Board in enforcing the compulsory attendance regulations that were introduced in 1876.

Table 5.1 *Performance of Reading School Board 1872-1902: Selected Years*

Year	School Board Places	Voluntary School Places	Total Places	% School Board Places	Average % Attendance (All schools)
1872	371	4,884	5,225	7·0	72·6
1882	2,110	4,716	6,826	30·9	76·9
1887	3,266	5,232	8,498	38·4	76·2
1892	6,423	5,613	12,036	53·4	84·6
1897	7,262	5,600	12,862	56·5	83·5
1902	9,552	4,458	14,010	68·2	85·7

Source: Reading School Board Reports, 1872-1902

As public provision increased with the access of the public authority not only to rate fund income and government grants, but also to easily available capital finance, the contribution to the elementary school provision of voluntary schools declined not only relatively but also in absolute terms. In some ways, these figures present a false division between the two sectors of education, for the School Board was responsible for enforcing standards in both. In enforcing attendance, for example, the board took its powers very seriously, commenting in its report for 1877 that 'regular and punctual school attendance is dependent upon the compulsory Powers of the Elementary Education Acts' when the attendance officers of the board 'ascertained parental neglect, or . . . wilful absence or irregularity on the part of the children'. In 1880 it noted that the increase in the number of pupils arose not only from the increases in the town's population and in the number of School Board places, but also from the activities of the board's officers in enforcing attendance in the voluntary sector. This accounted for 'a corresponding portion of the annual expenditure' and, the report added a little plaintively, 'this circumstance is too often lost sight of in the discussion of financial questions connected with the work of School Boards'. Some indication, moreover, of the board's view of its own responsibility for the encouragement and maintenance of educational standards may be inferred from the fact that in 1879 it joined other School Boards to press the Education Department to introduce 'some general test of efficiency [to be] applied to Private Adventure Schools'.

In 1880, moreover, the board drew to the attention of the proprietors of thirty-four private elementary schools the regulations of the Education Department. Although it welcomed the ending of the disqualification from employment of private school pupils who did not hold the board's certificate of proficiency, it urged proprietors and parents to present scholars for examination by the board. The board was willing to organize special examinations for fifteen or more such scholars, but its initiative produced little response from the private schools. Despite its assumption of a regulatory and monitoring role *vis-à-vis* the private sector, the School Board in 1887 emphasized that it worked 'in augmentation of and not in antagonism to the other . . . elementary Schools in the town', a view expressed (see below) when the board was resisting pressure from central government to provide additional school accommodation.

The School Board's activity was not restricted to the provision of elementary education, as its participation in the establishment and management of the Kendrick Schools, and the provision of scholarships to them, show. The provision of universal secondary, or higher elementary, schooling had to await the twentieth century, but in other areas of education the School Board was prepared to be innovatory. The concern of the public authorities in Reading with the needs of handicapped and disabled children ran ahead of national policy. Particularly in the case of what were then called 'defective and feeble-minded' children, the board complained in 1898 that the Education Department had published no practical guidelines advising upon how school authorities should deal with the problem, despite the fact that a Special Departmental Committee had reported in favour of legislation. In 1899 the School Board, although it had no power to spend money on special provision, set up a subcommittee in anticipation of the passage of legislation, to assess the extent of the problem in Reading. The subcommittee classified the children concerned as either mentally or physically handicapped or as blind or deaf, although in the cases of these two latter disabilities permissive legislation of 1893 allowed the board to make provision. In 1898 six children were maintained by the board in special institutions for the blind. When the report was received the board sought advice from central government on what practical provision might be made before legislation was passed and proposed to erect a special classroom on the site of Oxford Road School. A new Act was passed in August 1899 and although, as the board noted, it was permissive rather than mandatory, the local response to it would have far-reaching effects, not limited to the special needs of disabled and handicapped children.

The Education Department issued in February 1900 regulations governing the conditions to be fulfilled if special education was to qualify for grant. The requirements for the medical inspection of children were detailed and specific, demanding both a medical certificate from a general practitioner and an examination by a medical officer appointed by the board. The result was an expansion of the definition of the education service as the board appointed Dr Price as its medical officer, for his duties extended not only to the certification of defective children but also to the examination of the eyesight of all board schoolchildren, the issuing of sickness certificates and the quarterly inspection of the sanitary condition of all board schools. The first class for disabled children, the beginning of a service which would continue throughout the existence of a separate education authority for Reading and in which the town would be continually innovatory, was opened at Oxford Road School in September 1901, with an initial enrolment of seventeen out of twenty-seven children identified as in need of special teaching. It is worth noting that the provision of special education was one area in which the tendency of the board towards economy was counterbalanced by the presence of Socialist members more favourably disposed towards extending provision beyond what was required by law. On the board the pressure in favour of action in this field came, between 1897 and 1899, from J. F. Hodgson, a Social Democratic Federation member elected in 1895 along with G. H. Wilson.

Socialist members of the board were also concerned to extend the availability of evening instruction, another area in which the board acted beyond statutory requirements. The first evening school was opened in September 1891 and by 1899 there were four, and partly as a result of Socialist pressure they were open to all without age limit and without charge. In a time before education authorities were empowered to provide post-elementary education, these evening continuation schools were a means to extend education beyond the elementary level, but in 1899 rate fund expenditure on evening schools (and, where they existed, on higher grade schools) was challenged in the courts and declared to be unlawful. This challenge, resulting in the decision in *Rex* v. *Cockerton*, was part of a campaign to demonstrate the general ineffectiveness of the School Boards in the provision of education and to persuade the government to make elected local councils education authorities with a wider responsibility to include post-elementary education. In Reading, as the board said in its report for 1901, the judgement was seen as 'a subject of much contention and greatly to the embarrassment of the School Boards' for it raised the possibility that members of the board might be surcharged for the illegal expenditure. In the event, the costs for 1899-1900 were allowed by the Local Government Board and those for 1900-1 were met by the borough council, the judgement having been limited to the use of money raised by the School Board rate. Significantly the board seems not to have considered withdrawing the provision.

This brief account of the School Board years is completed by looking at the external relations of the board and at its dominant personalities and internal organization. Consideration has already been given to the relationship between the School Board and the borough council and it was noted that both institutions were subject to the same sorts of pressures from ratepayers and, especially in the latter part of the period, from new groups achieving representation for the first time. Similarly, both were affected by the increasing direction from the centre that came with an increased reliance on national government for direct financial assistance and borrowing approval. Education, however, was by far the most expensive service for which local authorities had assumed responsibility and the figures quoted above for the steady increase in the School Board precept tell only part of the story. Much of what the School Board did had to be done in a way that would ensure that it qualified for grant, and this relationship with the Education Department provided continuous opportunities for the centre to advise, regulate and prescribe. It also produced circumstances in which the search for economy at local level came up against central determination that provision should be increased or improved.

Government grants rose steadily throughout the School Board period and, because much of the grant was computed on the basis of average attendance (which, in Reading, was for much of the time higher than the national average), the grant regime militated in favour of the enforcement of national standards. Also, the inspection powers of the Education Department led, on occasion, to the exertion by central government of pressure for improvement of provision. In 1886, for example, because of overcrowding in its schools, the board applied to the Education Department for permission to reduce the space requirement from 10 square feet to 8 square feet per child, a concession that was granted only on the condition that by the end of the year the board could show 'that any deficiency in accommodation [was] being supplied with due despatch'. In this period, however, the board was in an economizing mood and it deferred the question of further building until after the triennial elections to the board in 1899, a ploy often resorted to by the corporation. The board took the view that since there were unoccupied places in voluntary schools in the borough, it need not incur further capital expenditure, but the Education Department insisted upon direct provision, either by the building of new schools or by the extension of existing ones. In the end, the board decided to respond both to the extension of the borough boundaries and to increasing housing development by building a new school in the west of the town and by providing a new central school for boys to serve the rest of the town. Similarly in 1897 the board was required to examine provision in Lower Whitley, but the extension of an existing voluntary school by its managers met the case. In 1898, when Swansea Road School was opened near the southern end of Caversham Bridge, the board's plans to convert an infants' school to a boys' school were countermanded by the Education Department. All of this was evidence of a closeness of supervision and control to which no other local authority service was yet subject.

For much of its existence, the School Board showed a high degree of continuity of membership. J. H. Wilson, the board's first chairman, served in that office for twenty-five years and was commemorated in the Wilson School in the west of the town which was replaced in 1972 by the Meadway Comprehensive. Samuel Preston, the Clerk to the School Board, served for the entire period of its existence and was subsequently Consulting Clerk to the new Education Committee. By the time of its dissolution, the board had provided itself with a committee system that formed the basis of the subcommittee structure of the new authority. In 1884, in order to conduct business between the monthly meetings of the School Board, there were appointed a General Purposes Committee and a School Attendance Committee and in 1889 a further reorganization, reflecting the growth in the board's responsibilities, set up an Attendance Committee, a Finance Committee, a Buildings and Works Committee, and a School Management Committee. In 1895 a Management Committee of the Whole Board and a School Visiting Committee were established. In 1901 on the eve of the board's demise, the Committee of the Whole Board was replaced by a School Accommodation Committee and a new Special Children's and Medical Officers' Committee was appointed in response to the board's policy departures in the field of special education and the provision of a school medical service.

In 1903 the Reading School Board passed over to the corporation its 'unfinished business' which the report of the School Board for 1902 listed as four capital projects for new or extended elementary schools and one for the erection of a higher elementary school, the capacity of education authorities to provide 'higher' or secondary education having been increased by the Education Act 1902. It is with the government and politics of secondary education in the years between 1903 and the merger of Reading's education system with that of Berkshire in 1974 that the remainder of this chapter is mainly concerned.

The foundations of public education in Reading were laid in the thirty years before the creation of the Education Committee of the borough council. The School Board's efforts had been concentrated on ensuring universal access to primary education, supplemented by senior standard schools or classes to provide education up to the minimum school leaving age of fourteen. As the *Rex* v. *Cockerton* judgement had shown, the boards had no power to provide 'higher' education, as it was called, and access to secondary education in the borough was both selective and strictly limited by the availability of places in the Kendrick Schools, Reading School and some charitable exhibitions to other post-elementary foundations such as the Blue Coat School. Throughout the seventy-two years of its existence, Reading Education Committee struggled intermittently with the question of the most appropriate and practical method of providing access to secondary education for the children of the town. At some periods, the policies chosen arose from the preoccupations of local politicians, at others from political philosophy, and at others again from the interplay of the ideas of professional officers and nationally determined priorities. As political priority and educational orthodoxy changed, the only fixed point in the town's secondary provision was the grammar school 'tradition' of Reading School.

As early as 1904, following an inspection of Reading School by the Board of Education, the corporation began to consider assuming full responsibility for the school. By that time, almost twenty years had elapsed since any payment had been received on the mortgage outstanding to the corporation, and on 27 July a motion by Councillors Venner and Clark proposed that 'any scheme for . . . higher education in Reading which shall include the Reading School and the Kendrick Schools . . . and which shall entail a charge upon the rates, shall make provision for any such school to be under the control of the Reading Education Authority'. Although the motion was lost, it was quickly followed by a resolution of the governors of the Kendrick Schools requesting that the corporation take them over because this was the only way to ensure that money would be made available for the 'increasing cost of maintenance and large expenditure . . . necessary to bring the school premises up to the requirements of the Board of Education'. The problem for all three secondary schools was the same: that their income was insufficient for their needs, especially in view of the increased powers of inspection and control assumed by the Board of Education under the 1902 Act. Although the council had in 1891 and again in 1899 considered the financial problems, particularly of Reading School, no solution had been found. In the early years of the century, it was Labour members in particular who frequently drew attention to the dependence on the rates of a notionally independent school.

In the years before the First World War the controversy about secondary education centred on Reading School, with the Kendrick Schools to some extent dragged along in the slipstream. The 1903 inspection of Reading School had been critical both of its facilities and of its management, the latter in the sense that the enlargement of the council in 1887 had rendered the 1867 scheme of government obsolete. The report was clear also on the need to relieve the school of its debt to the corporation and by 1905 the trustees had expressed their willingness to hand the school over to the corporation as a quid pro quo for writing off the debt.

In responding to the trustees' offer, however, the corporation was affected by one of the consequences of the co-ordination of education with other services provided by the corporation. This was to make expenditure on the service subject to exactly the same budgetary disciplines as others. It is true that the composition of the Education Committee differed from others in including co-opted and representative members from outside the corporation and that its composition required the approval of the President of the Board of Education at national level. None the less the education budget and the policies of the Education Committee had to be approved by the corporation and were, therefore, to some extent limited by the general scheme of priorities determined by the council. They were also limited as to capital expenditure, the eligibility for central government grants, and the opening and closing of schools, by the need to obtain the consent of the Board of Education. This system of constraints on the development of educational policy is clear in the attempts of the corporation, in the years before the First World War, to deal with the problems of secondary education in general and of Reading School in particular.

In 1905 the corporation proposed the amalgamation of Reading School with Kendrick Boys' School to provide a single secondary school to serve the entire town. For the corporation this would have produced obvious economies in that although new buildings would be required on the Reading School site, it would have been possible to sell the Kendrick School site in Queen's Road (or to use it for other purposes) and it would not have been necessary to incur expenditure there for repairs and maintenance. The difficulty for the corporation, both in 1905 when the merger plan failed and in 1914 when it succeeded, was that what it was proposing was what in the Stock Exchange would be called a reverse take-over. The point is made very clearly in the letter from the Board of Education, received by the Education Committee in February 1905, refusing consent to the merger:

> With the influx of 200 boys . . . of the kind who now attend Kendrick School . . . the School would be rather a development of the Kendrick School than an amalgamation of the two schools in any intelligent sense of the word. . . . Such a system [that is, differential fees and a division of the school into separate departments] . . . has not been found to work well in practice [and] . . . there seems no reason to think that such a plan should be encouraged at Reading.

The board went on to say that although they would regret a decision not to support 'a school of the type of Reading School' out of the rates they 'could not regard it as unreasonable'. Such a decision by the corporation would, of course, have led to the closure of the school if the corporation had also insisted on the payment of the outstanding debt. Finally, in a statement which perpetuated the anomaly of a quasi-independent school which was already *de facto* and would soon be *de jure* part of the public sector, the board said that it 'would regard the disappearance of the school, even though disguised under the name of amalgamation as . . . a serious loss to the cause of Education in Reading'.

Although the amalgamation was eventually effected in 1915, the opinions expressed by the Board of Education in 1905 contributed to the development of a legend of continuity in the nature and purpose of Reading School. At the same time, however, other Board of Education regulations were ensuring that its nature and purpose were changing significantly. The Education Committee, in a tone of complacent self-congratulation, might say in 1909 that 'the experiment of placing the control of a First Grade School in the hands of a popularly elected body has been in every way a success', but it also had to report that in order to qualify for government grant a proportion of the places must be available free of charge to boys from the town's elementary schools. During the second amalgamation controversy between 1912 and 1914, it would be alleged by supporters of Reading School that the question of public subsidies to the school was to a large extent irrelevant because the grants from both local and national sources were consumed by the 'free placers' and that if the corporation and the government had not become involved the traditions of the school could have continued without interruption or interference.

The final push towards amalgamation was, as in the first proposal, financial rather than educational. An inspectors' report in 1909 had declared the buildings of both Kendrick Schools to be inadequate and had required the Education Committee to provide new sites. Soon after, Kendrick Boys' School, after some delay, came under the direct control of the Education Committee, and the committee reported that if it could be provided with additional buildings and a sound financial base 'secondary education in the Borough would be complete'. In 1911, during the borough extension campaign, the capital expenditure on a new science, art and technical block at Reading School had exposed the corporation to some public criticism, and in 1913, in response to a request by the corporation, there took place in the Town Hall a conference involving the Board of Education, the corporation and the Berkshire Education Committee on 'The Cost of Secondary Education in Reading'.

Opening the case for the corporation at the conference, Town Clerk Clutterbuck was frank: 'The source of dissatisfaction is really the expense which Reading School entails to the ratepayers.' However, he also revealed that in resolving to call for the conference to be held, the corporation had been less than frank in that the resolution had omitted any reference to Reading School so as not to raise anything 'which would lead parents to think that there was anything wrong with the administration of Reading

School'. There seems little doubt that before the conference met, the corporation had decided upon what it wanted to achieve. The Town Clerk, referring back to the unsatisfactory outcome of a similar conference in 1904, told the delegates that the town council members attending had had a preliminary meeting to decide upon the points to be raised; and the chairman, an inspector from the Board of Education, concluded the proceedings by saying, in effect, that it was up to the corporation to decide how it wished to organize the provision of secondary education in the town.

There is no doubt that Reading School was costing the corporation a great deal of money, and little question that some of that money went to preserve its notional position as a 'first grade school' with a boarding element. A correspondent to the *Reading Standard*, which in 1913 ran a series of 'specially contributed' articles on 'The Future of Reading School', estimated that the cost to the rates by that time amounted to a total of £42,000 and that this contribution demanded that the school should be for Reading boys, a result that could be best achieved by the amalgamation with Kendrick School. Such an amalgamation would also, of course, solve the problem of the inadequacy of Kendrick Boys' School buildings. The *Reading Standard*'s special contributor, supported by many 'Old Redingensians', argued that 'the zeal of our city fathers in their efforts to keep down the rates is to be welcomed, but the passion for economy should only in the last resort be exercised in stultifying higher education in Reading, in destroying a school of such long and honourable traditions'. The council, however, precisely because it was a multipurpose authority, could not avoid the need to measure cost against benefit to the town and on 30 January 1914 the council voted by twenty-four votes to thirteen to amalgamate the schools. That decision was subsequently narrowly endorsed by a poll of the ratepayers and the amalgamation was completed in April 1916.

The merger of the two boys' schools on the Reading School site was, as the Board of Education had noted in 1905, a reverse take-over. For although the boarding element was retained, it was no longer a principal determinant of the character of the school. By using the Reading School buildings, however, the pretence could be maintained that its historical continuity and educational traditions were being preserved. In reality, the corporation had provided itself with a boys' grammar school whose place in the overall provision of education in Reading, even before the nature of secondary education became politically controversial half-a-century later, would always be problematic and sometimes anomalous. Such a conclusion, it should be emphasized, is quite compatible with a recognition that the school has, since 1916, provided an excellent standard of education for the small minority of the town's schoolboys who have attended it.

The influence of Reading School on the development of secondary education in Reading might have been less dominant had the corporation, like other county boroughs in the interwar years, established more grammar schools. In fact, in the economic depression following the financial crisis of 1931 the Education Committee's plans to build a grammar school in Caversham were continually postponed until the war and then overtaken by the postwar development plan. In the 1920s, however, Reading Education Committee was one of the most progressive in the country. Post-elementary education was provided by the opening of senior and 'central' schools which allowed for education beyond the age of 11, and in some cases beyond the age of 14, of children who were not thought suitable for a grammar school education at Reading or Kendrick, but who would benefit from some form of secondary education. As early as 1922 the committee could claim that in many respects it had acted 'in advance of statutory requirements'. By the time of the publication in 1926 of the Hadow Report on the Education of the Adolescent, reorganization on the lines advocated in the report was already in progress in Reading. In its report for 1923-4 the Education Committee had set out 'the policy which now governs the Committee's operations'. It described a tripartite system of elementary education: junior schools up to the age of 10; senior schools up to the school leaving age of 14; and central schools for 'selected pupils' up to the age of 16. Secondary education was by scholarship to Reading and Kendrick Schools (a new Kendrick School for Girls was opened in 1927) and by 1924 the authority was providing 216 free secondary places. The central schools provided 1,015 places and thus a total of 31 per cent of the town's children were receiving some form of advanced education. In its allocation of these places, the committee was clearly aware of its duty under the Education Act 1921 to provide 'any form of education by which [children] are capable of profiting' for it reported that 'the yearly examinations conducted by the

Examining Board have been and will continue to be . . . the means of assessing capacity to profit by higher education'. The four central schools were to be the precursors of the postwar 'bilateral' schools whose existence in parallel with the grammar schools would bedevil attempts at comprehensive reorganization until the demise of the county borough and beyond.

'By the end of the war', wrote one commentator on the development of education in the borough, 'Reading was something of an educational backwater' (Brand, 1966, p. 82). This judgement, though harsh, was not unfair. After fifty years of pioneering and innovation, often in the face of penny-pinching councils primarily concerned with the level of the local rates, Reading Education Committee in the 1930s found itself unable to resist the twin pressures of local economizing and the central restrictions on expenditure that came in the aftermath of the financial crisis of 1931 and which lasted until the outbreak of the Second World War. At the beginning of the war, therefore, the education system of the town 'was only just sufficient to meet the demands of the school population' (Burton, 1955, p. 5) and during the war demand was further increased not only by the effects of the steadily increasing birth-rate of the years between 1935 and 1938 but also by Reading's wartime status as a 'safe' or 'reception' town for evacuees from areas, particularly London, subject to enemy air raids. Evacuees increased the school population by about 55 per cent and it was the need to accommodate this influx – by overcrowding existing schools and by bringing into service other buildings, public halls and prefabricated classrooms – that provided the education authority with experience in coping with the postwar demand in the period between the approval of the development plan and the beginning of its implementation. As the period of reconstruction began Reading's education policy started to emerge from a combination of national pressure, local response and the demand created by both raised expectations and demographic change.

The most obvious source of national pressure was the Education Act 1944. This Act formed the statutory basis for the education service for the remainder of the life of the Reading Education Committee and beyond and it determined the legislative and planning framework within which the local education authority (LEA) and its professional officers had to work. The distribution of population in Reading was changing rapidly before the war as the housing policies of the corporation created new estates, both by direct provision of rented housing in the public sector and by planning policies and subsidies in the private sector, on the periphery of the nineteenth-century town. The worst slums in the centre were demolished using the corporation's clearance powers under the housing and public health Acts, and longer-term policies for redevelopment after the war implied a continuation of the housing programme with its consequent demand for schools to serve the new housing estates. The effects of the rising birth-rates of the 1930s and 1940s would be felt in the schools well into the 1960s and the resources of the education system would be stretched even further by the provision in the 1944 Act raising the school leaving age to 15.

The 1944 Act laid upon LEAs an obligation to submit to the new Ministry of Education, for approval, a development plan for all aspects of educational provision. These plans were both statements of policy and bids for grant aid and capital building approval and they compelled authorities to project their educational needs twenty years into the future. Development plans made education authorities take stock, often for the first time since the abolition of the School Boards, and to consider how their existing needs – in land, buildings and professional expertise – could be employed to meet the obligations placed on them by the new legislation. In producing its development plan, Reading Education Committee had a number of advantages.

First, one of the objects of the Act was the complete separation of primary and secondary education, an end to the system, largely a legacy of the School Boards, in which children remained in the same school throughout their period of compulsory education. Reading, with its tripartite system as described above, was well on the way to achieving this object and so, despite the lack of innovation in the 1930s, the town was, once again, ahead of statutory requirements. Second, the provision of scholarships to Reading and Kendrick Schools, as well as to other charitable and private foundations, gave the authority some measure of the demand for grammar school education in the town, for the demand for places regularly exceeded supply. The Education Committee Report for 1945-50 referred to the 'extreme shortage' of grammar school places and the report for 1950-5, written with ten years' experience of the new system, complained that for grammar schools 'the Education Act 1944 seemed . . . to give no advantage' while 'at the same time, never did so many parents give expression to . . . the value they place on a grammar school education'. (It is worth noting here that the form of secondary education was not, at the time of the preparation of the development plan, politically controversial. Indeed, as will be discussed later, bipartisanship in secondary education policy persisted in Reading well into the 1950s, so far as the process of selection for secondary education was concerned, and into the 1960s on the subject of the provision of grammar schools.) Reading's third advantage in implementing the 1944 Act was the appointment in 1945 of Percy S. Taylor, co-author of a standard work on the Act, as Chief Education Officer. The development plan was very much the Taylor plan and, as Brand comments, Taylor 'became known as the man who transformed the school system of the town' (Brand, 1966, p. 82).

In terms of the development of local policy, an absence of dispute between politicians inevitably increases the salience of officers' views. By the 1940s in Reading, as will become clear in Chapter 6, there was no shortage of political competitiveness on the borough council and in elections to it. That competitiveness was fully reflected in the internal organization of the borough council immediately after the war. In the Education Committee it took rather longer for the level of partisanship to rise to the point where debates were conducted between a controlling majority and an opposing minority. This was partly due to the presence of the co-opted members required by the Education Act, though by convention it was unusual for these members to vote upon politically controversial issues. The main reason, however, was the dominance, especially in the ten years after the war, of the problem of 'roofs over heads'. In other words, the energy and attention of members was, inevitably, concentrated on bricks and mortar, on the means of discharging the authority's statutory duty to provide education to the new minimum leaving age of 15, and on remedying the situation where Reading was almost the only county borough without a technical college, the lack of which was remedied in 1950. Only after basic obligations and needs had been met did educational provision in Reading become politically controversial.

Thus, despite the service of prominent and long-serving

councillors and aldermen as chairmen of the Education Committee, the driving force in the development of Reading's education system in the postwar years was the Chief Education Officer. Taylor's development plan, one of the earliest submitted to the ministry, was approved without any substantial change. It was both wide-ranging and innovative, especially in its vision of a secondary education system combining diversity and specialization with a maximum of parental choice. The fixed points around which the plan revolved were the town's two existing grammar schools and the six secondary modern schools, one of which was Roman Catholic. In the provision of secondary education they would be supplemented by a range of single-sex, paired bilateral schools built, in the main, on the town's periphery. The choice of sites was defensible both in terms of the likely availability of land and of the existing and prospective residential development of the town. Taylor's preference for single-sex schools was part of his vision that each school should develop its own specialisms. As the development plan put it:

> One school might develop alternative courses in engineering and agriculture, another in building and design. [For girls] . . . cookery, needlework, dressmaking, mothercraft and nursing . . . [but] in no case would courses be regarded as vocational.

This range of specialisms entailed the development of three types of bilateral school: the grammar/technical, the technical/modern and the grammar/modern. Such a system would work only if the borough were regarded as the catchment area for every bilateral school, with complete freedom of access and provision for pupils to travel, if they or their parents chose, daily from one side of the town to the other. It also relied on the continuation of selection at 11-plus. Selection in Reading in the postwar years was both philosophically preferred and administratively essential. Both major political parties were in favour of grammar school education, a preference which logically entailed some form of selection, especially since the development plan, following the Ministry of Education's (1945) advice in *The Nation's Schools*, envisaged that only 25-30 per cent of the secondary school places would be in grammar and technical streams. Secondary modern schools and streams would provide the balance of provision, despite the fact that, as the development plan put it, the committee 'could not discover any satisfactory definition of the aims and methods of modern schools'.

Taylor's new bilateral schools were mainly continuations and developments of the existing central schools but the restrictions on capital spending ensured that the completion of the schools promised in the development plan was delayed beyond the end of educational bipartisanship. Before the secondary education system was complete local politicians were actively debating further reforms to it, and despite the flexibility that local education authorities could exercise under the 1944 Act and the particular adaptability that Taylor claimed for his development plan, the immutability of the two grammar schools in the centre of the town acted as a check on both the capacity of politicians to effect change and on the ability of the peripheral schools to respond to changed perceptions of education. The development plan said of its proposals for secondary education:

> It should be emphasised that the Education Committee regard their proposals as experimental. They regard the organisation suggested as flexible enough to enable alterations to be made in the light of experience.

In fact, as with many long-term plans, Taylor's scheme was overtaken by events, but not before it had been implemented to an extent sufficient to make basic changes to the secondary education system of the town very difficult indeed. And, of course, its very existence could be used as an argument against departures from the kind of provision that it envisaged.

The end of educational bipartisanship in the 1950s, and Taylor's early death in 1962, were the main reasons why the ground of the debate moved away from the scheme envisaged by the development plan. It should be noted, however, that three aspects of the plan would have generated discussion and disagreement no matter how local politics had developed. First, as Brand points out, the 'free access' principles of the development plan did not foresee the rapid expansion of the town in the postwar period and the vast increase in traffic volume from the mid-1950s onwards. By the early 1960s when Brand's research was undertaken, 'the transport of children through the city had become a major problem'. By the 1970s when the Reading Labour Party proposed a change to 'Neighbourhood Schools', the first of the advantages claimed for such a system was that it would involve pupils in a minimum of travelling. There was also a cost implication of the maintenance of a secondary school system which assumed that a large number of pupils would travel fairly long distances to school, but this did not become a major issue until after Reading ceased to be an education authority. The second aspect of the plan which, even without the onset of the debate about comprehensive education, would rapidly have become controversial was Taylor's preference for single-sex schools. This proposal was controversial at the time of the plan's preparation, to the extent that the plan said that some of the new schools, like the former central schools and elementary schools, would be coeducational but because the authority had not decided which would be mixed, all were shown as single sex. The plan for pairs of single-sex schools had implications for capital allocations, for it was likely to be more expensive to build two schools on a single campus than to provide a single school. Also, the expectation that the paired schools would co-operate closely, even to the extent of sharing staff and accommodation, was not fulfilled, and it is difficult to acquit of naïveté those who raised it. Schools, like all institutions, become jealous of their autonomy. In the event, only three pairs of single-sex schools were built – Ashmead (boys) and Southlands (girls) in the south of the town, Stoneham (boys) and Westwood (girls) in the west, and Alfred Sutton Boys and Alfred Sutton Girls in the east. The paired concept was abandoned in the 1960s and the Alfred Sutton Schools were the last single-sex schools to be built by the Reading LEA. The long-delayed secondary school for Caversham was the town's first purpose-built comprehensive school (Highdown) and, just before local government reorganization in 1974, the Meadway Comprehensive School was opened in Tilehurst. Both are coeducational.

The third aspect of the Taylor plan that would have generated debate no matter how politicians had viewed educational provision may also be seen as the bridge between the period when education policy was dominated by the professionals and the period when educational debate was conducted by the politicians. As the quotation above about the lack of any clear view of the purpose of secondary modern schools suggests, this sector of Reading's provision did not attract the attention in the development plan that the number of places provided by it might have merited. All the secondary modern schools were in areas of the town that were declining rather than expanding, but their existence, despite antiquity and accelerating dilapidation, was a major contribution to putting roofs over heads. Thus it was inevitable that, in a period of scarce resources, they would be starved of the capital allocations by which they might have been modernized, as such allocations were applied to the construction of the new bilaterals, as well as to badly needed new primary schools. Reporting in 1966 on research conducted in 1962, Brand noted that among teachers in secondary modern schools 'there [was] a certain amount of feeling . . . that the bilateral schools [had] been developed at their expense'. This was at a time when the Labour Party, through a working party set up because the council under Conservative control would not agree to investigate the issue of selection at 11-plus, was developing a policy which would eventually commit it to a comprehensive reorganization of secondary education throughout the town. Thus the future of the secondary modern schools would have been pushed up the agenda as the completion of the bilaterals allowed official attention to be directed towards them. That process was accelerated by the increasing politicization of education after 1960.

The debate over comprehensive education and the organization of the town's secondary schools has lasted longer than any single issue since the drainage question in the mid-nineteenth century, and remains unresolved. (The long-running debate over a new civic centre differs from both in having been intermittent.) The course of the debate provides a vivid example of the discontinuousness of policy-making that may arise from the combination of political philosophy, central direction, local discretion and electoral volatility. In 1957, in its policy statement for the municipal elections, Reading Labour Party committed itself to the abolition of the selection of pupils at 11-plus. That commitment elevated to the status of an issue of principle what had hitherto been an administrative consequence of a system of secondary education which was not itself the subject of political division. At this stage the policy implications were not thought through, for there was no commitment to a reorganization of secondary education along comprehensive lines. Indeed, as late as 1962, a year after the Labour Party (in *Signposts for the Sixties*) had committed itself nationally to the introduction of comprehensive education, the municipal policy statement promised 'further improvements . . . to ensure that EVERY child that could benefit from a Grammar type education' would do so. Significantly in view of the course of the local debate, the reference to a 'Grammar type education' was dropped in 1963 in favour of a more general reference to the need for more places in the bilateral system. More significantly still, Reading Labour Party, also in 1963, defeated an amendment to the policy statement that would have committed the party to the immediate establishment of comprehensive schools.

These changes in the attitude of the Labour Party to the shape and nature of secondary education originated outside the council, in pressure exerted on the General Management Committee of the local party. Somewhat reluctantly, perhaps because this was a period when relations between the party and the Labour Group were rather strained, the Labour Group on the borough council took the matter up and suggested, in 1962, that the council set up a bipartisan working group of Labour and Conservative members to examine the question of selection. This suggestion was opposed by the controlling Conservative Group with the result that the Labour Group set up its own working party which was advised by Dr A. H. Halsey of Nuffield College, Oxford, Brian Jackson, editor of *Where* magazine, and Douglas Brown, senior lecturer in English at the University of Reading. The recommendations, which were endorsed by the Reading Labour Party and published in the spring of 1963, just as Labour took control of the council, were for an end to selection 'at the earliest possible time' and for 'a standard secondary school course' which would allow for transfer 'at the age of fourteen or fifteen to a grammar school course'. The report did not specifically mention 'comprehensive education' but it pointed clearly to a complete reorganization of secondary education in the borough.

Labour had been in control of the council between 1954 and 1960, and it is likely that the lack of any clear alternative policy to the implementation of the Taylor plan was due, in large measure, to Taylor's influence expressed through his advice that any major change in the system of secondary education would require a level of capital expenditure on new schools which, given the general restrictions imposed on the existing programme by central government, would be unlikely to win the approval of the Ministry of Education. The Conservative view, which informed their refusal to agree to a council working party, was to continue the implementation of the development plan. This was largely because, as the authority's settled policy, it was a substantial guarantee of the continued existence of Reading and Kendrick Schools. As Coombs (1970, p. 173) puts it, the Conservative attitude arose 'not so much from a philosophical opposition to comprehensive principles as from a practical belief in the virtues of the town's two grammar schools'. Both the development plan and the 'traditions' of the wholly selective schools were considerable obstacles in the way of any effort to change the direction of Reading's educational policy. Thus even when the Labour Party returned to power in the council in 1963 local effort alone would not be enough to ensure a change of course.

The return of a Labour Government in 1964 seemed to provide the extra support that was needed. Even before the publication in 1965 of Department of Education and Science Circular 10/65 requesting all LEAs to submit plans for comprehensive reorganization, the Labour controlling group had set up a working party to investigate the issue. The party's 1964 policy statement repeated the commitment to the abolition of the 11-plus and added a reference to the provision 'of all types of secondary education within an integrated system', but the working party, after publishing an interim report, suspended its deliberations, 'conscious of various unresolved difficulties'. In announcing its suspension, the working party, in a phrase redolent of the passions aroused by any proposal to interfere with the grammar schools, said that it wished 'to allay fears that a reorganisation was imminent which would be imposed without further consultation'. There was an echo here of the Labour Party's decision, when it considered the Labour Group working party report in 1963, to 'withhold the publication of item 4 of the recommendations [on the implementation of a reorganized system] until after the local elections as it could be misinterpreted to [the party's] electoral disadvantage'.

Labour's municipal policy statement for 1965, quoting almost verbatim from the council working party's interim report, prevaricated:

If selection at eleven must end, and new schools must be built, there is little alternative . . . [to] a fully comprehensive

system. . . . A massive reconstruction of our education
system will require detailed planning. . . . As the borough
boundaries are shortly to be revised . . . and as the Plowden
Committee's report on secondary education may influence
national policy . . . it is felt that detailed commitments cannot
be entered into.

By mid-1965 the uncertainties had been swept away by the
secretary of state's publication of Circular 10/65, but it is difficult
to resist the conclusion that the Labour Party's chances of
implementing a fully comprehensive system of education in
Reading were fatally damaged by its failure to press to a conclusion
the working party investigation of 1963-5.

Labour retained control of the council until the municipal
elections of May 1967. In March 1966 the revived working party
issued its report, *Secondary Education in Reading*, as the basis of the
authority's response to Circular 10/65. The recommendation of 'all-
through' schools for children aged 11-18 was unspecific about
Reading and Kendrick except in so far as they were not expected to
increase in size. Following further consultations the working party
recommended to the Education Committee that it should 'declare
its intention to integrate Kendrick and Reading Schools into a fully
comprehensive educational system'. On 19 September 1966 this
recommendation was approved by the Education Committee, but
the intervention of the May 1967 council elections ensured that
before the formal submission of a response to Circular 10/65 the
new Conservative majority would be able to rescind it. It did so in
July 1967. It is now clear that that decision was the one which
ensured that fully comprehensive education would not be introduced in Reading during the lifetime of the all-purpose county
borough authority.

The history of the education debate in Reading between 1967
and the demise of the county borough in 1974 reveals the degree to
which the policy-making autonomy of a local authority, even an all-
purpose one, is in large measure defined by its relationship with
central government. There can be little doubt that a Labour
response to Circular 10/65 would have been quickly approved by a
Labour secretary of state, for his response to the Conservative
council's formal submission said that it was unsatisfactory 'because
of the exclusion of the grammar schools and because there are no

plans to abolish selection at eleven-plus and achieve a complete pattern of reorganisation'. Equally, there was little chance that any proposal which the Reading Conservatives would make, which was bound to entail the preservation of the grammar schools, would be approved. Since the secretary of state was acting under the general powers of the Education Act 1944, he was unable directly to coerce the authority. He could, of course, use his power over capital allocations to prevent developments of which he disapproved but that was essentially a negative power, militating in favour of the status quo and limited by the need to ensure the capacity of the authority to replace obsolete buildings and to provide roofs over heads. A revised submission was made to the Department of Education and Science in late 1969, stating a long-term intention to replace both Reading and Kendrick Schools and expressing the view that 'the effect of parental options for schools once the new schools are erected will be to widen the entry to Kendrick and Reading schools'. This too was unsatisfactory, and its submission was clearly intended as a delaying tactic to prevent any major change taking place before a general election which might result in a change of government. In June 1970 the Conservative government came to office and almost immediately issued Circular 10/70 saying that 'authorities will now be free to determine the shape of secondary provision in their areas'. On 23 September the Education Committee confirmed that 'Reading and Kendrick [would] remain selective schools'.

The Conservatives remained in control of the council until 1972, so for five years the Labour Party's continuing, and hardening, commitment to abolish both the 11-plus and the grammar schools was pursued in the form of an opposition keeping its policies alive in anticipation of its return to power. Thus the Labour Party in 1969 invited the Socialist Education Association to prepare a report on the integration of Reading and Kendrick into a fully comprehensive system. (By this time, the Conservatives had abandoned the defence of the bilateral system and all were agreed on the closure of the secondary moderns of which only one remained: the grammar schools were the one point of fundamental disagreement. For Labour, their continuation compromised the whole notion of a comprehensive system.) The leader of the Labour Group, Councillor David Stoddart, wrote in 1968 to the Secretary of State for Education, in an effort to use the party political connection to accelerate a decision on the council's submission. In 1969 Councillor Bob Towner, who would succeed Stoddart as group leader on the latter's election to Parliament in 1970 and who subsequently served as the county borough council's last leader when Labour gained control in 1972, prepared a 'minority report' on secondary education which was submitted to the secretary of state to emphasize the practicability of amalgamating the two grammar schools as one coeducational school within the comprehensive system. In July 1971, as a protest against the indefinite continuation of the 11-plus, the Labour members resigned from the working party on secondary reorganization, which continued in existence because of the need to take decisions about allocation of secondary places and the consequences of the abolition of the last secondary modern school in the borough.

During Labour's last period in power, between the elections of May 1972 and the passage of responsibility for education to the new Berkshire County Council in April 1974, the county borough council was very much a 'lame duck' authority. It was, moreover, faced with a Conservative government at Westminster with Margaret Thatcher as Secretary of State for Education. At the first council meeting after the elections, in June 1972, a resolution in favour of abolishing the 11-plus and the grammar schools was passed and, subsequently, as part of the council's scheme to introduce a fully comprehensive system, the statutory notices to close Cintra School (the last secondary modern) and Reading and Kendrick Schools (as a preliminary to their amalgamation as a split-site coeducational comprehensive) were published. Not surprisingly, these notices were not approved by the secretary of state, and the Labour Group, and the council, could do no more in September 1973 than reaffirm their commitment to the reorganization of secondary education on the principles set out in the scheme submitted to the secretary of state. As between 1967 and 1972, the fact that the political complexion of the council differed from that of the government had made policy change impossible. Circular 10/70 notwithstanding, the Labour authority had been unable 'to determine the shape of secondary provision' in Reading.

For the greater part of the period covered by this book, and particularly in the years since the introduction of compulsory education, controversy in this field has centred round the provision of secondary education. There is a tendency for this fact to mask the more general impact of a service which quickly became the borough's biggest spender and which had an influence wider than that of putting roofs over heads and teachers in front of classes. The impact of education on the life of a community arises very directly from the fact that it is the only personal public service to which everyone is exposed. Everyone is affected by good drainage and pure water but these are background or environmental services which, at least in modern circumstances, tend to be taken for granted. And the direct effects of other personal services, such as housing and social services, are selective rather than comprehensive.

The School Board and the Education Committee, from the late 1870s onwards, were concerned not only with the inculcation of the three Rs but also with the physical well-being of the town's children. As early as 1878, the School Board noted the obstacles to education presented by 'want of clothing, temporary inability to pay the School Fees and unwillingness to apply to the [Poor Law] Guardians for their payment'; from 1907 school meals were provided because poorer children were 'unable through lack of food to take proper advantage of the education provided for them'. As was noted above, the board appointed a medical officer in 1900 and the school health service was progressively extended to cover dental health, the routine testing of children's eyesight and the provision of special schools and classes for pupils excluded from school because of their consumptive or verminous condition. In notifying infectious diseases, the school medical service was a valuable addition to the public health machinery of the borough and it was inevitable as well as sensible that the offices of the MOH and School Medical Officer would be combined after the assumption by the corporation of responsibility for education. The desirability of close contact between the various departments of the corporation was emphasized by the Education Committee in 1913. Under the Children Act 1908 the committee had set up a 'cleansing station' to deal with verminous children, but it pointed out that if their staff were to be successful in dealing with the problem 'they should have the assistance of the sanitary authority in cleansing the homes'. Here is an excellent example of the sort of co-operation that can achieve maximum effectiveness in a multipurpose authority.

In one area the wide definition of the education function put Reading far in advance of most other education authorities. The

Education Committee Report for 1945-50, commenting on its powers in the field of youth employment and careers guidance under the Employment and Training Act 1948 and the National Insurance Act 1948, may be forgiven the slight air of smugness with which it pointed out that having provided vocational guidance in the borough for thirty-six years it would continue to do so under the revised and nationally recommended scheme. In 1910 the committee noted that the Labour Exchanges were in some difficulty in finding skilled men for available vacancies and, in advance of the provisions of the Education (Choice of Employment) Act 1912, took this view of its responsibilities in the field:

> It would seem to be the duty of Education Authorities to consider . . . the formation of advisory boards in connection with their schools . . . to aid parents to find suitable employment for children when they leave school.

This was the genesis of Reading's Youth Employment Service which, through co-operation between the LEA and the Labour Exchange, allowed the committee to keep in touch with pupils between the end of their school life at 14 and their seventeenth birthday. The first scheme was introduced in 1912 and it was directed not only towards finding suitable jobs for school leavers but also towards finding, in the words of the committee's report for 1911-12, 'a way out of the "blind alley" for those who, on leaving school, had been able to find only temporary employment'. A Juvenile Employment Officer was appointed almost immediately and in 1923 the administration of both the Juvenile Employment Exchange and of the Unemployment Insurance Acts as they related to 16 and 17 year olds, were transferred from the Ministry of Labour to the Education Committee.

By 1947, when the school leaving age was raised to 15, the Youth Employment Service was firmly established. It was turning its attention, as it had at its inception, to the problem of 'unprogressive employment' and with the temporary slackening of the rate at which youngsters entered the labour market it could concentrate upon ensuring that those who did were guided into jobs essential to the progress of postwar reconstruction. As a greater number of pupils stayed on at school beyond the minimum leaving age the emphasis of the service changed to career guidance and broadened to include advice on higher and further education, drawing on the fund of experience and expertise built up as one of the pioneers in a service that became generally available only in the postwar years.

As local government's biggest spender (by 1970-1 the Education Committee Revenue Budget, stood at £6·2 million and required an education rate of 65 pence), the education service has often assumed not a dominant position within a local authority but a quasi-independent one. There are other factors that militate in the same direction. First, education is a highly professionalized service and its professionals tend not to move easily into other local government departments. Thus education departments often had their own architects, accountants and administrators. Second, the requirements that the composition of the Education Committee be approved by the responsible minister and that it include co-opted members with special knowledge of education places the committee on a different footing from most other council committees. In decision-making the Education Committee's wide delegated authority and its complex range of subcommittees, in Reading as elsewhere, together with its position as the operational institution of the corporation as the LEA, gave it a degree of autonomy from the council. At both ends of the period during which the borough council was the education authority for Reading, there was concern about the effect on the education service of its relationship with other services in a multipurpose authority. In 1903 many educationists regretted the end of the School Boards, fearing that the level of educational provision would suffer from the loss of independence, a fear, to quote Regan (1977, p. 237), that when 'education had to compete for funds with other services . . . administered by local authorities . . . it might not get a fair share'. In the late 1960s and early 1970s, when the orthodoxies of corporate management and corporate planning led to the designation of the Town Clerk as 'Chief Executive' with an explicit superiority over other chief officers, there were those who feared that the new decision-making processes implied by changes to management systems were 'just a cunning device to cut resources devoted to education' (Regan, 1977, p. 207).

An assessment of the general effect on education of its integration with other public services in Reading cannot be attempted here, though the account given in this chapter surely implies that, as with other services, effectiveness is increased when education is delivered by a multipurpose rather than by a single-purpose authority. As Regan points out (1977, pp. 235-8), Britain is unusual in not having retained separate education authorities, but the effects of integration have been conditioned by the status and influence of the Chief Education Officer. The influence of Percy Taylor on Reading's school system has already been considered, but it should be noted also that throughout the century of public education provision in Reading, the chief officers in charge first of the School Board and then of the Education Department have built up the authority that comes from long tenure of office. Samuel Preston served as Clerk to the School Board throughout its existence. The first Clerk to the Education Committee, Henry Pugh, served from 1903 until 1928. Pugh, at the time of his appointment, was a teacher in a Board school and a member of the corporation and his appointment caused considerable controversy. Pugh had strongly opposed the Education Act 1902 and he and E. P. Collier, a future chairman of the Education Committee, had in December 1902 initiated a council debate on the merits of autonomous school boards. His appointment, recommended to the council after a vote of eighteen to six at a Committee of the Whole Council, was vociferously opposed. Councillor Simmons asked whether it was usual to appoint to a £450 per year post without advertisement; Alderman Simonds observed that 'in future any gentleman who wished to be appointed as Town Clerk or Engineer or Borough Surveyor . . . would first take the preliminary step of getting elected to the Council'; the *Berkshire Chronicle* editorialized strongly against the appointment; and many members protested that the agenda for the Committee of the Whole Council had not made it clear that it was intended that an appointment would be made. Despite this dissension, the appointment was a successful one, and Pugh took the leading part in developing the foundations upon which his successors F. V. Merriman (1928-45) and Taylor (1945-62) would build. Taylor was succeeded by his deputy, W. L. Thomas, who served until Reading ceased to be an education authority in 1974. Thus in over a century the professional direction of the education service was in the hands of only five chief officers.

6

Party Politics and the Business of the Corporation

The ballot box is the power of the worker and he must support the cause of Labour against all parties.

>   James Keir Hardie MP, speaking in Reading, quoted in *Reading Mercury*, 22 July 1893

Representation on the Council cannot now be secured except by having the strong backing of a party.

>   *Reading Mercury*, 9 January 1926

It shall be the responsibility of the Labour Group . . . to take decisions on matters coming before the Council . . . it shall at all times endeavour to implement decisions taken by the local Labour Party . . . in so far as these decisions relate to Socialist principles as applied to local government.

>   Reading Labour Group, *Rules and Standing Orders*, 1962

For much of the nineteenth century contested municipal elections in Reading were the exception rather than the rule. When contests took place, they arose not from any continuing partisan battle but from intense short-term controversy over particular issues, usually concerning the level of council expenditure and the proper scope of government action. Thus, for example, both the Liberals and the Conservatives organized themselves for local elections during the Improvement Bill controversy of 1847-50, and although fighting elections on party labels did not become a common feature of the town's politics until the twentieth century, it was well known, through the efforts of a thoroughly partisan local press, which candidates were identified with which party. Again, during the period of the great capital expenditure on the sewerage scheme, as was indicated in Chapter 3, the council was clearly divided between Liberals and Conservatives, and many of the crucial votes on this highly contentious issue were on fairly strict party lines. However, on the few occasions during this period when elections were contested, the motive force was usually the Reading Ratepayers' Association, an 'economizing' force which, though closer to the Conservative view of local expenditure than the Liberal, cannot fairly be described as anything other than an independent organization. Indeed at many points in Reading's political history, Ratepayers' Associations have played a part in electoral politics, making common cause with Conservatives against Liberals in the nineteenth century and against Socialists in the twentieth, but they have always managed to remain autonomous.

If there was a continuing division in municipal politics in the nineteenth century, it was that between the economizers and the improvers. These categories, however, were for the most part proxies for Tories and Liberals and at times when municipal controversy was sharpest it was common for the local press to emphasize the point, sometimes in a way which simply identified the political complexion of the majority on the corporation and sometimes to express their own editorial opposition to the prevailing policies of the council in the guise of a public-spirited opposition to the malign consequences for public administration of the intrusion of party politics. In 1854, for example, in its disappointment at the failure of the Improvement Bill and the dilatoriness of the council as the Local Board of Health in executing a drainage scheme, the *Reading Mercury* commented that since 1835 the corporation had 'at all times . . . been more or less the victim of political partisanship'. In 1881, in deploring the fact that the Liberals had contested Castle Ward, the paper hoped that 'the defeat of the candidates nominated will lead to the cessation of the effort . . . to contest municipal affairs on political grounds – a state of things which has never yet benefitted any town . . . and from which, happily, Reading has hitherto been free'.

Thus newspapers which were themselves strongly partisan and which, as the *Berkshire Chronicle*'s vituperations against the Liberals in the 1860s and 1870s suggest, did not shrink from personal as well as political attacks on leading corporation figures, continued to propagate the view that partisanship in municipal government was both inappropriate and harmful. As late as 1926 there was a tone of regret and a feeling of bowing to the inevitable but undesirable march of time in the *Mercury*'s comment that 'representation on the Council cannot now be secured except by having the strong backing of a party'. But by that time, the scene had indeed changed. Elections were openly and routinely partisan. Council debates and the distribution of power on council in the form of committee memberships and chairmanships were ordered party politically. Even elections to the aldermanic bench and to the mayoralty were affected by the change in the basis of organization of municipal government and politics. The first part of this chapter examines the process by which this change took place.

Despite the occasional sharp dispute upon particular issues and the public identification of most members of the corporation with one or other of the national political parties, the corporation for most of the nineteenth century was homogeneous enough to conduct its affairs so that the internal organization of the council was not dominated by partisan divisions. Whether members were Tories or Liberals, economizers or improvers, they came from a restricted social range. They were, in the proper sense of the term, an élite. They were the 'fit and proper persons', suited by background to the task of government and made eligible for the task by a restrictive municipal franchise based upon a fairly high property qualification. They were also people who, in the political culture of a time before universal suffrage, were expected to feel a duty to serve. Cook (1970, p. 11) expresses the point well:

> Throughout the nineteenth century, there was a strong feeling that the men running the most important firms in the town should take part in its general government. And there were other . . . factors like an independent income, ownership of land and property, and a 'good' education, which equipped a man to take a leading role in local affairs.

For most of the sixty-five years between the passage of the Municipal Corporations Act and the end of the century, members of the town's main commercial and industrial families served on the council. The biscuit-making Palmers, directors of the closely associated tin-box manufacturers Huntley, Boorne & Stevens (whose managing director, in a connection between local industry and politics which was by then less common, served as

Conservative leader on the borough council between 1945 and 1955), the brewing and banking Simonds, the seed-producing Suttons and, of course, the lawyers and entrepreneurs of the Blandy family, served as councillors and then as aldermen, often for very long periods uninterrupted by the inconvenience of contested elections. In a very important sense, these men were self-selectors, motivated by a sense of civic duty and a lively perception of their own acumen. Recruitment, as a mechanical and clearly identifiable process, is difficult to pin down. Sometimes it was dynastic, as the continuous presence of members of the same families and firms would suggest, and there were at least two examples of son following father on the council. At other times, members of the corporation, together with other influential members of the community, actively sought out 'economic and social leaders' and persuaded them to put up for election. Whatever the pattern of recruitment, however, the common social backgrounds, in an important sense transcending the political divisions which, in any case, were defined by attitudes to national political issues from the Corn Laws through parliamentary reform to questions of the Empire and Irish union, led to an easy acceptance of the conventions by which the corporation was run.

The most important principle which governed the distribution of power, authority and influence within the council was seniority. The Mayor was almost invariably the most senior member who had not already held the office. Aldermanic vacancies were automatically filled by the election of the most senior councillor. Committee chairmanships were held, overwhelmingly, by the aldermen who, by definition, were the longest serving members of the corporation. Most of the committee work was undertaken by the aldermen too, with the councillors, other than the most senior ones, serving on only a few committees, and discharging their civic obligations by their service on the full council and on the frequently employed Committees of the Whole. Cook (1970, p. 177) identifies a further subtle effect of the seniority principle: the tendency for junior members to serve on the general committees and for aldermen and senior councillors to specialize. This is an important distinction, for the general committees were largely concerned with routine business and the implementation of national requirements while the specialized committees dealing with quasi-commercial services such as the waterworks and the tramways, major local projects like the Municipal Buildings, and important local initiatives such as the implementation of the sewerage scheme and the extension of the borough boundaries, offered much more scope for local power, influence and initiative. The reliability of seniority as the organizing principle of the corporation's decision-making structure depended on continuity of membership, and for much of the nineteenth century continuity was ensured by the absence of contested elections, and the recruitment of new members by the processes described above. Seniority relied also on its general acceptability, the absence of challenge to it and the readiness of new members to serve their time and to climb the ladder of influence slowly. As the century wore on there were signs that these conditions were becoming less easy to take for granted. As the corporation did more, spent more and, most significantly, raised more in rates, the social selectivity which characterized the recruitment process in the twenty to forty years after the Municipal Corporations Act became more difficult to maintain. More people were affected by the council's activities and, as has been implied before, it was those without property and therefore ineligible until 1882 to participate in the local electoral process who were the clearest beneficiaries of the expenditure on public health improvements after 1870. At the other end of the social scale, in the strata from which members of the corporation were overwhelmingly drawn, the impact of increased rates was easiest to bear. In between, there were the 'lesser men', the tradesmen, small businessmen and shopkeepers whose profitability and standards of living were directly affected by rising rates, and who sought, with increasing frequency, to join the council from 1870 onwards. Most of these men accepted the prevailing norms of behaviour and organization within the corporation. Occasionally, however, they responded to their exclusion from positions of influence by acting in ways which brought down upon them not only the patronizing contempt of their senior colleagues, but also the wrath of the local press.

An unwillingness to be bound by the traditions of the institution is often the first sign of profound change. In the 1870s James Belcher, a small builder, was a continual irritant to the more established members of the council, often being reprimanded by the Mayor, who warned him on one occasion, when he attacked the personal interest of one of the richest members of the corporation in the matter under discussion that he was speaking 'at a public meeting and all that he says may be taken down by the press'. At other times, he resigned from the council because of the 'contumely' he had received from most of the members, voted against a resolution of regret at the retirement of a senior alderman, and was removed from the Survey Committee for 'insulting and unruly conduct'. Cook (1970, p. 173) describes Belcher as a 'forerunner of the kinds of men whose entry to the Council was made possible by the 1882 Act' which removed most of the property qualifications for election. His behaviour also anticipated that of the Socialist and Labour members whose arrival on the council at the beginning of the twentieth century represented the first sustained and eventually successful challenge to the conventions which underpinned the organization and operation of the corporation.

The first precondition for a change in the organizing conventions of the council was, of course, a change in its composition. As we have seen, changes had begun to occur as early as 1870 and from 1882 onwards the access provided by the absence of property qualifications brought the middle and lower-middle classes on to the council in greater numbers. However, the fact that contested elections were still exceptional (when the boundary extension of 1887 led to an increase in the number of wards from three to ten, only half of the new wards were contested at the first elections) suggests that no fundamental challenge to the values underlying civic administration was perceived. The 1880s and 1890s, despite extensions to the powers and duties of the corporation, were a time of retrenchment and containment of expenditure, with no major scheme comparable to those of the 1870s embarked upon. In the 1890s, as Socialists began to contest elections to the Poor Law Guardians and the School Board and then to the borough council, the Reading Ratepayers' Association had perhaps its most successful period, and by 1897 it could claim to have placed nine men on the corporation. The increasing incidence of contested elections in the mid-1890s owed much to the efforts of the Ratepayers' Association and the various Socialist and Labour electoral organizations that were established for the primary purpose of seeking Labour representation on public bodies. An 'Independent Labour' candidate was elected for Battle Ward in 1894 and although as a representative of the Trades and Labour Council which had been formed in 1874 he attempted to persuade the council to stipulate the payment of trade union wage rates and the use of local materials in council contracts his connection with the Labour movement did not survive his six years as a councillor. At his re-election in 1897, he was supported by the Ratepayers' Association against a Socialist candidate. As Cook remarks, 'Labour representatives . . . could be tolerated' but Socialists were extremists 'to be watched with suspicion'.

It was not until after the formation of the Labour Representation Committee in 1900, as the precursor of the Labour Party, that Labour candidates were elected to the borough council. S. G. Jones was elected in 1900 and Patrick Connolly in 1901. These two councillors were re-elected in 1903 and 1904 respectively and they were joined by Herbert Watts in 1904 and by John Rabson, who was elected, unopposed, in Minster Ward in 1906. Another Socialist, under the banner of the 'Labour League' had been elected when Thomas Waters won a seat in Minster Ward in 1902. Although no further successes were recorded until the election of Lorenzo Quelch in a by-election in May 1914, the number of Labour candidates was indicative of a major change in the electoral politics of the town. The effect which the Labour members had on the business of the council, particularly in relation to unemployment relief and the wages of council employees was clearly an additional pressure towards a more aggressively partisan approach to municipal elections by other political groupings.

The minutes of the Reading Conservative Association for this period show a mood of growing partisanship, though the myth of non-political local government was strong enough to prevent the party from fielding *official* Conservative candidates for another forty years. In November 1906, just after the municipal elections, the Executive Committee considered a resolution from the Castle Ward Conservative Committee stating that they would 'in future nominate and work for their own candidate for . . . the Town Council' and requesting 'that the Central [*sic*] Committee . . . ask all Ward Committees to do the same'. The Executive Committee responded by appointing a subcommittee which would ensure that there was a Conservative candidate in every election and which would have power to organize and give assistance to candidates at its discretion. The object, in the words of the Executive Committee resolution (17 December 1906) was 'the return of more

Conservative . . . representatives to the Borough Council'. By October 1913 the Labour threat was thought to be strong enough for the Conservatives to consider entering an informal agreement with the Liberals to prevent the nomination in certain wards of two anti-Socialist candidates. In October 1914, after a meeting of the agents of the Conservative, Liberal and Labour parties to agree an electoral truce for the duration of the war, the Conservative Association's Municipal Elections Committee felt it necessary to resolve that if Labour did not agree to extend the truce beyond 1915, it would come to a separate agreement with the Liberals 'with a clause binding the two parties to combine against any Labour candidate opposing the spirit of the agreement'. The Elections and Registration Act 1915, by suspending municipal elections for the duration, made a local agreement unnecessary, but the foundations of later united action by Conservatives and Liberals had been laid.

The relations between the Reading Conservatives and Liberals when normal electoral politics resumed after the war may have been affected by the continuation at national level of the wartime Coalition government and the electoral arrangements between the two parties for the general election of 1918, for Blondel (1959, p. 104) suggests that the question of the coalition was not a controversial one in Reading, even after the town's Tory MP became an anti-coalitionist in 1922. In September 1919 the Conservative Municipal Elections Committee responded favourably to an approach from the Liberal agent suggesting 'that it was desirable to arrive at an agreement to fight Labour at the forthcoming municipal elections'. (Such an agreement had been reached for the Poor Law Guardians elections earlier in the year.) The Liberal executive would instruct its ward committees not to contest six Conservative-held seats if the Conservatives did not put up candidates in four Liberal seats, with each party free to go its own way in the three seats being defended by Labour. This was the most comprehensive 'stand-off' agreement yet arrived at, and neither party put up candidates against the sitting Labour members. It was adhered to by the Conservative executive even when it came under pressure from the Redlands Ward Conservatives who were keen to put up a candidate because the sitting Liberal had announced his retirement from the council. The executive also decided that it would support the Liberal candidates in the Liberal wards to which the agreement applied. The following year the Conservatives and Liberals came even closer together by the publication of a joint address to Conservative and Liberal electors.

These moves, and the reiterated opposition in the next few years to three-cornered fights against the Labour Party, were part of a polarization of electoral politics that could not fail to affect the internal operations of the corporation. The aim of the Conservatives was clearly stated by their chairman when he appealed to all members in 1920 'to do all in their power at the coming municipal elections to keep out the nominees of the Socialist Labour Party'. In 1925 the Municipal Elections Committee referred to the executive of the Conservative Association a suggestion that anti-Socialists in Reading should follow the London example and run under one label, and although the executive strongly recommended to the Reading Conservative and Unionist Party 'that it is advisable to form a Reading Municipal Society', the plan foundered because the Liberal Party refused to be associated with it on the grounds that it would be political, by which they presumably meant Conservative-dominated. The Conservatives, however, felt strongly enough about the need to maximize the anti-Labour effort that the matter was referred to a subcommittee 'with a view to finding someone outside politics who would take the lead'. The policy of not opposing Liberal candidates was continued until, in 1929, the Reading Municipal Association (RMA), composed of all anti-Socialist members of the corporation, was formed for the purpose 'of securing greater cohesion and unity in the Council Chamber'. That the internal organization of the corporation had changed profoundly can be inferred from the decision of the Municipal Elections Committee on 20 September 1929, that the Municipal Association should hold private meetings before council meetings 'to decide beforehand their course of action and thus help to ensure complete unanimity'. The association was, in effect, the Conservative Group on the borough council and it was aware that the practice of holding private group meetings was already followed by its Labour opponents. It survived as such even after the decision in 1947 to nominate official Conservative candidates in the municipal elections.

From the moment of their arrival on the council, Labour

members chafed under the weight of long-established convention. Their early attempts to focus the attention of the corporation on issues that it had not hitherto considered attracted the contempt of long-serving members of the corporation and savage criticism in the press. In 1902, for example, when Jones put down a motion seeking the resignation of another member because of an alleged conflict of interest, he was told by the Mayor that a motion of that sort 'lowers the dignity of the Corporation' although the Mayor 'hardly saw his way clear to rule it out of order'. The *Berkshire Chronicle*'s view was that Jones's conduct was 'neither honourable nor dignified'. In 1902 Jones's demand for a balance sheet of the Mayor's expenditure on the town's Coronation festivities was similarly deplored and in 1904, when so many members left the Chamber during consideration of a motion by Thomas Waters on unemployment as to render the meeting inquorate, Waters threatened to 'adopt a policy of obstruction'. A similar response to a similar motion was reported by the *Chronicle* later in the year with the remark that 'Mr Waters occupied considerable time in developing socialist doctrines', and a motion to prescribe trade union rates in council contracts was condemned by the paper as 'an objectionable proposal'. Jones and Waters had together run foul of council tradition in 1903 when they moved and seconded a motion to pay a minimum wage of £1 10s 0d per week to the corporation's tramway workers. The corporation minutes recorded that 'in moving and seconding this motion the mover and seconder used language of such an improper character that nearly every member of the Council withdrew from the meeting, and the Mayor left the chair'. The last straw was apparently an allegation that the council's policy was one of 'enslavement'. Even John Rabson, who was by then senior enough to have become Chairman of the Public Health Committee, provoked a walk-out in 1910 by alleging mismanagement and poor safety standards in the tramway undertaking.

All these incidents, and many more, revealed that social and political homogeneity could no longer be relied upon to oil the wheels of the corporation's decision-making machinery. However, formal challenges to the distribution of power and influence on the basis of seniority rather than representativeness were infrequent, although as early as 1903 Labour members had objected to the fact that none of them had been appointed to the Education Committee at the time of its establishment. In the years before the electoral truce of the First World War, two significant changes were made in the conduct of the corporation's business, and both arose from an unusual convergence of the interests of working-class and lower-middle-class members who, especially after the election of a number of shopkeepers at the turn of the century, could not afford to subsidize from their own pockets the costs of public service. The first was the decision in 1903 that the monthly meetings of the corporation (though not yet the statutory quarterly meetings) should be held in the evenings. The second, in 1907, was the decision to pay an allowance to the Mayor to cover at least part of the expenses of a year in office. The allowance was initially fixed at £300 per year and the council agreed to it despite the warning of a former Mayor, A. H. Bull, that it would eventually lead to the payment of members. In supporting the payment, which had been proposed on previous occasions without success, Councillor Jones revealed that despite the seriousness with which he clearly approached the representation of working-class interests he was not without a sense of humour. He told the council (10 January 1907) that he had heard no opposition to the proposal among the ratepayers 'apart from a little chaff from my own class as to which house in Bath Road I was going to occupy when I had the £300 a year'. More seriously, the office of Mayor was of considerable symbolic importance, and a remark by Councillor Creed, when the possibility of paying an allowance to the Mayor was first discussed by the corporation in 1894, was particularly relevant to the new Labour members. Creed said that it was 'a most unfair thing that a gentleman who took upon himself the office of Mayor should not only give perhaps the larger portion of his time but also have to put his hand in his pocket and spend a large sum of money'.

The selection of the Mayor and the deference due to the holder of the office were first called into question by the Labour Group on the council as Labour representation increased in the 1920s. Labour participation in the elections became better organized after the establishment in 1918 of Reading Labour Party and, indeed, there is no doubt that the electoral pact between the other two parties was stimulated by the higher profile adopted by the party in the elections of 1919. In 1920, the joint address from the Liberal and Conservative chairmen referred to the fact that 'the Parliamentary Candidate for the Labour Party had been addressing a series of meetings' in support of Labour candidates for the borough council. It was in 1921, however, that Labour mounted a successful challenge to a long-standing convention regarding the mayoralty, that the outgoing Mayor ought not to be opposed if he sought re-election to the council at the end of his term of office as Mayor. The convention reflected the view that the Mayor was, for his year of office, 'above politics', partisan or otherwise, and that part of the reward for his service should be his unopposed re-election, on the infrequent occasions when demission of office as Mayor coincided with the end of an incumbent's three years on the council. It also ensured that a related convention (and one that is still followed) could be adhered to – the appointment of the immediate past Mayor as Deputy Mayor for the ensuing council year. The decision of the Labour Party to nominate Alice Jenkins against Mayor Denys Egginton in Katesgrove Ward was deplored both by senior members of the council and by the newspapers, and her victory threw the council into temporary confusion as it had to defer the appointment of a Deputy Mayor to allow Egginton to return to the council a month later at a by-election. The vacancy was created by the resignation of one of the retiring Mayor's colleagues, partly to facilitate his return but partly also as a protest against the action of the Labour Party in opposing him. Much was made by the Conservatives, then and on subsequent occasions, of any departure from the practice of giving the Mayor a free run in an election, but the challenge was evidence that the Labour Party was not bound by conventions which it believed to be defended in the partisan interests of its opponents.

The next challenge to convention was both much more significant and more clearly reflective of how deeply partisan intra-council politics had become. In 1926 the mayoralty was the subject, for the first time, of a contested election in the Council Chamber. The convention governing the mayoralty was, as has been indicated, seniority. The mechanics of choice and nomination, however, were also important, especially where there was equal seniority or any doubt that the senior councillor would be willing to serve. There was, therefore, a Selection Committee of former Mayors who would make recommendations to a private meeting of the corporation where, if necessary, a vote would be taken. The individual nominated would then be elected by acclamation and apolitical ceremony at the annual Mayor's Day.

In 1926 the seniority principle pointed clearly to two members, one of whom was John Rabson, the long-serving and by that time highly influential Labour alderman. No minutes of the Selection Committee were presented to the council, but in 1926 the matter of the mayoralty became public when the Labour Party held a protest meeting over the decision to nominate Councillor William Henry Short rather than Rabson. Labour anger arose from the fact that Short was not the other 'candidate' originally considered by the Selection Committee. That candidate (revealed by the private reports of the Selection Committee to have been Alderman A. J. Maker who, despite an astonishing sixty-one years on the corporation, 1906-67, broken by only a one-year absence, never became Mayor) had indicated his unwillingness to serve and at a subsequent meeting of the Selection Committee Short was chosen. Labour's view was that if Rabson had been a serious possibility the first time around, he should have been the automatic choice when the question had to be considered again. The political atmosphere in 1926 was highly charged and at the protest meeting Lorenzo Quelch alleged that the decision not to elect Rabson to the mayoralty was because 'there was one terrible fact against him – the General Strike in which he had sided with his fellow trade unionists'. At the same time, Labour alleged that in the reorganization of the council committee system that had been agreed by the corporation, their committee representation had been reduced because, once again, they had put up a candidate against the outgoing Mayor seeking re-election.

After the protest meeting, the Labour Group decided to contest the mayoralty in the Council Chamber. The debate was well-mannered, adhering closely to the convention that no ill should be said of individuals nominated for ceremonial office, but it was clear that Labour believed that the actions of the Selection Committee justified their dramatic breach of the convention of unanimity at mayor-making. In the event, Short was elected over Rabson by twenty-nine votes to eleven. Rabson became Mayor the next year and served for two terms, but by contesting the election the point had been made that Labour would not adhere to convention when its own interests were at risk. It was not until 1951 that the mayoralty was again publicly contested and that occasion is considered later in this chapter.

In the late 1930s, however, as the Labour leader Councillor Kersley told a private meeting of the council on 19 September

1944, the parties appear to have reached an 'implied agreement . . . [that] a member of the Labour Group would be selected . . . on a one [year] in three basis'. That agreement was not questioned between 1938 and 1943 because in the 'exceptional circumstances' of the war Councillor William McIlroy served five successive years as Mayor. The Labour challenge to the mayoral nomination of Alderman Newham, an Independent, on the basis that he would be the third successive non-Labour Mayor, failed by twenty-eight votes to eight. In the course of the debate however, the Conservative leader, Alderman Bale, said that had it succeeded it would have 'establish[ed] for all time that the election of the Mayor . . . is entirely a political matter [and] that would be a very great pity indeed'.

Aldermanic elections did not become seriously controversial until 1945. In the period now under discussion, however, the principle of seniority and nomination by the Selection Committee was challenged frequently by Lorenzo Quelch's nomination in opposition to candidates with longer service on the council. No debates took place publicly on these elections to the aldermanic bench and the minutes of the Conservative Association for the interwar period contain no references to them. It is likely, however, that they were evidence of Labour's reluctance to allow Conservative nominations always to go unchallenged. Quelch eventually became an alderman in 1933 and in the same year, Edith Sutton, whose sex and from 1920 her adherence to the Labour Party presumably explain why the seniority principle failed to secure her election to the aldermanic bench until 1931 (when only Labour votes seem to have been cast in her favour, with the Conservatives abstaining), was belatedly elected Mayor.

The seniority principle was also questioned during this period for reasons of area representation rather than political partisanship. In May 1919 a meeting of Caversham electors presented a protest to the corporation against the appointment to a vacancy on the aldermanic bench, caused by the death of one of the Caversham representatives appointed at the time of the 1911 extension, of the senior councillor, George Stewart Abram, who represented a Reading ward. Although Abram's election was not publicly contested in the Council Chamber, a Caversham councillor had, at the private meeting which received the Selection Committee's recommendation of Abram, nominated another Caversham member for election as alderman. Although this incident was hardly comparable to the challenges mounted by Labour, it is further evidence that controversial change – in this case the incorporation of Caversham – is likely to be followed by challenges to established convention.

That the corporation was becoming more clearly partisan was revealed during the First World War, when great bitterness was engendered when the anti-Labour majority on the council used its power to co-opt to fill casual vacancies in a way which Labour believed did not reflect the political opinions of the electors in the wards concerned. In 1916 vacancies in the strongly Labour Minster Ward, on both the council and the Poor Law Guardians, were considered by the Municipal Elections Committee of the Conservative Association and a subcommittee was formed to select a candidate for the council vacancy. On 17 February the Executive Committee was informed that Dr Fielding Clarke had been chosen 'in accordance with the feelings of the Minster Ward Committee' and on 2 March, after Rabson and Quelch had nominated a Labour candidate, the council legitimized a choice that had clearly been made by the Conservative Party. It is probable that the refusal of the corporation and the Poor Law Guardians to co-opt Labour nominees to fill vacancies in Labour-held seats strengthened the determination of the Labour Party to contest as many elections as possible, both to and within the council. As Cook (1970, p. 346) says, the Conservatives' actions under the Elections and Registration Act 'caused great bitterness and emphasised the indispensability of electoral strength for the achievement of a share in the exercise of power'.

The culmination of this period of contentiousness about the operation of the council was the eventual recognition in 1926 that the allocation of committee places should be in proportion to the strength of the parties on the council. Labour's objection to the number of places they were allotted by the Conservative-controlled Selection Committee probably arose from the fact that the less formal selection methods employed by the council up to 1926, with members, generally speaking, selecting their own committees subject to the operation of the seniority principle for appointment to the most powerful and specialized committees, had probably given the party more representation than their position on the council could justify. But having contributed to the process of politicization the Labour Group was hardly in a strong position to object to its consequences.

By 1945, when the Labour Party first secured a majority on the borough council, the politicization of the institution was all but complete. The only remnant of the historic view that the corporation was for 'fit and proper persons' was the continued refusal of the Conservative Party to contest municipal elections under their party designation. That pretence was abandoned in 1947, although the suggestion that only Labour candidates were party political appeared again in 1949 when the Reading Municipal Association placed an advertisement in the local newspapers declaring that its object was 'to retain in the hands of Reading Borough Council the maximum control of municipal affairs, in the interests of the citizens of Reading as a whole, as distinct from any policy directed by Party considerations'. The statement went on to say that the Reading Municipal Association maintained close co-operation with 'any Conservative or Liberal Association . . . whose policy conforms with the objects of this Association'. This was despite the fact that between 1945 and 1947 negotiations with the Reading Liberal Association had proved abortive. The Liberals, who had all but disappeared from the council in the 1920s, refused to consider 'a broad anti-Socialist platform'. This refusal led directly to the decision that candidates should contest the 1947 elections as Conservatives. As Coombs (1970, p. 99), whose partiality as a member of the Conservative Group sometimes compromises the reliability of his account, candidly points out, the absence of any mention of Socialism in the objects of the RMA raised 'no great likelihood of misunderstanding' that their objective was the promotion of the Conservative cause in local elections.

The Conservatives were badly shocked by their comprehensive defeat in the 1945 municipal elections, especially when it was compounded by the decision of the triumphant Labour Group to replace four Conservative aldermen with Labour nominees. That decision effectively ended the tradition of seniority in the appointment of aldermen, although as early as 1934 the corporation had approved a Selection Committee report that said 'we have come to the conclusion that seniority . . . should not be the only factor taken into account'. Nevertheless the issue remained controversial throughout the remaining years of the county borough. Election to the aldermanic bench was non-controversial only when political control of the council was not at stake, and there were several occasions when the controlling group allowed the opposition to fill a vacancy caused by the death of one of their members. For most of these years council majorities were small enough for the aldermanic seats to make a difference and for this reason it is not surprising that in 1957 the Labour Group rejected outright a proposal conveyed to them by the Town Clerk on behalf of the Selection Committee that the allocation of aldermen between the parties be proportional to the party strengths among the elected councillors, for with aldermanic elections taking place only every three years there was no way of ensuring that strict proportionality could be continuously maintained. An agreement to maintain the status quo between the parties on the aldermanic bench when casual vacancies occurred might have taken the heat out of a continuing dispute but, particularly from 1955 onwards, the Labour Group was under insistent pressure from Reading Labour Party to maximize its advantage on council by taking aldermanic seats whenever it had the voting strength to do so.

The minutes of the Labour Group and the Labour Party for the postwar period reveal that the politics of the Council Chamber in relation to the aldermanic elections were directly affected by perceptions of the prevailing political climate in the town. The elevation of a councillor to the office of alderman would necessitate a by-election and the operation of the seniority principle, even if it applied only within a party group rather than to the corporation as a whole, might cause a by-election in a ward that the party was not sure to win. In 1958 after a complete redrawing of the ward boundaries, Labour lost three seats in the new Minster Ward to the Conservatives. On 12 May the Labour Group decided that having suffered the unexpected loss of three experienced councillors they had 'the opportunity to set the matter right by appointing three members of the Group to the Aldermanic Bench in place of the three Tories who retire'. In justifying this decision, the group agreed with its officers' view that:

> The original reasons for the creation of aldermen no longer apply. Continuity is assured and seniority has long since ceased to be the major factor. . . . The Aldermanic Bench has been used for many years past as a political instrument and there is no reason why we should seek to alter the position.

It was noted that the Reading Labour Party had expressed the view that the group should elect only Labour aldermen and that it expected 'the Group to be as anti-Tory on the Council as they profess to be at election times'. The group decided to choose three of its senior members 'having regard to the safety of the seat so vacated in any ward'. In the event, Labour retained all three seats in the subsequent by-elections.

The report which formed the basis of these Labour Group decisions is the clearest statement available of the politicization of the office of alderman. On 30 June 1958 the Selection Committee resolved, after receiving the Labour Group's formal rejection of what had been described at a group meeting on 2 June as 'a Tory suggestion' that the distribution of aldermanic seats be on a basis of proportionality to party strengths among elected councillors, to 'express regret that . . . it is not possible to make any agreement between the respective parties on these matters'. After 1958 appointments were almost always made by the controlling group and in the last aldermanic elections in 1970 the Conservatives removed all but one of the Labour aldermen, reappointing only the 'Father' of the council, who had served continuously since 1935.

One further stage in the use of indirect elections to the aldermanic bench for party advantage should be recorded. In the 1958 report the Labour Group considered the possibility of appointing aldermen from outside the council. Under the Local Government Acts anyone qualified to be a councillor was eligible for election as an alderman (or, indeed as Mayor, a procedure used only once in Reading, when Martin John Sutton, head of the seed firm, was elected Mayor in 1904) but the Labour Group rejected this course on the grounds that it would create 'an undesirable precedent'.

In 1966, with an overall majority on the council of only two, the Labour Group clearly felt that immediate survival was more important than the undesirability of any precedent that might be set, for it filled a vacancy from outside the council, albeit by the appointment of a former councillor. In so doing the group acceded to the wishes of Reading Labour Party which, in a year when a general election had preceded the municipal elections by only a month, clearly wished to avoid a by-election, especially one which, if lost, would deprive the party of overall control of the council.

There is little doubt that the politicization and manipulation of

the aldermanic bench in English borough councils contributed to
the decision, implemented in the Local Government Act 1972, to
abolish the office. In Reading the disputes remained local, despite
the decision of the Conservatives in 1955, at their group meeting
before the annual meeting of the council at which four Conservative
aldermen were removed, to make sure 'that a member of the
national press be present on Mayor's Day'. In other towns, as Jones
shows in his study of Wolverhampton (Jones, 1969, pp. 325-45),
manipulation of the aldermanic bench was employed to try to
ensure a majority for a party that had been clearly defeated in the
municipal elections, and in Wolverhampton itself the issue was
finally settled in the High Court. Few borough politicians regretted
the demise of the aldermen whose position, anachronistic enough
with the coming of universal suffrage in local elections, became
increasingly anomalous and troublesome as institutions organized
themselves on party political lines. In Reading the anomaly was
heavily underlined by the results of the last elections to the county
borough council in 1972, when Labour won eleven of the fourteen
seats contested but, because there were twelve Conservative
aldermen, had an overall majority of only two.

The question of the mayoralty became publicly controversial
only once in the postwar period, although it took several attempts
at inter-party negotiations before a formal agreement was reached
in 1962 that in each three-year period the controlling group should
nominate the Mayor for two years and the opposition in the third
year. The Conservatives were more anxious to reach agreement
than was the Labour Group, perhaps because it was they who had
in 1951 acted in such a way as to precipitate a contest for the
mayoralty on the floor of the Council Chamber. The position in
1951 was that it was the end of the third year of Conservative
control and in line with a 'gentlemen's agreement', the Selection
Committee had recommended that a Labour councillor, A. E.
Smith, should be Mayor for 1951-2. Given the Conservatives'
attachment to historical convention, an additional complication
arose from the fact that one of their members, T. W. Knight, was
the senior councillor. The Conservative Group was informed on 15
March 1951 that 'central office' (presumably of Reading
Conservative and Unionist Association) had advised against opposing the Labour nominee and after a debate during which a number
of councillors argued 'that the understanding hitherto respected

should be ignored', it was decided to adhere to the 'gentlemen's agreement'. That decision was reversed at a group meeting two weeks later on the grounds that the Conservatives' position on the council, with a majority of thirty-four to seventeen over the Labour Party, entitled them to the mayoral nomination for three years rather than two. L. V. Smith, the leader of the group, clearly saw the matter as both party political and personal, saying that 'if we [are] to survive as a party in Reading, we should have nothing to do with Councillor Smith'. Alderman Bale, however, seemed more alive to the implications of rejecting the nomination of the Selection Committee and he suggested that in future the Mayor should be chosen by the council itself. Knight's name was substituted for Smith's at a specially convened meeting of the Selection Committee and he was eventually elected Mayor by thirty-four votes to Smith's fourteen. As with John Rabson a quarter of a century before, Smith became Mayor in 1954 and served for two years.

Coombs (1970, p. 98) rightly describes this contest as 'the low point in these dealings' about the mayoralty, but a close reading of the Conservative Group (Municipal Association) minutes to which he had privileged access and of the minutes of the Selection Committee does not support his version that 'T. W. Knight was elected despite opposition from the Socialists whose candidate . . . contested the election in the Council Chamber'. It is clear that the Conservatives used their majority to overturn the original recommendation on the Selection Committee. It is accurate only in the technical and procedural sense to say that it was the Labour Group which contested the election of the Mayor. The *Berkshire Chronicle* (25 May 1951) may have been right when it justified the Conservatives' actions by saying that Labour objections 'sounded strange when it is remembered how the anti-Socialist aldermen were treated in the full flush of the Socialist victory of 1945'. The struggle of the political groups on the council to reconcile their deepening partisanship with the exercise of patronage in respect of offices created in a less political age convey an unmistakable flavour of tit-for-tat and the paying off of old scores. In 1952 the Conservatives removed the Labour leader, H. V. Kersley, from the aldermanic bench and in 1955 the Conservative leader, L. V. Smith, was among four Conservatives removed by Labour.

The growth of formal partisanship in municipal elections and in the internal organization of the council was not, of course, purely procedural and it would be mistaken to see it as simply a process by which one organizing principle, seniority, was replaced by another, party politics. As we have seen, the change was facilitated by the liberalization of the municipal franchise in 1882, the effects of which were strengthened by the pressure towards working-class, Socialist and Labour representation in the 1890s. As with the Socialist members of the School Board (see Chapter 5), the Labour and Socialist members who arrived on the corporation from 1900 onwards came not simply to represent but to promote the interests of their class. In other words, they wished to change the conditions of the working class and the achievement of that aspiration depended on their changing the business of the corporation. They did not have a definite programme, indeed as late as the 1950s the Labour Group on the council objected to the publication by Reading Labour Party of a municipal policy statement, preferring to keep control, within the context of corporation agendas, of their own policy priorities. They were, however, determined to turn the attention of the council to matters of special concern to the working and poorer classes of the town, and they believed that the town council, with its ever-widening powers and duties, could be used as an instrument for the improvement not only of the physical environment but also of conditions of life and work.

The corporation was by 1900 a substantial employer of labour both directly and indirectly by the award of contracts for building and road improvement. It also stimulated employment by the use of its powers to compel the owners of houses unfit for human habitation to improve and rebuild. The acquisition of the tramway undertaking and the expansion of the water and sewage works further increased the corporation's workforce. It was not surprising, therefore, that Labour members concentrated their early efforts on the improvement of the wages and working conditions of council employees. These were matters over which the council still had autonomous control, for it was not until after the First World War that the negotiation of the wages of public service workers began to be undertaken nationally and applied locally by local authorities as the immediate employers.

As well as moving resolutions on minimum wages and unemployment, as noted above, Labour members were concerned to press the corporation towards improvements in conditions of employment, in particular by reducing hours of work, providing employees with one day off in seven, and the payment of overtime rates for Sunday working. The tactics employed by Labour members, who were in a very considerable minority in the corporation, reveal how the standing orders of the council could be used to ensure both the formal consideration of matters uncongenial to the majority and, through the press, publicity for them. As the Mayor's response to Jones's motion on the Coronation festivities expenditure indicates, it was difficult to rule out of order any motion that bore upon the business of the council. Thus, if Labour members failed, through their activities on the committees which met in private, to get any change in council policy, they could raise the matters that concerned them at the public meetings of the full council. There, the only tactic remaining to the majority, if they wanted not simply to vote a proposal down but to prevent debate, was to walk out, and although this was occasionally done, it was a last resort to be used sparingly and only when it could be argued to be in response to intemperateness on the other side. Motions in council, however, had to be related to the business of the corporation. In 1904 the Mayor ruled out of order a motion condemning the use in South Africa of Chinese labour and when the ruling was challenged by a motion opposing the Mayor's power to rule in this way, the corporation took counsel's opinion to confirm that the power existed. Clearly the majority was concerned at the possible disruption to council business that might arise from the use of the agenda for propaganda purposes. Where motions related to the responsibilities of the corporation, no matter how unpalatable their content might be to the non-Labour members, they had to be considered. Sometimes consideration would be deferred by the reference of the issue to an appropriate committee and, although this usually meant that Labour proposals would be killed, it also guaranteed another public debate when the committee reported back to the council. Sometimes, too, insistent pressure eventually paid off, as when the corporation, after failing to act for seven years, conceded in 1911 pay increases, reduced hours and one rest day a week for the tramway employees of the corporation.

The arrival of the Labour members and their activities on behalf of the section of the town's population which they regarded as their constituency provoked editorial hostility from the press as well as an increase in partisanship and electoral organization on the part of other political groups. For much of its municipal history, Reading Corporation has demonstrated an exaggerated concern with the level of the rates, and the Labour members appeared on the council at a time when the increase in the corporation's activities, especially by the assumption of responsibility for education, made the local newspapers apprehensive about the costs of municipal services. Throughout the 1890s the corporation was made aware of the continuing costs of improvement, especially in view of the enlargement of the borough in 1887. By 1891 the borrowing powers of the corporation under the 1881 and 1887 Acts were almost exhausted, only £485 remaining under the former and £2,942 under the latter, and in a motion moved by John Justins Brinn, a brewer and dedicated economizer who remained on the council well into the 1920s, the council resolved to finance current paving works out of the rates. This was seen as a more reliable way of controlling expenditure and therefore the level of the rates, because, as Brinn said, it was 'immoral the way the Council borrowed money, and as long as they could get it they would go on spending it'. The clear implication was that when expenditure was directly dependent on raising the rates members would be less likely to commit the corporation to it. In the same year Alderman William Berkeley Monck, who had seconded Brinn's motion, resigned as Chairman of the Finance Committee because he disagreed with the council's borrowing policy. Arthur Hill was elected as his successor but he declined to serve, and George William Palmer was persuaded to take on the chairmanship. This led to a tightening of control over the estimates of the spending committees, with Palmer telling the rate-fixing meeting of the council on 5 May 1892 that 'it was the duty of the Finance Committee to thoroughly examine the estimates of all committees and recommend that a certain rate should be made'. Proceedings on the estimates were interrupted by ratepayers demonstrating in the gallery and they were told by the Mayor that 'their time to act [would] come in November' at the municipal elections. In the event, the council rated for an amount that was £4,000 lower than the sum of the committee estimates and the Finance Committee was given power to direct the spending committees on the detailed approval of their estimates.

In 1893 the corporation rejected an appeal for financial support from the Thames Side Improvement Association and was complimented by the *Berkshire Chronicle* because it had 'proceeded to throw out two or three schemes of a very expensive character and was thus able to separate with the satisfaction that is derived from the possession of a good conscience'. In 1896 John Wessley Martin told the council that 'a large number of gentlemen are of the opinion that the School Board expenditure is alarming' though he stressed that 'the Education Department was the greatest culprit', and that until central government acted to curb the department's activities 'there would be no check on the expenditure'.

In addition to the continuing local concern about levels of expenditure, the press and members of the corporation could point to the alleged extravagance of those authorities on which Labour had gained control. On 15 November 1902, for example, the *Berkshire Chronicle* expressed the view that 'it would be a bad day for the town if the Labour Party should obtain a controlling influence on the Council and inaugurate a policy like that which has proved so disastrous at West Ham, where the rates have risen to over ten shillings in the pound'. At that time, however, Reading still had a long way to go, for the total of the borough and general district rates stood at only 6s 4d.

In the first decade of the century as Labour candidates appeared in growing numbers at municipal elections and so provoked the opposition into a higher level of organization, the small number of Labour councillors raised issues of a broader concern to the working class, unemployed and poor of the town. Although the Labour Group was small it was strengthened in the presentation of its arguments by the frequent submission to the corporation of petitions and memorials by the Trades and Labour Council, acting in a pressure group role in a more determined way than had been the case with any other organization, with the exception of the Ratepayers' Associations. From the 1890s onwards the Trades and Labour Council had put constant pressure on local institutions to institute public works to help the unemployed. That pressure scored some successes when the council either accelerated work it had already planned or resolved to take other action, such as the decision in 1895 to set up a Labour Bureau and a register of the unemployed which would help employers to find labour. It also provided a method of recruitment to local politics, with some of those who were prominent in delegations to the corporation later becoming candidates and councillors.

Labour councillors supported Edith Sutton in persuading the

council to consider the issue of votes for women (despite an attempt to rule the matter out of order as 'political') and they placed on the council agenda motions on free meals for needy children (1904), with the council agreeing from 1908 onwards to pay any costs not raised by public subscription; the possibility, which was rejected, that the School Medical Officer might visit sick children in their homes; the provision of municipal cemeteries; a resolution in favour of a by-law (1904) to require all newly built houses in the town to have a bath installed which, though carried, was not followed up by the making of the necessary by-law. They were unsuccessful in attempts to instruct the School Medical Officer to make a return of children's ailments to the council, but successful in changing the rule whereby the marriage of a woman school-teacher was regarded by the education authority as the equivalent of three months' notice of termination of employment. Concern was expressed at the medical costs of childbirth as early as 1910, although it was not until 1917 that the corporation decided to introduce a maternity care scheme which led in 1919 to the acquisition of the Dellwood Maternity Home.

The significance of these Labour campaigns lay not so much in what they achieved as in what they revealed about changing conceptions of local government. It was noted in Chapter 3 that in the 1870s and 1880s, with the improvers in positions of great influence on the council, the years after the institution of the sewerage scheme saw the end of the notion of limited municipal government, with the corporation committed as much to the creation of a better environment as to the suppression of particular nuisances and hazards to health. In the 1890s, and with greater impact after the election of Labour councillors between 1900 and 1906, the representatives of the working class provided a counterweight to the forces of economy which, as the costs of improvement, municipal buildings, street construction, waterworks and borough extensions began to be felt in an increasing municipal debt, kept up an insistent and generally successful pressure for limitations on corporation expenditure. Between 1891 and 1901 the combined borough and general district rate rose from 4s 9d to 5s 10d, a fairly modest rise, especially in view of the facts that in the period the council adopted permissive acts to allow it to levy additional rates for the provision of recreational and museum facilities and, as the Mayor would note in 1898, was subject to the effects on its work of an increasing amount of new legislation.

Between 1888, when Reading became a county borough, and the beginning of the First World War, the business of the council was increased not only by local pressure but also by the acquisition of new powers and duties as a consequence of national legislation. In 1898 the newly elected Mayor, William Wellman, noted that the work of the council 'was continually growing, and no sooner did they get used to administering one Act of parliament than another was passed, and it required all their care and ability to keep pace with the new acts they had to administer'. This growth in the responsibilities of the corporation was a direct consequence of the preservation of the borough's municipal independence in 1888, for when new legislation, whether permissive or mandatory was passed, the powers granted were, by definition, available in their entirety to the county boroughs, whose unitary structure ensured that, with the exceptions of the School Boards until 1903 and of the Poor Law Guardians until 1930, there was no competing local authority upon which new powers could be conferred. The contrast, after the passage of the District Councils Act 1894, was with the county areas where the two-tier structure ensured that some functions went to the county councils and some to the district councils, with the resulting need for inter-authority liaison of a kind that did not come to Reading until 1974.

The Labour representatives on the corporation and the School Board during this period often had to push the authorities to implement legislation passed nationally with the object of assisting and improving the conditions of the working classes. At other times, especially after the election of the Liberal government of 1906, national legislation directly facilitated the work of Labour in the localities. It was because of their sense of working-class representativeness that Labour members objected to their exclusion from the Education Committee in 1903 and, as was discussed in Chapter 5, it was the Labour members of the School Board and subsequently of the corporation in its role as LEA who pressed hard for the extension and improvement of the ancillary medical and welfare services which the education authority was permitted but not obliged to provide. The passage in 1905 of the Unemployed Workmen Act, in 1908 of the Old Age Pensions Act and in 1911 of the National Insurance Act led to the statutory establishment of committees whose membership included council members as well as those outside who were thought by the appointing body to have special knowledge of the subject matter of the legislation. Here again, as with the pressure applied to the corporation by Labour organizations, the work of the Distress Committee, the Local Pension Committee and the Local Insurance Committee extended the work of the public authorities and provided another route to public service, as appointed members sometimes progressed to become elected members of the corporation. All of these new acts, by dealing with matters on which Labour organizations had campaigned, gave added legitimacy to the efforts of Labour members of the council to place related issues on the agenda of the corporation.

Perhaps the service that was of most direct interest to the working classes of the town was housing. In this field corporation activity can be traced back as far as the Public Health Acts of 1872 and 1875 but, as was noted in Chapter 3, these Acts were permissive and, despite the efforts of Reading's MOH, progress was both fitful and slow. Reading was no different from other towns in this respect and the inaction of local authorities was revealed in 1890 by the Report of the Royal Commission on the Housing of the Working Classes. In the same year the Housing of the Working Classes Act empowered local authorities to develop improvement schemes and to begin the direct provision of working-class houses. It was not until 1897, however, that the corporation established the Housing of the Working Classes Subcommittee to report to the Sanitary Committee on any action taken under the legislation. Very little was achieved and the Mayor, after his election at the annual meeting of the council in November 1898, attributed the slow progress to the fact that the Act was 'so cumbrous and difficult' to implement, thus making comprehensive clearance and redevelopment of slum areas very difficult to achieve. Once again, Reading was not alone. Briggs (1952, p. 85) quotes the president of the Birmingham and District Trade and Property Association as claiming in 1907 that 'for ten years the 1890 Act was practically a dead letter . . . as it has been in most of our towns and cities to this day'. Despite a further Housing Act in 1903, it was not until 1906 that the corporation considered going further than the piecemeal exercise of its powers to close unfit houses, require owners to improve their rented properties, and inflict fines on defaulters. In 1902 Councillor Jones, as part of his general campaign to focus attention on the conditions of the working classes, spoke of the 'insanitary conditions of some of the poor slum areas of the town'. His forecast that 'the public would soon demand vigorous action on the part of the Council in clearing these slums, and erecting for the people cheap and decent dwellings' said more about his own preoccupations than about the capacity of public opinion to press action on a corporation still dominated by the search for economy. In 1906 the Housing of the Working Classes Subcommittee asked the Borough Surveyor to report on the costs of providing municipal housing at economic, or self-supporting, rents, but no action was taken and the question was not actively considered by the corporation until 1914, when an intention to proceed to build a council housing estate to relieve overcrowding created in part by the exercise of the corporation's powers to close unfit dwellings, was overtaken by the war.

At the end of the war the council set up the Housing and Town Planning Committee in anticipation of the Housing and Town Planning Act 1919. This decision marked the effective beginning of council housing in Reading and the emergence of the corporation as a housing authority, although concern about the housing problems of the town had been expressed in the war years when the subcommittee had proposed, but the council had referred back, the purchase of sites in Southampton Street for working-class houses. In 1917 the council commissioned Ewart Culpin, Secretary of the Garden Cities and Town Planning Association, to prepare a report on the housing of the working classes. His report assessed the suitability of various sites, most of which were in the ownership of the corporation, for development for housing purposes. It also addressed the 'question of principle' of whether, to make up a housing deficiency estimated by the MOH at 500 dwellings, the corporation should build small numbers of homes on 'in-fill' sites in the existing developed area or build a new estate on the outskirts of the borough. Given Culpin's institutional affiliation, it was not surprising that he concluded that 'from every point of view . . . it would seem that a comprehensive scheme is advantageous' and on 28 February 1918 the Housing Committee recommended that the borough embark upon a comprehensive scheme for 500 houses 'on the Garden City Principle' in the southern part of the town. The original proposal to build on land at Manor Farm which had been acquired as part of the land assembly for the sewage farm was vigorously opposed by Labour members and by Labour organizations in the town on the grounds that the land was low-lying and damp. In January 1919 on a motion by Labour members Quelch and Rabson, the decision to build at Manor Farm was rescinded by twenty votes to two, and the corporation then decided to build on two of the other sites identified by Culpin, at Shinfield Road on the southern outskirts and on part of the Norcot Estate in the west. By 1921 101 houses had been occupied.

Throughout the 1920s and 1930s the council's efforts to solve the housing shortage were hampered by a number of factors, some national and some local. Nationally recurrent financial restrictions caused postponements of the council's plans, and despite Quelch's protest that such restrictions amounted to 'one of the most callous and criminal acts the government has perpetrated on local authorities', they were supported by economizers on the council who wished to resist any further extension of municipal enterprise. The economizers, not surprisingly, welcomed and enthusiastically implemented the 1923 Act which allowed councils to advance money to private builders, a policy vigorously opposed by Labour because, as Quelch put it, 'the way to get houses is to build them; giving money to people is not building homes'. The supporters of the advances scheme, however, did not seem to consider that by borrowing money to finance it the council was adding to what John Rabson in 1927 would call 'the deadweight debt of the Borough' just as it would have done by building for rent. The dispute between the supporters of these two competing ways of remedying the housing shortage was essentially political, and had much in common with both the issue of municipal enterprise in the nineteenth century and the question of council house sales later in the twentieth. In the short term, however, the balance was tipped in favour of direct provision by the Housing Act 1924 which, by the introduction of exchequer subsidies, made the building of houses for rent a more financially attractive option.

Although the influence of Labour members on housing policy was considerable in this period, the infrequent council debates on the subject revealed much about the continuing conflict between those who saw the duty of the corporation as the satisfaction of basic needs and those who saw it as the improvement of working-class standards of living. In 1919 the Chairman of the Housing Committee had expressed his philosophical preference for private enterprise by saying that although some council initiative was unavoidable in view of the acute postwar housing shortage, the corporation must be careful not to compete with the private sector: 'The most wasteful and extravagant of all systems is state management: the next wasteful [*sic*] is municipal management.' In 1925 Councillor Newham, a Labour member whose adherence to the party had lapsed by the time he was nominated as Mayor in 1944, moved in council the rejection of the Housing Committee's proposal that some of the houses to be built on the Norcot Estate should be of the 'non-parlour' type, having a living-room, kitchen/scullery and bedrooms, but no sitting-room. Newham argued that the non-parlour houses already built at Shinfield road were 'prospective additions to the slums', but Councillor Palmer (Conservative) argued that because the rents of parlour-type houses were two-thirds higher than the non-parlour ones, people who rented them 'would have to go without kippers or bloaters for breakfast'. Councillor Wooldridge, a Labour member supporting the motion, inquired of those who opposed parlour-type houses whether they 'sat with the servants in the kitchen'. At the time of the debate there were 1,318 applicants on the corporation's housing waiting list of whom 874, according to the Chairman of the Housing Committee, wanted non-parlour accommodation. The chairman went on to say that the council should build 'neither slums nor palaces'. The debate, which ended in the rejection of the Labour motion, like many on council housing, generated more heat than light, but it revealed that neither side had any monopoly on paternalism.

The planning powers of the council were increased by legislation after the First World War and the exercise of these powers, especially after the passage of the Housing Act 1903, put further pressure on the town's housing stock. Between 1931 and 1939 the corporation declared thirty-five clearance areas, mainly in and around the town centre, thus creating a demand for housing to accommodate the people displaced. In 1937 draft planning schemes were adopted covering most of the borough. Much of the work to implement these schemes was delayed by the Second World War and, as was noted when looking at education and the proposed extension of the borough boundaries, the capacity of the town to solve its housing problems was compromised after the war by the changed emphasis in planning policy which led to the designation of Reading as a location for up to 12,000 people 'overspilled' from London. After 1945, until the later 1960s and the 1970s, the housebuilding programme was seldom particularly divisive between the parties, although there were disputes about rent policy and the use of direct labour as opposed to private builders in the construction of new estates. It was not until the disputes over the Rent Act 1957, the Housing Finance Act 1972 and the question of the sale of council houses in the late 1960s and early 1970s that housing policies were vigorously debated in council. In 1960, in anticipation of a move by the Conservatives to make the sale of council houses an election issue, the Labour Group decided by a small majority to come out in favour of the policy on the grounds that, as Councillor David Stoddart told the group on 21 March 1960, 'conditions had changed and we now had a sufficiently large stock to allow us room for manoeuvre [and] in any event, I do not think that a large number of houses will be sold'. Thus, for part of the postwar period there was no division on principle on the question of council house sales.

In 1950 the issue of council house rents reached the High Court when a group of tenants challenged the decision of the controlling Conservatives to raise rents in 1948. The case was resolved in favour of the corporation and the Labour Group attempted to persuade the council not to press for full payment of the arrears accrued by the plaintiffs. At the same time, Reading Labour Party, with the help of the town's two Labour MPs, sought national support. In the end, the costs were paid by public subscription and the principal plaintiff, Percy Belcher, later became a Labour councillor. The case of *Belcher* v. *Reading Corporation* established that in setting rents the corporation had to balance the welfare of its tenants against the interests of the ratepayers as a whole, an indication that the power of an authority to make rate fund contributions to its housing revenue account in order to keep rents down was not unlimited.

The increasing partisanship of the corporation and the changes in both the nature and the extent of its business came together after the Second World War to produce an important change in the process of decision-making, as the locus of decision moved out of the formal structure of committees, subcommittees and full meetings of the corporation into private meetings of the controlling political group.

Group organization was common to both parties by the end of the 1920s, but it was not until after 1945 that group meetings became an integral and significant part of the council's policy-making process. Until then, the behaviour of the political groups had been largely reactive, their private consideration of corporation business largely confined to the examination of the minutes of the committees before their presentation to council, and the determination of the general line to be taken on any controversial items. After 1945 the minutes of both the Labour Group and the Conservative Group show them to have been more actively concerned with the making of policy, and there was a trend towards the use of the committee system as a means of formalizing and legitimizing decisions taken by the controlling group meeting in private. In this Reading was following a pattern common in many urban local authorities.

The change in the tone of the Conservative Group meetings coincided with the decision of the Conservative Party to nominate official candidates in the municipal elections of 1947, in which they gained control of the corporation after two years of Labour rule. During their period of power, which lasted until 1954, the Conservatives routinely determined policy at group meetings. The Municipal Association held monthly 'policy meetings' at which they debated, in advance of committee consideration, such matters as housing policy, the estimates and the rates, expenditure on the Festival of Britain, the site for the proposed new civic centre, the sale of council houses, transport policy and, of course, their attitude to the mayoralty and elections to the aldermanic bench.

By far the most important of these issues, for a party committed to economy and the containment of the level of the rates, was the annual estimates. Every February the Conservative Group debated and decided upon the budget to be presented first to the Finance and General Purposes Committee and then to the rate-fixing meeting of the council. In 1949, for example, the group decided that an anticipated deficit for 1949-50 would be eliminated by 'round figure reductions . . . in an endeavour to maintain the rate at last year's level'; and in 1950 Alderman Bale, Chairman of the Finance and General Purposes Committee, told the group that he was 'very disturbed over the estimates for the financial years 1950-53' and it was decided that economies should be suggested to the spending committees by the Rates Subcommittee in an effort to prevent unacceptable rises in the rates. In 1954 on the eve of the elections in which the Conservatives lost control of the council, the group debated suggested reductions in the estimates which, while keeping the rate increase to 1s, might necessitate a similar increase the following year. An alternative course was to raise the rates by 1s 6d in the hope of avoiding any increase the following year. Having considered possibilities that would not be put to any formal committee meeting the group accepted Bale's recommendation of an increase of 1s.

With decisions on the level of the rate made at group meetings, the formal rate-fixing meeting of the corporation became more ritualistic and formal, with debates taking place as part of the process of public accountability rather than of real decision-making. This change, of course, demanded that the group be able to rely on the solidarity of its members when the final formal decision had to be made. In this respect, Reading's Conservatives when in control seem to have taken for granted that group decisions would determine the actions of members in the Council Chamber, for it was not until they were in opposition that the group considered the question of discipline and whipped voting, although on at least one occasion, in 1951, there was a reference to the issue of a 'three-line whip' to all Conservative members of the Highways Committee. On 1 June 1955 the group rejected a resolution which would have bound members 'on all occasions to accept and follow the decisions of the majority . . . on all matters of Conservative principle after due discussion and a show of hands'. In April 1956 it was agreed that 'members should retain the privilege of voting as they wished but should declare their intention at the time of discussion'.

For the Conservatives specific policy initiatives were usually governed by their antecedent decision on the level of the rates. In this respect they maintained a non-programmatic approach to civic government which differed sharply in substance from that of Labour. In procedural terms the approach of Labour was the same as their opponents, with group policy determined in private and implemented through the formal machinery of the council. In the Labour case, however, the decision-making process in group was more formalized, with the detailed consideration of policy under-taken by the Executive Committee of the group, a small body comprising the leader, deputy leader, secretary and two or three others elected by the group at its annual meeting. Policy determination, in respect of both the continuing business of the corporation and specific new policies proposed by the group for consideration in committees, was the responsibility of the full group, but debates were invariably structured round the recommendations of the executive which was, on occasion, accused of usurping the functions of the group itself. On some matters, such as secondary school reorganization (see Chapter 5) and policy on the aldermanic elections, the reports of the executive, and of working parties appointed by it, were detailed and specific, with the group acting in a genuinely innovative way in the formation of local public policy. In 1956 the group endorsed detailed recommendations from the executive on the structure of council committees and the policies to be considered by them. The attitude of the group to its role in municipal policy-making was clearly indicated by its adoption of over seventy items of policy and its acceptance of a statement by the executive that:

Each committee should go ahead as quickly as possible with these schemes and . . . heavy responsibility rests with the chairmen. It will be the job of the chairmen to see that these and other schemes reach fruition and group is recommended to call for reports as to progress from time to time.

Labour's attitude to discipline has always been more rigid than that of the Conservatives, and it is complicated by a continuously uneasy relationship between elected public officials and their local party organization. Both Conservative and Labour groups on Reading Corporation, during the 1950s and 1960s, experienced periods when their relations with their respective parties were far from happy. In the Conservatives' case matters were invariably resolved locally, but in 1960 a rift between Reading Labour Party and the Labour Group over the removal from the party's panel of municipal candidates of three members who had voted against a group decision in the Council Chamber was resolved only by referring the matter to the National Executive Committee of the Labour Party. (In 1952 bad relations between party and group had led to the intervention of a Labour Party regional official.) A year later the NEC recommended the reinstatement of the three members. On a very few occasions the Labour Group decided to allow a free vote for its members, but otherwise members were expected to defy the whip only on matters of conscience and then only after receiving the permission of the group to do so.

One further consequence of the growing importance of the party groups in municipal policy-making should be briefly noted. Attempts by the controlling party to co-ordinate council policy-making inevitably entailed changes in the relationship between members and officers. It was not until the reorganization of local government that it became commonplace for professional local government officers to advise party groups, and in the period under discussion, Reading's Town Clerk and other chief officers did not do so. As early as 1951, however, the Conservative Group decided that committee chairmen should discuss the estimates with the Borough Treasurer before their final consideration by the spending committees and the subsequent decision on the level of the rate by the group meeting. The members of both parties, in anticipation of the widespread moves towards a more corporate approach to local policy-making that characterized the late 1960s and early 1970s, revealed a wish to ensure that co-ordination at officer level be imposed by clearly designating the Town Clerk as head of the borough's officials. In 1960 the Conservative Group considered the difficulties in obtaining liaison between heads of departments and the Town Clerk, and in 1966, when considering the appointment of a successor to the retiring Town Clerk, George Darlow, the Labour Group decided that the duties of the new Town Clerk should 'include that of senior co-ordinating officer with overall control of town hall departments'. In the event, when Deputy Town Clerk Harry Tee succeeded Darlow in 1967, he was designated Town Clerk and Chief Executive Officer.

7

'Having Powers in All Matters . . .'

It is a matter of great importance to the town that all its public undertakings are, to use a common phrase, controlled 'in a ring fence', the Corporation having powers in all matters.

Reading Illustrated: A Concise Guide, 1899

The Burgesses of Reading can congratulate themselves on having a very progressive municipal government, but under moderate control, pledged to retrenchment of expenditure.

Reading Chamber of Commerce, *Reading, England: The Ideal Town for Factory Department*, c.1936, p. 6

It had become obvious that there was an immediate need for new administrative buildings.

Reading Labour Group, *Executive Committee Minutes*, 29 June 1956

With the passage of the Local Government Act 1929, which abolished the Poor Law Guardians and transferred their powers to local councils, the county boroughs reached the peak of their powers. As an all-purpose authority, Reading Corporation was responsible for a range of services that included education, welfare and social services, housing, town planning, public transport, water supply, drainage and sewerage, libraries, recreation and other amenities, highways and bridges, police, fire protection and public and environmental health. In consortia with other authorities it maintained the Berkshire Lunatic Asylum at Moulsford and the Brentry Colony at Westbury-on-Trym, originally set up so that the authorities could discharge their duties under the Inebriates' Act, but later used as a training facility for the mentally handicapped. It was represented on statutory committees of the kind discussed in the previous chapter and on the Thames Conservancy, the body responsible for the management of the river until the establishment in 1974 of the Thames Water Authority. Its population by 1931 had grown to 97,149, and the town was very clearly the dominant authority in the area, once again overflowing its boundaries with evidence accumulating which would form the basis of the unsuccessful application for extension in 1947.

For British local government as a whole the 1929 Act, supplemented by the Local Government Act 1933 which consolidated a body of statute that had been growing for a century, represented the apogee of its power and influence. In addition to the personal and environmental services that had accrued to local authorities, this was the heyday of municipal trading, with many councils running electricity and gas supply companies (Reading Corporation acquired the Reading Electricity Supply Company in 1933) and some operating municipal banks, restaurants and theatres. In 1935 many authorities celebrated the centenary of the Municipal Corporations Act by publishing accounts of their achievements, and in a collection of essays sponsored by the National Association of Local Government Officers and edited by three of the foremost academic students of government and administration, leading figures in local government looked back on *A Century of Municipal Progress* (Laski, Jennings and Robson, 1935). Reading Corporation considered the possibility of publishing a collection of short reports on the work of the various departments but proceeded no further on grounds of cost.

By the 1930s, then, local government in Reading was simple to understand but complex to administer. Its simplicity was inherent in the structure of the all-purpose, unitary authority. Local government came from the Town Hall. A century after its passage the value of the Municipal Corporations Act was clear: by democratizing the corporations it had ensured the existence of a natural institutional home for any new powers conferred by Parliament on sub-national bodies and it had provided a base for structural and functional consolidation, first for rating and then, with the abolition of the separately elected School Boards and Poor Law Guardians, for the planning and provision of services.

Its administrative complexity arose from the combination of the heterogeneity of the range of services for which the corporation was responsible and the departmental structure by which it was organized. The expansion of service provision in Reading was, as everywhere else, incremental. Powers, duties and responsibilities were conferred on the corporation and, in general, the corporation responded by creating new committees, new departments and new chief officer posts. Some officers, as we have seen, were required by statute. Others, such as Chief Education Officer and Director of Social Services, became so as the degree of central intervention and supervision of local authorities increased, and the transfer and acquisition of powers from other authorities and institutions presented the corporation with ready-made departments. This happened in the case of water supply, tramways, electricity, education and the Poor Law. This chapter considers attempts by the corporation to co-ordinate its services so as to ensure that it was more than a convenient location for a large group of practically autonomous authorities, each with its own committee and chief officer.

The most obvious source of co-ordination was the need to levy a rate to finance the services planned and delivered by committees and departments. The rate, which until 1928 was usually levied in two half-yearly instalments in May and October, had to cover both the current expenditure of the corporation and the loan charges arising from capital work financed by borrowing. As was discussed in Chapter 3, the earliest moves in the direction of financial co-ordination took place in the 1870s and 1880s, and it was noted in Chapter 6 that, as a result of concern about the effect of loan charges on the rates, the council accepted in 1892 that committees should be given greater guidance and instruction by the Finance and General Purposes Committee in both estimating and spending. The central purpose of this form of co-ordination was not the planning but the containment of local expenditure with a view to limiting the level of the rate. In the pursuit of this objective, the trading activities of the council, in particular the tramways undertaking but also, to a lesser extent, the waterworks and the sewage farm (which raised livestock and harvested several crops of hay each year), brought receipts which, if the council so chose, could be transferred to the rate fund and so effect a corresponding alleviation of any rate increase necessary to keep the borough fund in balance. But here again, the absence of interdepartmental co-ordination, at least until the organization of the council on partisan lines, limited the capacity of the Finance and General Purposes Committee to manage the finances of the corporation in a comprehensive way. Departmentalism creates power centres, and the alliance of a strong professional chief officer and an influential chairman, together with an administrative culture which laid much emphasis on 'business-like' management, often led the tramways undertaking to resist any disposal of its surpluses, preferring to retain them for further investment in plant and machinery. In 1908, for example, the Chairman of the Finance and General Purposes Committee, John Wessley Martin (who presented twenty-seven successive annual budgets to the corporation, a continuity which, in itself, might be regarded as a contribution to co-ordination) proposed that a modest £500 be transferred from the Tramways Account to the rate fund. He was opposed at the rate-fixing meeting by the Tramways Chairman, Alderman Field, on the grounds that such a transfer would be 'injudicious', arguing that it was important to build up a reserve for the use of the undertaking. In later years, the power of party ensured that this sort of inter-committee disagreement would not see the light of public debate. In 1949 the Conservative Group decided, at its policy meeting on the estimates, that a surplus of £13,000 generated by the transport undertaking should be 'utilised in reduction of the rates', and in the modern period of party-based local government surpluses (and deficits) on trading services are regarded as an integral part of the financial profile of the corporation and not as separate accounts held by separate 'businesses'.

By 1920 the combined borough and district rate had risen to 13s in the pound, and in January 1921 a motion to prevent further rate rises was referred by the corporation to the Finance and General Purposes Committee. The outcome of this referral was a decision in March to embark upon what Cook describes (1970, p. 386) as an economy campaign. The recommendation from the Rates Subcommittee via the Finance and General Purposes Committee to the council led to a further move along the road to more centralized co-ordination of expenditure and therefore, at least by extension, of corporation policy. The report to the council noted that even without any new policy departures, corporation expenditure in the following year was likely to increase but expressed the view that attempts should be made to ensure that there would be 'no increase in expenditure from the Borough and District Funds'. In other words, the corporation was committing itself formally to a policy of rate limitation which, given the extensive and varied responsibilities it now had to discharge, depended upon a degree of direction from the authority's financial centre of the spending policies of its committees and departments. The council decided that any variations in the estimates of committees should be scrutinized by the Rates Subcommittee and then by the Finance and General Purposes Committee, which would then make recommendations directly to the council. This change implied that after the annual estimating exercise committees would lose control of their overall budgets, with their estimates functioning as bids to the financial committees of the corporation. It was opposed by Labour members, with Lorenzo Quelch attempting to ensure that any changes proposed by the Rates Subcommittee should be referred back to the appropriate committees before going to Finance and General Purposes. Only four members of the council voted for Quelch's motion, and by accepting the new budgeting procedure the corporation, for neither the first nor the last time, committed itself to economy and rate limitation, a policy to which it adhered throughout the interwar period.

The adoption of these new procedures was a significant stage in the development of the council as an all-purpose authority. As the range of functions and the number of departments increased, a policy of rate limitation depended upon more than the exhortation of the 1870s and 1880s and the guidance of the 1890s. The decision-making processes of the corporation had become inadequate to give effect to the policy preferences of the majority and change became inevitable. The opposition of the Labour members was evidence of the procedural consequences of a political stance which favoured expansion rather than retrenchment. Such a stance would be better served by a decision-making process that maximized the influence of the service or spending committees as opposed to the resource or controlling ones. Thus views of the committee system began to reflect the tension between those whose top priority was the containment of rate levels and those who were more concerned with service levels. None the less the principle of central co-ordination was established and the autonomy of committees and departments was correspondingly reduced. In substantive terms the innovation was a success and the rate did not again rise to 13s until 1945.

Rate reductions in the interwar period were further facilitated by a review in 1927-8 of the capital expenditure and borrowing policies of the corporation. In August 1927 the council passed a resolution, moved and seconded by John Rabson and Harold Coster Dryland, in favour of an investigation of 'the deadweight debt of the Borough'. Between 1918 and 1927 the borough had borrowed about £1·75 million, of which about 40 per cent had been for housebuilding and housing advances, and the report on capital expenditure received by the council in July 1928 noted that assuming no further borrowing the debt charges would amount to a maximum of £89,000 (the equivalent of 1s on the rates) in 1930, decreasing by 1937 to £65,000. The report also said that £1 million 'could usefully be expended on capital account during the next ten years'. As a result of the adoption of the report, the corporation provided itself with a further mechanism for the control of expenditure and budgeting, with the appointment of a Finance Advisory Subcommittee with a brief to examine, in advance of commitment, the financial implications of capital expenditure projects.

On the officer side, the major innovation in the field of financial policy co-ordination was the decision in 1946 to bring the position of Borough Treasurer 'in house', with the appointment of the serving Borough Accountant, G. C. Jones, as Treasurer. As the financial business of the corporation expanded after the Second World War, the influence of the Treasurer inevitably increased. That influence was both recognized and resisted by the politicians. In 1951 the Conservative Group resolved to make arrangements for the chairmen of committees to discuss their estimates with the Borough Treasurer before they were brought to committee. In 1959 the Labour Group discussed a proposal from the Borough Treasurer to the Finance and General Purposes Committee which would have obliged any committee which proposed to incur any capital expenditure to receive a report on its financial implications, particularly its effect on revenue expenditure and rate levels. According to the Labour Group this suggestion had caused 'grave disquiet among certain members . . . for it was implicit . . . that the Borough Treasurer could become a virtual financial dictator'. The group was also told that certain chief officers were apprehensive about the proposal and it was resolved that it would be thrown out when it came to committee. The Labour Group's attitude demonstrated both a concern that members might become dominated by officers and a fear of the effect on service levels of reducing the autonomy of committees and departments. From the Treasurer's point of view, however, it was simply good management practice to ensure that policy-makers were aware of the longer-term implications of their decisions. At about the same time, moreover, the controlling Labour Group was conducting a review of the borough's capital programme which was clearly directed towards the kind of medium-term financial planning that was implicit in the Treasurer's suggestion.

It was indicated at the end of the previous chapter that the growing partisanship of the council (itself a powerful source of co-ordination) led to a concern to enhance the co-ordinating role of the Town Clerk. It will be remembered, moreover, that as early as 1879 the creation of the Finance and General Purposes Committee and its designation as 'the consulting committee of the Town Clerk' has ensured a close relationship between the Town Clerk and the most influential and powerful committee and its members. After the demise of Thomas Rogers and Robert Dryland, relations between Reading's Town Clerks and the corporation were generally amicable and, at least in public, there was no recurrence of the acrimony that had characterized the late 1860s and early 1870s. Nevertheless the power and influence of the Town Clerk, and the capacity of the holder of the office to co-ordinate the business of the council, steadily increased. The competence of Town Clerks Day and Clutterbuck in the extension campaigns of 1887 and 1911 was noted in Chapter 4, as was the influence in 1947 of Town Clerk Darlow, who was himself appointed, with the approval of the council, an Assistant Local Government Boundary Commissioner dealing with a review in Nottinghamshire. In 1915 when the council received a petition signed by 3,042 ratepayers protesting against a proposed increase in the Town Clerk's salary, the Mayor, L. G. Sutton, described the Town Clerk as 'the managing director of one of the largest business concerns in the town'.

Until recently, however, the co-ordinating functions of the Town Clerk arose from convention and practice rather than from any specific grant of authority. By virtue of his position at the centre of the administration of the council, he was *primus inter pares*, but it was not until the 1960s that the parties on the council began to move towards the formal designation of the Town Clerk as the head

of the paid staff of the corporation. The culmination of that
process, which was given additional impetus first by the Maud
Report on Management in Local Government (Maud, 1967) and
then, as part of the process of reorganization between 1971 and
1974, by the Bains Report (Bains, 1972), was first the designation
of the Town Clerk as Chief Executive Officer and then the
temporary separation of the two posts with the appointment in
1973 of Borough Secretary to discharge the legal and administrative
duties formerly undertaken by the Town Clerk. When the Borough
Secretary moved to another authority in 1977, the post was
abolished and the joint office of Chief Executive and Town Clerk
re-established. In terms of the decision-making processes of the
corporation, however, the most important change was the designation of the Chief Executive as the council's principal policy adviser.
This, together with the appointment of a Policy Committee to
replace the Finance and General Purposes Committee, demonstrated a commitment to the central co-ordination of the formal
stages of policy determination. These developments, and the shift
in the locus of political decision into the private meetings of the
controlling group (to which the Chief Executive would sometimes
give advice), consolidated the position of the Town Clerk and Chief
Executive in a way which would be of considerable significance
when, for ten years after reorganization, no party on the council
had an overall majority. This point is considered in the next
chapter.

As the politics and policy of the corporation became more
deeply partisan, politicians became increasingly aware of the need
not only to co-ordinate policy, but also to co-ordinate its
presentation to the public via the press. Until the decision in 1972
to open all committees except the Policy Committee to the press
and public, the procedure of the corporation inhibited rather than
facilitated the communication of detailed information to the public.
This was so for four interconnected reasons. First, Reading's
system of delegation to committees, especially after the major
review of committees' terms of reference set in train by Town Clerk
Darlow in 1950, was unusually extensive with the result that, even
more than in Darter's day, a century before (see Chapter 2), most
of the business of the corporation was done in committee. Second,
the fact that committees met in private made it impossible to use
the committees themselves for the direct communication of

information and, in any case, both major parties were anxious to present themselves and their policies in the most favourable light, a concern that led them to oppose, until 1972, the admission of press and public. Third, the procedure at full meetings of the council of the minutes of committees being presented by their chairmen and approved *en bloc* unless specific amendments were moved and debated, presented opportunities for the controlling group to highlight some issues and pass over others. Fourth, and to some extent as a counterweight to the last process, council standing orders gave the opposition an opportunity to stage a debate on any part of the controlling group's policies that was referred to in the minutes or, by tabling a separate motion, they could initiate a wider debate on some aspect of council business. In conveying information, these procedures were at best haphazard, relying as they did on the presence of the press at council meetings and the availability of news space in the issues of the newspapers appearing after the monthly (or later, six-weekly) meetings of the council.

Between 1945 and 1972 both the major political parties tried to increase their capacity for news management. In 1949 the Conservative Group decided that any information to be released to the press should be approved by the chairman of the appropriate committee. Similarly in 1957, after a meeting with the editor of the *Reading Standard* at which the officers of the Labour Group had alleged that the paper's 'reporting was often coloured, biased, and ill-informed and that editorials were sometimes so naive that it was obvious that the editor had not taken the trouble to ascertain the true facts', the Labour Group recommended that committee chairmen should give more relevant information to the press. In 1959 the controlling Labour Group, concerned at the publication in one of the local newspapers of details of proposed arrangements between the corporation's transport undertaking and another bus operator, decided to introduce regular press conferences between the publication of the agenda for each council meeting and the meeting itself. The Labour Group proposal was that all the press conferences should be attended by the Mayor, the group leader and one other member from each side of the council and by 'chairmen of committees who were involved in important items on the Minutes'. The response of the Conservative Group at a meeting in April 1959 was a decision that the Conservative members should boycott the press conferences 'as the Labour Party will undoubtedly use them for fostering Socialist policy in the Council'. Also, with more consistency than political judgement, the group decided not to hold its own press conferences. Conservative hostility to the Labour majority's attempts to improve the public relations of the corporation went further. From May 1959 to November 1961 the borough published a bi-monthly newsletter entitled *Civic News* and at a meeting of the Conservative Group on 29 February 1960, Councillor Badnall was nominated to be responsible for 'vetting' the publication in search of Socialist bias.

In 1962 the Liberal Party gained representation on the corporation for the first time since the 1920s and from 1965 a Liberal member and future Mayor, Jim Day, annually proposed a motion to admit press and public to committee meetings. He was supported by the *Evening Post* but when the paper noted (25 October 1965) that 'some council members are worried that if the press is admitted to committees discussion will be inhibited and council officers discouraged from giving advice freely', it did not recognize that more openness would reduce the capacity of members of the corporation to control the flow of information. In 1973 after six months of the new open system, a leading Conservative member said, 'The public are over-informed and therefore confused'. The Labour Group's cynicism on the subject may be inferred from the fact that having resolved throughout their period in control to oppose Day's motions, they decided in 1967 'that now we are in opposition, it would be advisable to abstain from voting on the resolution'.

During the 1960s weekly press briefings were given by the Town Clerk and reporters would follow up with interviews with leading members. The final decision to open all committees except the Policy Committee was taken by the Labour Group on 25 May 1972 'for a period of six months in the first instance', during which period the Local Government Act 1972 was passed, making compulsory the admission of the public to committee meetings in the reorganized system of local government. Until then, Labour and Conservatives had been at one in refusing to support the Liberal proposal.

The reluctance of local politicians to open the decision-making process to public scrutiny was probably related to the highly competitive nature of party politics in Reading in the postwar period. Control of the council, with majorities often inflated by the political manipulation of the aldermanic bench, changed four times between 1961 and 1972. Two studies of the attitudes of members of the controlling Labour Group at different times during this period (Gregory, 1969; Alexander, 1974) suggest that members believed that because of this competitiveness and the possibility that a very small shift of opinion could have a crucial effect on the party balance on the council, even a marginal impact of local issues might be important enough to raise concern about the quality of information reaching the public. It is significant that Labour's concern in 1959 came at the height of the public controversy over the Labour Group's decision to build an Olympic-sized swimming pool in the town, a decision which eleven of the twelve members interviewed by Gregory mentioned as having had a marked effect on Labour's performance in the elections of that year. Gregory is sceptical about this, but his analysis demonstrates the degree of concern that local politicians had about the public presentation of their policies. That the Conservatives seem to have been less concerned about their public image as presented through the press was due to the fact, as Coombs (1970, p. 146) points out, that local press reports on the party's activities were, for most of the postwar period, 'extremely full and extremely favourable'.

The comment by Mayor John Okey Taylor, quoted at the head of Chapter 2, about the slowness of decision-making in Reading was, no doubt, an oratorical exaggeration. The point remains, however, that in the twentieth century two major projects first proposed before the First World War were not completed until after the end of county borough status. One of these, the new borough library, lies outside the scope of this study, for although it was intimately connected with the long saga of the new civic offices, its eventual completion was under the control of the county council as the library authority in the reorganized system of local government. The other, the provision of a new administrative centre, as a physical contribution to the co-ordination of the business of the corporation, completes the account of the borough's response to the expansion of its responsibilities, particularly in the period after the local government legislation of the 1930s.

It was noted in Chapter 3 that the corporation's decision in 1869 to provide itself with a new administrative centre arose from a recognition that the effectiveness of the borough in discharging its constantly widening responsibilities required the concentration of its departments in a single building. In the twenty-five years after the opening of the new municipal buildings in 1876, the further expansion of the corporation's activities rendered them inadequate, and in 1901, arising out of a need to provide a new police station and magistrates court building, the council decided in principle to concentrate the public offices on a single site. This decision led to a long negotiation to buy out the leasehold interest of Reading University Extension College in the ancient Abbey Hospitium building at the rear of the municipal buildings. In 1902 the corporation received plans for the extension of the municipal buildings on their existing site which involved the incorporation of the Hospitium into the Town Hall complex. A further plan for expansion and internal modification was submitted in 1914 but was overtaken by the outbreak of war.

It was not until the 1930s that the corporation again turned seriously to the question of its office accommodation and by that time the acquisition of education, welfare and other functions discussed elsewhere had ensured that the borough offices were scattered all over the centre of the town. The Municipal Buildings Committee examined a number of sites, as well as considering the possibility, which their consultant architect strongly advised against, of a staged redevelopment of the existing site, supplemented by the acquisition of a house, used for commercial purposes, at No. 1 Friar Street, sandwiched between the Town Hall and St Laurence's Church. The major difficulty in the way of redevelopment of the Town Hall site was its small area, compounded by the fact that the presence of the church and churchyard made expansion to the south and the east impossible.

An understandable preference to continue in use a range of buildings which was barely sixty years old led the corporation in 1936 to make the first of a long series of subsequently rescinded decisions about its headquarters. To extend the existing site, it was decided to build on the north-west corner of the Forbury Gardens. Not surprisingly, since this was the one major area of open space within easy reach of the town centre, the proposal raised great public controversy, and after receipt of a petition against the plan, the decision was reversed in 1937. The Forbury Gardens decision had been made after the corporation, in referring back the Municipal Buildings Committee's proposals, approved the committee's decision not to consider further a site at Hosier Street, St

Mary's Butts and Castle Street where, forty years later, the new civic centre was eventually built.

The other sites considered in the mid-1930s were at Hill's Meadow, on the north bank of the River Thames (rejected because of difficulties of access and the danger of flooding), on Prospect Park in the west of the town (not seriously pursued because of distance from the town centre) and on a parcel of land about three-quarters of a mile from the existing municipal buildings, bounded by London Road, Sidmouth Street, Eldon Road and South Street. When the whole proposal was deferred in 1939 'until the national and financial position is easier', this last site had been chosen.

In the immediate postwar period, as the political control of the corporation alternated between Labour and the Conservatives, so also did the council's official preference for its new home. The St Mary's Butts site, which had become available as a result of the clearance of some of the town's worst slums, was approved in principle by a Committee of the Whole Council in May 1946. The committee's report described the site as 'the very core of Reading', a description justified by its proximity to the centre of the ancient town, just on the fringe of the modern business, commercial and shopping area. Because of its position, however, it was also thought, particularly by the Conservatives, to be a prime site for commercial development, and in January 1952 the Conservative Group decided that the St Mary's Butts site was 'not suitable', and in April the council resolved to seek an alternative site. In December the council rescinded the St Mary's Butts decision in favour of a return to London Road. This change had been made easier by the decision of Berkshire County Council in 1949 not to participate in the development of a new range of public buildings, but the move in favour of London Road was an indication that the Conservatives had in mind a more modest project than that recommended by the Municipal Buildings Committee in 1947, which included an assembly hall, new magistrates courts, a municipal theatre and an arts centre.

The planning of the new civic centre was also affected by considerations of cost and, in the period of reconstruction after the war, the high priority demanded by housing and educational building projects. In 1950 the Municipal Buildings Committee was disbanded because it was considered 'unlikely that further progress will be made for some time to come'. It is likely that the fact that the council continually returned to the question of its office requirements arose from the growing dissatisfaction of its staff with the cramped accommodation in which they had to work and their perception of the inefficiency inherent in the continued dispersal of the offices of an all-purpose authority. On 29 June 1956 the deputy leader of the controlling Labour Group, told the Executive Committee of the group that in discussions with Town Hall officials 'it had become obvious that there was an immediate need for new administrative buildings but [that] the question of siting was involved'. The Executive Committee decided 'that there was every reason why . . . the site at London Road should be abandoned' in favour of St Mary's Butts, and the chairman of the appropriate committee was instructed to take the necessary steps to rescind the decision of December 1952. By 1959 the Conservative Group, still in opposition, had accepted that it was necessary to build a civic centre, with a town hall, library and art gallery under one roof, and throughout the planning and construction stages between 1960 and the opening of the Civic Offices in 1976 and of the Hexagon multipurpose assembly hall in 1977, the approach to the project was generally bipartisan. Most of the delays were caused by central government's restrictions on public expenditure and on several occasions the corporation had to seek ministerial approval to continue the planning and preliminary work on a project that had been under consideration for more than thirty years.

The preservation of a bipartisan approach to what was the borough's biggest capital project was facilitated by the corporation's decision, in 1959, that all matters concerned with the Civic Centre should be referred to the Selection Committee. This committee, originally set up to consider nominations to the aldermanic bench and the mayoralty, was unique among the corporation's standing committees in that its minutes were not submitted to the council. Its decisions were made either under delegated authority or on the basis of reports submitted to the Finance and General Purposes Committee (later the Policy Committee). This highly confidential treatment of a project involving the expenditure of a huge amount of public money may be viewed in two ways. First, it is certainly true that financial matters of great delicacy, involving not only the negotiations with contractors and consultants, but also the effect of a major development on land and rental values in the area, had to be considered. There was thus some risk of compromising the public interest if decision-making on this project had been subject to the same level of scrutiny that applied to other council business. On the other hand, confidentiality could also have been maintained, especially given the exclusion of the press and public from committee meetings, by the resuscitation of the Municipal Buildings Committee, subject to the generally applicable procedure that, in reporting to the council, contractual details remain confidential until agreements have been reached. Such a procedure, it may be argued, would have better preserved the principle of public accountability, because it would have been difficult for the corporation to justify the exclusion of such a committee's minutes from the council agenda. At the very least, there must be a question mark over the use of a committee whose minutes remained confidential because it dealt largely with the exercise of the corporation's patronage powers, in respect of which it was generally agreed to be essential to preserve an appearance of unanimity, for the consideration of matters which might be a source of legitimate public controversy.

By the time of the completion of the Civic Offices, Reading had ceased to be an all-purpose authority. Local government reorganization transferred to the county council the borough's powers in education, highways, social services and strategic planning. The Reading Police Force had become part of the Thames Valley Police in 1968, but the new Reading Divisional Police Headquarters, together with a range of magistrates courts, were accommodated, as had originally been planned, on the Civic Centre site. A Berkshire and Reading Fire Authority had been set up in 1949. The corporation's powers in the personal health services and hospital management were removed by the National Health Act 1948 and most of its remaining public health functions were transferred to new health authorities established in 1974. Reading's autonomy as a water authority had ended with the creation of the Thames Valley Water Board in 1959 and the establishment in 1974 of the Thames Water Authority. The final chapter considers the reorganization of local government in 1974 and examines its consequences for the government of the Borough of Reading.

8

The End of Independence

The needs of the population must be defined, and plans made to meet them over areas in which the needs have got to be satisfied: and the authorities which make the plans must be in a position to see that they are carried out.

> Redcliffe-Maud, Royal Commission of Local Government in England, *Report: Vol. I*, Cmnd 4040, 1969, para. 88

The former county boroughs . . . – which have a long and distinguished history of local autonomy – have resented the fact that they were deprived by the 1972 Act of many of the functions they had previously exercised.

> Department of the Environment, *Organic Change in Local Government*, Cmnd 7457, p. 5

One fundamental condition of every good system of local government must surely be that the town which is inhabited by a genuine community should have an independent council.

> William A. Robson, *The Development of Local Government*, 1931, p. 182

Reading lost its municipal independence on 31 March 1974. For the first time since the grant of its first charter in 1253 part of the responsibility for the local government of the town was held by another local authority as the corporation's powers in some of its most important policy areas passed to the new Berkshire County Council. Like all the other county boroughs, Reading fell victim to the discontinuousness of the national policy process as it applied to the reorganization of local government, a process in which first one national governing party and then the other sought to maximize its advantage in determining the shape of the new system.

In some important respects Reading typified the problems of the local government system that led, in 1966, to the appointment of the Royal Commission on Local Government in England. As the application for extension in 1965 had emphasized, the town had vastly outgrown its jurisdictional boundaries. In that year the population of the county borough was 123,310 and the corporation's submission to the Local Government Commission argued that previous reports of the commission, after reviewing local government boundaries in other parts of England, suggested that the determining factor in deciding on boundary changes in urban areas should be a judgement on 'what really is or will be the area of the town'. By 1965 the 'area of the town' in all but jurisdictional terms had extended well into Woodley and Earley in the east and south, into Caversham Heights and Mapledurham in the north, and into Tilehurst in the west. These areas were, as the Selection Committee reported to the corporation in May 1965, 'part and parcel of Reading for every purpose except that of local government administration', and their inclusion within the borough would have increased its population by more than 40,000 and almost doubled its area. A look at the local government position in Woodley and Earley underlines the problems that had arisen for a structure established in 1888 and 1894 operating upon boundaries not revised since 1911, and in the case of this south-eastern fringe of Reading, not since 1887. That part of the town which was outside the south-eastern boundary had a population of 28,483, mainly housed in the continuous urban areas of Woodley and Earley. These areas were within the jurisdiction of a rural district council, Wokingham, which, at the time of local government reorganization, with a population of well over 100,000, was the fourth most populous rural district in the country.

  The important point about the condition of the local government system in the mid-1960s, and one which Reading's position vividly illustrates, was that its major fault lay in its boundaries and only secondarily in its structure and distribution of functions. As the Royal Commission Report put it in 1969 (Redcliffe-Maud, 1969, para. 85): 'Local government areas no longer correspond[ed] to the pattern of life and work in England. Population has long since over-run many of the old boundaries.' That was certainly true of Reading, where there was clear evidence of the obsoleteness of the borough boundaries and equally clear evidence, as there was in the other county boroughs, of the functional effectiveness of the single-tier, all-purpose, local authority. In other words, if local government was ineffective or inefficient, these deficiencies arose more from the lack of fit between jurisdictional areas and the distribution of the population than from any weakness in the basic institutional structure of urban government.

The contention here is that local government in Reading is now less effective than it was before the reorganization of local government. This is not to suggest that what the borough still does it does less well. Rather it is to suggest that it would do better what it does, if it still did other things. It would be mistaken to assert that the municipal independence of the borough before 1974 made contact, co-operation and liaison with other authorities entirely unnecessary. However, when the corporation had to treat with its neighbours it did so on a basis of equality or superiority. It was in no sense a subordinate authority. In its White Paper anticipating the legislation to reorganize the local government system, the Conservative government said that 'it would be quite wrong to use the terms "upper" and "lower" tier authorities' (Cmnd 4584, 1971, para. 15), but there can be no doubt that the functional arrangements in the new system undermine the accuracy of any such assertion. Quite apart from those major services, such as education and social services in respect of which the borough has no power and very little influence, the working of agency arrangements, by which the borough executes some work, principally in the construction and maintenance of major roads, on behalf of the county, emphasizes its reduced status. Local government no longer comes only from the Town Hall or Civic Centre.

Much more importantly, however, the informal interdepartmental liaison between closely related personal services which was part of the normal processes of administration and decision-making in the county borough is now the subject of more formal, more uncertain, more extended and more expensive liaison arrangements, at both member and officer levels, between separate and separately elected local authorities, each of which jealously guards its own limited autonomy. This point is made by considering how, in an all-purpose authority, the separateness of departments and committees is modified by a number of processes which, in the case of a two-tier local government structure, have to be specifically negotiated and formally organized. First, in the county borough, members would be appointed to several committees and these cross-memberships served to ensure liaison between particular policy areas. Second, chief officers and their staffs would attend meetings, not only of their own controlling committee, but also those of related departments. Thus, for example, the Director of Housing would attend meetings of the Social Services Committee and the Director of Social Services would go to meetings of the Housing Committee. Third, the various co-ordinating mechanisms discussed in the previous chapter – party groups, Policy Committee, the role of the Town Clerk – offered a continuous opportunity for liaison, negotiation and trade-offs between committees and departments. Such administrative devices as that which ensured the reference between committees of items for comment where the interests of more than one department were involved was a more effective process than that necessitated, for example, between one council as the housing authority and another as the social services authority. The difficulties in Berkshire's new local government structure in devising an administrative system for dealing with the problem of homelessness provide a clear example of reduced effectiveness which, in Reading's case, arose from the end of county borough government (Alexander, 1982, pp. 53-4).

As the new local government system came into operation, Reading Borough Council retained direct responsibility for housing, its transport undertaking (though the responsibility of public transport co-ordination was given to the county council), local planning and development control, local roads and refuse collection. In all of these services, there was a need for liaison with other authorities, principally the county council, but also the neighbouring districts of Newbury, Wokingham and South Oxfordshire. Like twenty-six other county boroughs, Reading became a district council (styled a borough council under a provision of the Local Government Act 1972 which recognized the dignity but not the authority of ancient corporations) without any change to its boundaries, although a small area of South Oxfordshire came into the borough as the result of a Boundary Commission review in 1977. Thus, the major fault of the old system was carried forward into the new and it was compounded by the administrative arrangements introduced by the new Berkshire County Council whereby the borough council's area constituted an educational and social services division. In the case of education these arrangements have added to the complexity of dealing with secondary school provision in the borough. The issue of comprehensive education remains unresolved and it has been further complicated by the fact that the change in jurisdiction has given Reading children a right of access (or at least of application) to Berkshire schools in those parts of the suburban fringe that have never been part of Reading's jurisdictional area. Thus administrative complexity is compounded by the need to process secondary school choices which cross the boundaries of educational divisions.

In public transport the existence of a continuous urban area of which only the centre is under the jurisdiction of the transport authority, and with the responsibility for co-ordination in the hands of the county council, has emphasized how the boundary conservatism that characterized the planning of the new system made the provision of adequate service more difficult rather than less. Co-ordination of public transport involved the county council in long and sometimes acrimonious negotiations to determine which routes within the Reading area would be served by Reading Transport (generally acknowledged to be one of the most efficient local authority transport undertakings in the country) and which by the local branch of the National Bus Company. There can be little doubt that the provision of this service would have been more effectively undertaken if Reading had been the centre of one of the new, enlarged unitary authorities recommended by the Royal Commission Report or if, in designing the two-tier structure introduced by the 1972 Act, the boundaries of Reading District had been extended, along the lines proposed by the borough in 1965, to include a major part of the suburban fringe. On this last point it may be argued that a major planning opportunity was lost when jurisdictional arrangements failed to recognize that the completion of the M4 motorway in 1971 provided Reading with what it had always lacked, a 'natural' southern boundary. As things have turned out, all of the problems of fit just considered have been exacerbated since reorganization by the development, within the area of Wokingham District Council, of major new residential areas between the borough's southern boundary and the northern side of the motorway. This development has created demands for public services – in transport, traffic management, education and social services – with which the institutional structure of the area is ill-designed to cope. As this is written, the borough council has before the Boundary Commission an application to extend into Woodley and Earley and, once again, these territorial ambitions are being vigorously opposed by neighbouring authorities in a way that would not have been possible if the changes had been made as part of a nationally ordered reorganization.

When the Conservative government's plans for the new local government system were announced in 1971, there was little scope for the borough to campaign, as it had done in 1888, in defence of its municipal autonomy. While the Royal Commission was at work, the corporation had not submitted separate evidence but it had associated itself with the evidence presented to the commission by the Association of Municipal Corporations (AMC). This evidence was in favour of a system of provincial councils responsible for regional planning and urban-based local authorities responsible for the direct provision of most local services. After the rejection by the Labour government of the recommendation of the commission in favour of provincial councils, the AMC proposed the establishment of 130 unitary authorities (the commission had proposed 58, together with a two-tier structure in the major conurbations), a structure that would have defended the municipal independence of Reading and other boroughs but which had little else to recommend it. With the decision of the Conservative government to implement a two-tier structure, MPs for borough constituencies were pushed back to a damage-limitation exercise which, by securing the introduction of agency arrangements, retained some functional departments in the former county boroughs but at the price of adding further complications to the liaison process in the new system.

In 1976-7 Reading was among a group of about twenty medium-sized boroughs (that is, those having populations between 100,000 and 200,000) which campaigned in favour of what the Labour Secretary of State for the Environment, Peter Shore, called 'organic change' in the local government system: the return to some of the larger districts in urban areas of some of the powers they had lost in 1974. The Labour government published a White Paper (Cmnd 7457) in 1979, the proposals of which would have given Reading responsibility for social services, highways and traffic management, and most aspects of planning, but not education. No legislation was introduced before the Labour government lost office in 1979 and Reading entered the 1980s with no choice but to make the best of the existing distribution of functions. Any major change will now depend on the policy preferences of national political parties, none of which is likely to give a high priority to further radical reform of the local government system.

Reorganization in Reading coincided with a significant change in the political behaviour of the town. With the exception of a brief period between May and November 1960, when the party strengths had been equal, there had been no time since the politicization of the corporation was completed in 1945 when the council was without a controlling majority. Throughout the 1960s and early 1970s, however, the economic and political composition of the town had been changing. Partly because of the planning policies of the borough council, partly because of national policy on the relocation of offices and industry from London, and partly because of the effect on Reading's already advantageous position of the completion of the M4, the economy of the town was becoming predominantly commercial and administrative, with major companies such as Metal Box, Foster Wheeler, and several insurance companies moving national or regional headquarters there. Huntley & Palmers had ceased making biscuits in the town and Suttons had moved its seed business to the West Country. During this period the local political system experienced a weakening of two-party domination and at the last elections to the county borough council, the Liberals increased their representation to five, still not enough to deprive the Labour Party of its small overall majority, but an indication that, at least in the western suburbs of the town, the third party was increasing in strength. The new borough council, which was composed entirely of directly elected members, the office of alderman having been abolished, had forty-five members and it was not until 1983 that any party, in this case the Conservatives, secured an overall majority.

For an authority that had grown used to clear majorities with strong partisan direction, its status as a 'hung' authority presented considerable difficulties in internal organization. In decision-making the great advantage of partisan organization is its predictability. Whether policy initiatives arise from professional officers or from party programmes, all participants in the process of decision know that once the controlling group has made up its mind, the remaining stages are more about accountability and democracy than about substantive policy choice. Without a majority an authority risks discontinuity of policy, lack of coherence between the objectives of departments, and the uncertainty of decision-making, as opposed to policy confirmation, at meetings of the whole council. In the latter years of the county borough, agendas for committees were drafted by the appropriate chief officers and, before the committees met, the individual chairmen were briefed by the officers and they could have some influence on both the timing and positioning of agenda items. This procedure was predicated upon the capacity of the chairman to deliver a majority on his committee and, therefore, was inappropriate for a council with no overall political control.

In dealing with the new situation, the borough's Chief Executive secured the agreement of the political parties to the constitution of 'management groups' for each committee. This innovation was a development of the county borough's 'urgency member' system by which, if decisions had to be made between meetings of a committee, they were referred to the chairman, vice-chairman and one member nominated as 'third urgency member' by the minority party. In the last years of the county borough, Liberal representation was recognized by giving the party an entitlement to an 'urgency member' position in respect of one committee. On the new borough council the management group for each committee was composed of one member from each of the three party groups. Meetings of the management groups took the place of the chairman's briefing meeting and the management group also constituted the 'urgency members' of the committee. These groups had no executive or decision-making powers except in matters of urgency, their role being consultative and advisory. But they made it possible to identify which agenda items were likely to be the most controversial and, since they gave a preliminary indication of the views of the parties, they allowed officers to gauge the likely outcome in circumstances where any two of the three parties could combine to produce a majority. This procedure could not, of course, reach the level of predictability provided by a controlling majority. It did, however, have two valuable consequences. First, it reduced uncertainty by providing an early opportunity for compromise; and second, it encouraged a close relationship between members of all parties and the officers of the authority. The innovation was regarded as successful enough to be adopted by Berkshire County Council when it, too, found itself without a majority group in 1981. In Reading, despite the Chief Executive's view that it could operate profitably even in a majority council, the management group system was abandoned when the Conservatives secured a majority in 1983.

There is no doubt that the reorganization of local government reduced the capacity of the borough council to affect the life of the town. Despite this, however, its continued existence as a corporate body, albeit without the comprehensive power of its predecessor, provides a focus for the municipal identity of a major provincial town. The Mayor still takes precedence over any other civic or municipal dignitary, and the preservation of borough status has ensured a ceremonial continuity which, in the future, could provide a basis upon which to build a more effective and more rational local government structure. In common with other former county boroughs, Reading has never regarded the Local Government Act 1972 as the final stage in its institutional history. Nor does it regard itself as subordinate to the county council in the life of the town. The point remains, however, that with the decline in the significance of local authority housing, the exclusion of the borough from direct participation in the provision of the major personal services of education and social services, and the progressive limitation by central government of the autonomy and independence of sub-national institutions, Reading celebrates the 150th anniversary of democratic local government in the knowledge that the achievements of the past are unlikely to be matched in the future.

A Note on Sources

In the interests of maintaining the continuity of the narrative specific references have been kept to a minimum. The purpose of this note is to indicate the main documentary sources which have been drawn on in the preparation of this study. Secondary source material is listed in the Bibliography.

Public Records

At the time of the reorganization of local government in 1974, Berkshire County Council became the Archive Authority for the county. The minutes of Reading Corporation and of most of its committees for the period 1835-1974 are housed in the County Record Office at Shinfield Park. These form the comprehensive record of the decisions of the corporation, though the manuscript minutes of the nineteenth century are fuller than the printed minutes of the twentieth. In the case of the latter, the reports on which many decisions were based are frequently not reproduced in the corporation minutes, and sometimes not in the minutes of the appropriate committee. No formal minutes were kept of sub-committees whose recommendations were made to the parent committee in the form of reports which were, for the most part, brief and to the point. Also, because the meetings of committees were private until 1972, the background to particular decisions has sometimes had to be inferred from press reports of debates at full council. Only intermittently were reporters provided with copies of reports, and the full briefing of the press did not become routine until the 1950s.

The County Record Office also holds a deposit, still largely uncatalogued, of about one thousand boxes of 'Town Clerk's Papers'. These boxes are uneven in quality, their content apparently dependent upon the intelligence and idiosyncracies of generations of filing clerks. For one part of this book, they proved invaluable: it would have been impossible to piece together the story of the two extension campaigns (Chapter 4) had it not been for the magpie instincts of the Town Clerks of the time and their staffs. Archives are very much the Cinderella of local government. If this large corpus of papers could be properly catalogued – that would require more resources than the Record Office now has – it would form the basis of much scholarly work on the history of official Reading.

Some sensitive and confidential papers – most notably the minutes of the Selection Committee and notes of private meetings of the corporation for the period 1933-74 – are held by the borough, mainly in a vault at Tilehurst Library. I am grateful to the Town Clerk for allowing me access to these papers, for they have enabled me to analyse important parts of the process by which the organization of the corporation became dominated by partisanship.

Political Parties

I am grateful to the agents of Reading Labour Party and Reading Conservative Party for allowing me access to the following records:

Labour Party: Minutes of Reading Labour Party (Executive Committee and General Management Committee), 1947-65
Minutes of Reading Labour Group, 1956-74 (the minutes for 1945-56 have been lost).
Conservative Party: Minutes of Reading Conservative (and Unionist) Association, 1906-48
Minutes of Reading Municipal Association (Conservative Group), 1949-61.

Reading Local Collection

Reading Borough Library (administered since 1974 by Berkshire County Council) has an extensive local collection of printed material, manuscripts, pamphlets and other ephemera, corporation reports and internal correspondence, guide books and directories. Especially for the nineteenth century, this collection is of great value, and it is to be hoped that accessibility to it, and the reliability of its catalogue, will be improved when the long-awaited new library is opened in 1985.

Newspapers

For the entire period the *Berkshire Chronicle* has been published at least weekly, although from about 1920 its emphasis moved decisively towards county rather than borough news. For the period thereafter, at various times the *Reading Mercury*, the *Reading Standard* and the *Reading Observer* have provided reports of corporation business and, since 1965, the daily *Evening Post* has become an important source of information, though its reliability varies with the experience and enthusiasm of its municipal reporters.

Bibliography

Alexander, A. (1974), 'Procedure, partisanship and public participation in urban politics' (paper presented to the European Consortium for Political Research, Strasbourg).

Alexander, A. (1982), *Local Government in Britain Since Reorganisation* (London: George Allen & Unwin).

Ashworth, W. (1954), *The Genesis of Modern British Town Planning* (London: Routledge & Kegan Paul).

Bains, M. A. (1972) (Chairman, Working Group on Local Authority Management Structures), *The New Local Authorities: Management and Structure* (London: HMSO).

Barber, B. J. (1980), 'Aspects of municipal government', in D. Fraser (ed.), *A History of Modern Leeds* (Manchester University Press), pp. 301-26.

Berkshire Chronicle (1871a), *A Little Book* ... (Reading: *Berkshire Chronicle*).

Berkshire Chronicle (1871b), *Another Little Book* ... (Reading: *Berkshire Chronicle*).

Blondel, J. (1959), 'The Conservative Association and the Labour Party in Reading', *Political Studies*, vol. 6, pp. 101-19.

Brand, J. (1966), 'Reading', in D. Peschek and J. Brand, *Policies and Politics in Secondary Education* (London School of Economics), pp. 79-109.

Briggs, A. (1952), *A History of Birmingham, Vol. II* (London: Oxford University Press).

Burton, K. G. (1955), 'A reception town in war and peace: some aspects of life in Reading, 1938-1950', *Planning Outlook*, vol. 3, pp. 1-23.

Buckley, J. K. (1926), *Joseph Parkes* (London: Methuen).

Childs, W. M. (1910), *The Town of Reading during the Early Part of the Nineteenth Century* (Reading University College).

Command Papers (1945), *Local Government in England and Wales During the Period of Reconstruction*, Cmd 6579 (London: HMSO).

Command Papers (1971), *Local Government in England: Government Proposals for Reorganisation*, Cmnd 4584 (London: HMSO).

Command Papers (1979), *Organic Change in Local Government*, Cmnd 7457 (London: HMSO).

Cook, A. F. (1970), *Reading 1835-1930: A Community Power Study* (PhD thesis, University of Reading).

Coombs, S. C. (1970), *The Conservative Party in Reading 1945-1970* (MPhil thesis, University of Reading).

Corley, T. A. B. (1972), *Quaker Enterprise in Biscuits: Huntley and Palmers of Reading, 1822-1972* (London: Hutchinson).

Daltry, R. W. (1933), *A History of the Public Health of the Borough of Reading* (MA thesis, University of Reading).

Darter, W. S. (1888), *Reminiscences of Reading* (Reading: Blagrave Street Steam Printing Works).

Finlayson, G. B. A. (1966), 'The politics of municipal reform', *English Historical Review*, vol. 81, pp. 673-92.

Fraser, D. (1976), *Urban Politics in Victorian England* (Leicester University Press).

Gilbert, E. W. (1934), 'Reading: its position and growth', *Trans. S. E. Union of Scientific Societies*, pp. 81-90.

Gill, C. (1952), *A History of Birmingham, Vol. I* (London: Oxford University Press).

Gregory, R. G. (1969), 'Local elections and the "rule of anticipated reactions" ', *Political Studies*, vol. 18, pp. 31-47.

Hennock, E. P. (1973), *Fit and Proper Persons* (London: Edward Arnold).

Hinton, M. G. (1954), *A History of the Town of Reading* (London: Harrap).

James, R. H. (1954), *The Development of the Public Health Movement in Reading 1785-1872* (MA dissertation, University of Durham).

Jones, G. W. (1969), *Borough Politics* (London: Macmillan).

Laski, H., Jennings, I. and Robson, W. A. (1935), *A Century of Municipal Progress* (London: George Allen & Unwin).

Lee, William (1850), *Report to the General Board of Health: A Preliminary Enquiry into the Sewage, Drainage and Supply of Water, and the Sanitary Condition . . . of Reading* (London: William Clowes & Sons).

Maud, Sir John (Chairman), Committee on the Management of Local Government (1967), *Vol. I: Report* (London: HMSO).

Ministry of Education (1945), *The Nation's Schools* (London: HMSO).

Reading Corporation (1908), *Representation of the Mayor . . . to the Local Government Board*.

Redcliffe-Maud, Lord (Chairman), Royal Commission on Local Government in England (1969), *Vol. I: Report*, Cmnd 4040 (London: HMSO).

Regan, D. E. (1977), *Local Government and Education* (London: George Allen & Unwin).

Wykes, A. (1968), *The Queen's Peace* (Reading Corporation).

Young, K. (1983), *National Interests and Local Government* (London: Heinemann).

Index

HIST